Apartheid
Narratives

STUDIES IN LITERATURE 31

Series Editors
C.C. Barfoot - A.J. Hoenselaars
W.M. Verhoeven

Associate Editors
P.Th.M.G. Liebregts - A.H. van der Weel

Apartheid Narratives

Edited by
Nahem Yousaf

Amsterdam - New York, NY
2001

The paper on which this book is printed meets the requirements
of 'ISO 9706:1994, Information and documentation
- Paper for documents - Requirements for permanence'.

ISBN 90-420-1516-0 (bound)

Printed in The Netherlands

CONTENTS

APARTHEID NARRATIVES

Nahem Yousaf

In February 1990 F. W. de Klerk asserted: "The season of violence is over. The time for reconstruction and reconciliation has arrived," and Nelson Mandela's release from jail was announced.[1] De Klerk intended his statement as an endorsement of a new South Africa battling through the political fog at the end of many seasons of apartheid policy. Kenneth Parker writing "Apartheid and the Politics of Literature" in 1986 was clear then that apartheid would soon be replaced but foresaw problems with the "manner of replacement."[2] Consequently, Parker places inverted commas around "South Africa" throughout his article in order to illustrate that the region has historically been a white construct and that the appellation has never reflected the fragmented communities it sought to contain. Many critics remain loath to remove the scare quotes from the "new South Africa" until it has proved its existence in more than words and emerged from what Nadine Gordimer long ago described as a "state of interregnum." Extrapolating from Gramsci, Gordimer describes the impasse "not only between two social orders but between two identities, one known and discarded, the other unknown and undetermined."[3]

Debate about the necessity for a literature of commitment continued throughout the 1990s, with Albie Sachs adding his voice to that of Njabulo Ndebele who advocated a return to the "ordinary" in fiction and wished for a demise of what he called the "spectacular": a mode of writing characterized by its focus on oppression and squalor, and its aim to re-present the "obvious" horrors of apartheid, an example of which might be protest writ-

---

[1] F. W. de Klerk quoted in Jo-Anne Birnie Danzker, "Organizational Apartheid," *Third Text* 13 (1990/1991), 85.
[2] Kenneth Parker, "Apartheid and the Politics of Literature," *Red Letters* 20 (1986), 12.
[3] Nadine Gordimer, "Living in the Interregnum," in *The Essential Gesture: Writing Politics and Places*, ed. Stephen Clingman, London, 1988, 269-70.

ing, with its attendant demand for an emotional response by the reader.[4]
Sachs, in "Preparing Ourselves for Freedom," advocated at an ANC Conference that the slogan "Culture is a Weapon of Struggle" be banned, together with all culturally symbolic uses of guns and spears (the spear is one of the symbols of the ANC itself, of course).[5] Sachs has remained consistent over the years in his desire to emphasize non-violent alternatives in struggle.[6] But his paper raised a whole range of responses and they came at a time when the ANC was only just announcing the official suspension of the armed struggle, after the release of Mandela. The problem is really the extent to which the oppressors' violence and consequent armed resistance can fade into the background with the end of apartheid, as the Truth and Reconciliation Commission has shown. Apartheid was not ended by armed resistance alone but came about more through a gradual wearing away and crumbling of the architecture of the system, although murders, massacres, confrontations, demonstrations and assassinations preceded its demise. Those committed to the struggle for a free and democratic South Africa have participated in the struggle in any way possible, but the role of the writer has also been that of a reporter fully prepared to report events in an unflinching manner, no matter how gory or unpalatable those events may be. Indeed, in his address to the delegates at the 1986 Stockholm Conference for African Writers, Sipho Sepamla — renowned for incisive works like the "Soweto novel" *Ride on the Whirlwind* (1981) — made it quite clear that the South African writer was "confronted with such devastating material" that he or she had no need to "embellish it by exaggeration."[7]

Writers in apartheid South Africa for a long time occupied a space that was dangerous and incredibly necessary. Their position was dangerous because the writers' words were often considered on a par with the actions of those who were politically active, and important because they might help to give a voice to those who found themselves beaten into silence, but not into submission. As Annamaria Carusi points out in her discussion of the writings of Don Mattera:

---

[4] See the essays collected in Njabulo Ndebele, *South African Literature and Culture: Rediscovery of the Ordinary*, Manchester, 1994.

[5] Albie Sachs, "Preparing Ourselves for Freedom," *Red Letters* 29 (1991), 8-10.

[6] See, for example, his discussion of violence in Albie Sachs, *The Jail Diary of Albie Sachs*, London, 1990, 102-105.

[7] Sipho Sepamla, "To What Extent Is the South Africa Writer's Problem still Bleak and Immense," in *Criticism and Ideology: Second Africa Writers' Conference, Stockholm 1986*, ed. Kirsten Holst Petersen, Uppsala, 1988, 186-92 (p. 187).

> The attitude towards literary production ... is one which sees a structural similarity between what writers do in their poetry and stories and what political or trade union activists do in the political and economic fields.[8]

Censorship, banning, detention, house arrest, solitary confinement, shooting, torture — such were the royalties that awaited the writer/activist who dared to write/act against the State during the apartheid years. The writer was to be crushed by the white racist regime because he or she dared to "express a sensibility and an outlook apart from, and independent of, the mass direction."[9] However, the Nigerian Wole Soyinka's sentiments, as applied above to writers across modern African states, cannot be uncomplicatedly attributed to the South African situation since "the mass direction," or common consensus among the people, was quite specifically that which wished to see the dismantling of the apparatus of apartheid, and subsequent liberation for all to speak with voices that would represent the "sensibility" of the *mass*, not the minority. Although the anti-apartheid South African writer may not have expressed particularly different views from those of the "mass direction," writers still found themselves in a precarious position *vis-à-vis* a state that the Kenyan writer and activist Ngugi has described as a "nervous fascist outpost."[10] Allied to the removal of liberty is the banning of an author's works, whereby nothing that the author said or wrote could be reproduced in apartheid South Africa as a direct result of the Suppression of Communism Act of 1950 and the Publications Act of 1974.[11] Politically active African, colored and Indian South African

---

[8] Annamaria Carusi, "Post, Post and Post: Or Where Is South African Literature in all This?" in *Past the Last Post: Theorizing Post-Colonialism and Post-Modernism*, eds Ian Adam and Helen Tiffin, Hemel Hempstead, 1991, 97.

[9] Wole Soyinka, "The Writer in a Modern African State," in *Art, Dialogue and Outrage: Essays on Literature and Culture*, London, 1993, 16.

[10] Ngugi wa Thiong'o, *Writers in Politics*, London, 1981, 73. See also Etienne Balibar's essay "Racism and Nationalism," in Etienne Balibar and Immanuel Wallerstein, *Race, Nation, Class: Ambiguous Identities*, London, 1991, in which Balibar equates South African apartheid with German Nazism.

[11] T. T. Moyana, "Problems of a Creative Writer in South Africa," in *Aspects of South African Literature*, ed. Christopher Heywood, London, 1976. Moyana has shown the insidious nature of apartheid-constructed legislation designed to restrict the creative output of the artist: "The following carry the most restrictive provisions: the Bantu Administration Act (1927), Riotous Assemblies Act (1956), Entertainment (Censorship) Act (1931), Suppression of Communism Act (1950), Criminal Law Amendment Act (1953), Customs Act (1955), Extension of University Education Act (1959), Prisons Act (1959), Unlawful Organizations Act (1960), Publication and Entertainments Act (1963), General Law Amendment Act (1963), Criminal Procedure Act (1965), Terrorism Act (1967), General Law Amendment Act (1969)," 87-88.

writers inevitably found themselves in positions where they could not produce "art for art's sake." They felt politically obliged as well as empow-
ered to produce work that would provide the outside world with a detailed
exposé of the daily oppression faced by the black majority at the hands of
the white minority that exploited it. Consequently, the act of writing can
be understood as a form of resistance against the rulers of that same "fascist outpost."

For example, Wally Serote in his address to the African Writers' Conference of 1986 stated that a writer under apartheid should aim to produce
work that would:

> record the story of the people of South Africa, to portray the people of this
> country, to contribute to the betterment of their lives, to inspire these same
> people to reach their aspirations, and to give lasting, sustaining hope, so that
> their lives can be ruled by optimism.[12]

Anti-apartheid writing had the power to offer ideas to the people; it could
play a part in representing the people's views and potential routes to rebellion. In such a volatile political situation words have a political function
and a task to perform, as Lewis Nkosi, who proved most vocal on this issue over a number of years, has explicated:

> sometimes words by writers help to bring into clear focus feelings of frustra-
> tion and resentment which have long remained inchoate and unfocused for
> the general mass of the public. It is by embodying the unspoken thoughts
> and emotions of their people that writers and poets perform a national
> duty.[13]

The revolutionary power that literature may contain is a feature that could
not pass unnoticed by the apartheid regime. Alex La Guma pointed to the
fact that by 1969 the South African government had banned some 13,000
books. The government was in the regular habit of altering posters advertising those American films that showed black and white people together.[14]
Under the apartheid regime politically active writers and poets were
banned or exiled. One need only remember the names of Nat Nakasa, Ar-
thur Nortje, Dennis Brutus and Lewis Nkosi who were, among others,
forced to flee their country. In exile a number continued to write about a

---

[12] Wally Serote, "Power to the People: A Glory to Creativity," in *Criticism and
Ideology*, ed. Kirsten Holst Petersen, Uppsala, 1988, 194.
[13] Lewis Nkosi, "Art Contra Apartheid: South African Writers in Exile," in his
Home and Exile and Other Selections, London, 1965, 94.
[14] Alex La Guma, "The Condition of Culture," *Presence Africaine* 80 (1971), 119.

remembered South Africa whilst others, most notably Nakasa and Nortje, could not countenance the alienation entailed in exile. They committed suicide, perhaps because they felt impotent that they could not be *there* to fight the oppressor on home ground.

In *Culture and Imperialism*, Edward Said argues that it is not possible to examine the work of politically committed writers without taking into account the fact that such work is "embedded in its political circumstances, of which the history of imperialism and resistance to it is surely one of the most important."[15] In Said's view, resistance is a two-part action: the first part is "primary resistance" which he defines as "literally fighting against outside intrusion." But it is also possible to see how literature works to present a new ideology, the second part of the resistance equation, which Said characterizes as encompassing those efforts made to "reconstitute a shattered community, to save or reinforce the sense and fact of community against all the pressures of the colonial system."[16]

In the apartheid context the Nationalist party's policies existed to cement segregation into the national fabric of the Republic. To this end the existence of small "political" groups like the Coloured Peoples Organization, or the Indian Congress was not perceived as a *major* threat to South Africa — unlike the Communist Party of South Africa which disbanded before it could be banned in 1950. It was only with the Congress of the People that the government saw the real danger that mass mobilization could bring, so it sought to hinder the meeting, allowing the delegates and speakers a platform on the first day before moving in on the second day arresting those involved and seizing all papers. The function of Congress of the People was primarily for discrete racial groups to ratify the Freedom Charter and to accept it as a manifesto for *all* South Africans, and this they did. This was an historically momentous event because it represented the real possibility of all oppressed South Africans fighting the racist government with a united front.

The writers examined in this volume of essays combine to produce a socially- and politically-committed body of work that defied governmental pressure not to write, and often sought to mobilize the oppressed. The writing sought to represent the barbarity of the judicial system; to expose the quotidian realities of life for a population, often, relegated to ghettos

---

[15] Edward Said, *Culture and Imperialism*, London, 1993, 288.
[16] *Ibid.*, 252-53.

and sprawling "homelands" on the fringes of white "society." In effect, apartheid writing gave voice to a voiceless population.

David Schalkwyk takes Mikhail Bakhtin's concept of the chronotope as his starting point in a discussion of prison narratives by women writers. He suggests that prison writing is especially suited to this kind of Bakhtinian reading because the narratives "bear the representation of time and space and the gap between the narrative and narrated chronotopes as a special burden, since the passage of time and the restrictions of space are themselves the very substance of the story." His examination of Ruth First's *117 Days*, Helen Joseph's *If This Be Treason* and Jean Middleton's *Convictions: A Woman Political Prisoner Remembers* reveals a structural absence of black people while he demonstrates that in *Strikes Have Followed Me All My Life* Emma Mashinini, conversely, finds the presence of whites an "unbearable intensification of her imprisonment and suffering." Through a discussion of interior and exterior selves, Schalkwyk argues that white political female writers' strategies for survival within the confines of prison are fundamentally different to those of their black counterparts. Nahem Yousaf reads the colored political activist and writer Alex La Guma's second novel, *And a Threefold Cord*, as an important development in the author's movement towards expounding communitarian values over individualistic sensibilities. He argues that "South African apartheid and capitalism operate as interchangeable practices" responsible for keeping blacks in overwhelming poverty. Yousaf also draws on Bakhtin together with the work of the so-called Bakhtin circle (V. N. Volosinov's *Marxism and the Philosophy of Language* and P. N. Medvedev's *The Formal Method in Literary Scholarship*) to examine consciousness-raising as a dialogic activity manifested in a character who understands his social status as a product of apartheid.

Rather than accept traditional interpretations of silence as representing either complicity or defeat, Mike Marais in "Disarming Silence: Ethical Resistance in J. M. Coetzee's *Foe*" argues that silence "enables an ethical authority that is to be distinguished from political power." By drawing on Emmanuel Levinas' *Totality and Infinity: An Essay on Exteriority* and his papers on "Philosophy and the Idea of Infinity" and "Freedom and Command," Marais makes a compelling case for viewing Friday's silence as resistance: "the resistance of that which has no resistance [...] his utter helplessness *demands* responsibility from Susan Barton, it *demands* that she care and 'be for the other' rather than for herself." Furthermore, by examining the reader's subjective relation to the text,

Marais is able to demonstrate how readings of Coetzee that regard him as a non-political writer are ultimately reductive. Kelwyn Sole focuses on political fiction to trace the changing fortunes of Mtutuzeli Matshoba who he suggests was, at one time, "the most influential fiction writer in South Africa." In "Political Fiction, Representation and the Canon," Matshoba's links with Black Consciousness philosophy are examined and Sole argues that the writer's ideological project consistently extolled the necessity for black unity in overcoming the apartheid system. Matshoba charges the reader to examine important issues of political oppression, social injustice and economic exploitation and the stories collected in *Call Me Not a Man* "enact the intertwined process of individual and communal self-fashioning Black Consciousness suggested for black South Africans." While Matshoba, rather like Alex La Guma, may be deemed outmoded or dated post-apartheid, Sole joins Yousaf in calling for apartheid writers to be revisited and reappraised.[17]

Vasu Reddy's chapter in this volume focuses on writing produced by authors of Indian descent: writing "shaped by questions of history, memory and politics." Reddy provides an overview of works produced across the major genres of prose, poetry and drama before providing a reading of Deena Padayachee's *A Voice from the Cauldron* to investigate the idea of marginalized communities working together to overcome oppression: "the 'I' never shows itself to be an autonomous entity, divorced from the community, but [is] one that speaks with and for the collective." With this idea in mind, Reddy examines *Coolie Doctor: An Autobiography* focusing on the author's political activism and underlining that the spurious racial boundaries set by the state deserved to be transgressed. He moves on to Ronnie Govender's Cato Manor stories and an examination of the implications of the Group Areas Act on an established multiracial community.

In an examination of biographical writing, "Constructing Lives: Black South African Women and Biography Under Apartheid," Desiree Lewis demonstrates how authors can be complicit in reproducing stereotypes about agency, power, knowledge and race, key factors associated with apartheid. She shows that biography or life-writing is not "neutral" when written by white women. Through two detailed readings of Shula Marks' *Not Either an Experimental Doll* and Elsa Joubert's *The Long Journey of Poppie Nogena*, she uncovers how the biographer can manipulate the wit-

---

[17] For a fuller discussion, see Nahem Yousaf, *Alex La Guma: Politics and Resistance*, Portsmouth, NH, 2000.

ness-subject to authenticate a negative reading of events or issues. Lewis' chapter provides the reader with an important reminder of the politics of representation, and, indeed, from her reading of Joubert one is cautioned that the biographer can take on the role of colonial interlocutor.

Judie Newman's chapter addresses the important question of whether South African writers have now, in a post-apartheid context, lost their essential subject: apartheid. Newman examines the nuances of two different debates about culture and storytelling: providing the reader with an overview of the positions held by Albie Sachs ("Preparing Ourselves for Freedom") and Njabulo Ndebele ("Turkish Tales and Some Thoughts on South African Fiction") before moving on to examine Nadine Gordimer's short stories. For Newman, it is against the background of the Sachs/Ndebele debate that Gordimer plots her path toward post-apartheid writing: deploying "a strategy which both recognizes the necessary connection between art and its social or political objectives, and also offers a critique of art as merely a weapon of struggle." She provides a critical review of responses to *Jump and Other Stories* concluding that what reviewers and critics fail to appreciate is that Gordimer's stories actually function as "jump stories," that is stories "designed to make the audience jump, quite literally." Or, put another way, stories deriving from paradigms established via oral traditions that demand physical (re)action. Newman believes that "jump stories" are particularly appropriate in the South African context since the content of the stories "allows a satiric purpose" — exposing horrors — whilst the structure "dramatizes the post-apartheid reversal of roles from victimizer to victim." Continuing the examination of short stories in this volume is "Discontinuity-in-Relationship: Apartheid in the Short Fiction Cycle" by Sue Marais. Marais contends that in short fiction produced at the height of apartheid, geographical locations "accrue a politically-motivated impetus as an expression of solidarity and cultural cohesion/value which transcends or eludes the imposed confinement and derogation of ghettos." For Marais the short story cycle — simply defined as stories that may have linked episodes — is a particularly appropriate genre/mode in the apartheid context, in its demonstration of the tensions between segregation and unity.

While Vasu Reddy is interested in transgression in specific relation to Indian writing, Craig Mackenzie examines this concept as potentially liberatory in his reading of Bessie Head's *The Cardinals*. A novel labeled "an immature work by an immature writer" is saved by Head's "bold individualism," a feature usually associated with her later work, but which for

Mackenzie is clearly evident from the beginning of her writing career. In Mackenzie's view, much of the fiction produced in apartheid South Africa during the 1970s and 1980s — protest writing — now seems dated but Head is redeemed from this fate due to her then "unfashionable" focus on the individual over the community. In "Bessie Head's South Africa," he argues that Head chose to locate the action of her novel "inside the consciousness of her central character, thereby implicitly questioning the arrogation of moral and epistemological value to the collective rather than the individual." Bessie Head, along with Miriam Tlali, Zoe Wicomb, Gcina Mhlope and Ingrid de Kok, is also the focus of Gina Wisker's "'A Gesture of Belonging': Creativity and Place in South African Women's Writing." Wisker argues that despite the overwhelming horrors of apartheid, her chosen writers "combine often dichotomous responses and forms to a creative imaginative end" and that they achieve this through "investigating and embodying the shifting relationship between identity/self and place/location." The major focus of her piece is Head's Serowe experience.

In 1994 the African National Congress achieved victory in the first free South African elections and thus overturned the white nationalists and apartheid rule which had dominated since 1948. Despite the state's best efforts, since 1948, and indeed, earlier if one thinks of missionary-sponsored writing, the literary and cultural history of South Africa has flourished. The mid-1990s saw the emergence of the Truth and Reconciliation Commission with its aim to heal the rifts and traumas of the past. Under the chairmanship of Desmond Tutu, the Commission encouraged cathartic confession in an effort to purge South Africa of its past nightmare. However, it is my contention that the Truth and Reconciliation Commission's work was begun much earlier: by writers. Tutu himself referred to the testimonies presented to him as "stories": "The country has taken the right course in the process of healing to hear these stories."[18] Although I do not claim that the writers covered in this collection correspond to an exhaustive list of those who produced creative work since 1948, I do believe that the range of writers, from the well-known to those who have been critically neglected, is indicative of the breadth and resilience of apartheid writing.

---

[18] Desmond Tutu quoted in *Negotiating the Past,* eds Sarah Nuttall and Carli Coetzee, Oxford, 1998, 19.

CHRONOTOPES OF THE SELF
IN THE WRITINGS OF WOMEN POLITICAL PRISONERS
IN SOUTH AFRICA

David Schalkwyk

To read the accounts of their imprisonment by women political prisoners in South Africa from the Treason Trial in 1956 to the release of Nelson Mandela in 1990 is to be confronted by a myriad of differences: of historical sensibility and material condition; between white women and black; between women, black or white, and male prisoners; in length of incarceration; between detainees, those awaiting trial, and convicted prisoners; between those kept in solitary confinement, isolation, or communal cells; in prisoners' relationships to a wider community; in family status and ties; in culture, language, and education; and in the relationships to jailers, including different regimes of interrogation and torture. All of these differences shape the prison narrative in ways that constitute what Bakhtin has usefully called a chronotope: the distinctive molding together of space and time into representational form and substance.[1]

Prison narratives more than any other bear the representation of time and space and the gap between the narrative and narrated chronotopes as a special burden, since the passage of time and the restrictions of space are themselves the very substance of the story. How does one convey the endless, eventless passage of time whose characteristic quality or value is precisely its *lack* of "content," "substance," or "event"? How does one convey space which is both empty and totally restricted? Jean Middleton very aptly conveys the paradox of prison time, which drags interminably while it is being experienced, but which, precisely because it is almost totally empty of the events which give daily living its impetus, seems in retrospect to have passed very quickly:

> During my three years and nine months in prison, I counted every day of my detention and every day of my sentence. Both dragged unbearably. Now,

---

[1] Mikhail Bakhtin, *The Dialogic Imagination*, trans. Caryl Emerson and Michael Holquist, Austin, 1981.

> when I look back on them, they seem surprisingly short, because they were empty of innumerable kinds of experience that go to pack ordinary life: locking and unlocking the door, catching the bus to work, walking down the street, shopping for food, cooking it, choosing what to wear, reading the newspaper, meeting friends, meeting new people.[2]

In the representation of the experience of prison time and space, the differences listed above play a determining and irreducible role: how and why does one prisoner take up almost two hundred pages to convey the passage of a hundred-and-seventeen days, while another allows an equal measure of time to flit by in two or three paragraphs? How does a cell appear to one prisoner as "homely" while a similar one appears to another as utterly bleak and alienating? Why does one prisoner welcome the absence of companions within the space of the cell, while to another it constitutes the worst kind of psychological torture? Why does one prisoner constitute the passage of time through the "events" of an interior consciousness, while another's chronotopes are almost devoid of any kind of interiority, restricted to material occurrences in "real" time and space? What roles, if any, do race and gender play in the experience and construction of the time and space of incarceration?

I shall be addressing these and related questions in my analysis of the writings of five women who spent some time as political prisoners in South Africa between 1960 and 1990: Jean Middleton, Helen Joseph,[3] Ruth First,[4] Caesarina Makhoere,[5] and Emma Mashinini.[6] Encompassing differences of race and class, generation, political persuasion, education, periods, places and conditions of incarceration and historical moment, these books provide an ideal opportunity for the exploration of the chronotopes of incarceration and the ways in which such chronotopes are informed by historical and ideological pressures. Helen Joseph's *If This Be Treason*, published, like Ruth First's *117 Days*, in 1963, covers an earlier period of imprisonment than the latter. It is a white woman's insider account of the infamous Treason Trial, which lasted from December 1956 to March 1961, and includes an account of her detention in 1960, along with

---

[2] Jean Middleton, Convictions: *A Woman Political Prisoner Remembers*, Johannesburg, 1998, 129.
[3] Helen Joseph, *If This Be Treason*, Johannesburg, 1998.
[4] Ruth First, *117 Days*, London, 1988.
[5] Caesarina Kona Makhoere, *No Child's Play: In Prison Under Apartheid*, London, 1988.
[6] Emma Mashinini, *Strikes Have Followed Me All My Life: A South African Biography*, London, 1989.

other trialists. It is the earliest of my selected accounts of incarceration: it records a very specific moment in the history of the opposition to apartheid, and in effect marks the last celebration of a major *legal* victory over the state.

Joseph's book focuses on the trial and the trialists, rather than on herself. Her incarceration is incidental to the main story, which is systematically interpellated with the voices of the major actors in the lengthy trial. As narrator she is thus seldom alone; there appears to be little opportunity or cause for the kind of self-reflection and examination that constitutes so much of Ruth First's memoir, for example; time itself has a completely different quality as the days and nights in gaol serve merely as punctuating stops and pauses for the main story of a comradely sharing with others in the communal excitement of the trial itself. They take tea together at the restaurant across the road from the court, eat shared lunches in the courtyard, collaborate in preparing evidence, relish the communal singing in the van on the way to the court, and Joseph herself acts as an active commentator and conduit for the events in the court, re-presenting as a kind of sounding-board verbatim evidence and statements of her fellow accused. In this way the experience of imprisonment and of the trial share similar features, not all of them oppressive or even unpleasant. Joseph's personal voice is difficult to find in the overwhelmingly communal mode of her narrative, itself signaled, characteristically, by her citation of an anonymous comrade in *New Age* about the exclusive nature of that community:

> The end of the trial is in sight – after more than three years. We do not know what the end will be nor when it will be, nor if others will come after us, to sit on those same wooden benches, to ride in that same bus, to listen, as we have listened to thousands of documents and speeches, to many hours of legal arguments. We have lived in a sealed circle, the thirty of us, we have our own language, our own jokes, our own games. (56)

It is clear that Joseph was incarcerated before the later, much harsher regime of real deprivation and isolation, at least as far as white women prisoners were concerned. This makes all the difference to her representation of prison space which, though restrictive, is not totally alienating. Her various cells, isolated and shared, are transformed into colorful, almost homely spaces, with none of the intense gloominess, anxiety and sensory deprivation of later detentions. There is the "pastel-painted cell" with its bed covered with a "pink coverlet and sheets" (75), which in Joseph's words she was soon able to "transform [...] into a bedsitting-room," and once Joseph is permitted to join her friend and fellow-detainee, Hannah, the two women are able to recreate a comforting if not exactly comfortable domesticity:

> Early in the afternoon my cell door was opened and I was told to take out my things and to my joy the move began into Hannah's cell. We arranged our new home, our little house, and there was just room for our two narrow beds, two lockers and Hannah's table and two chairs, even though we do have to move the chairs about when we have to move ourselves. I'm de-lighted to find that by standing on my bed, I can just see out of the window, and actually see right across Pretoria. It's a Room with a View [...]. The time goes quickly now, and it's all exciting because we are no longer alone. Even our food tastes better when we eat it together. (96)

Much of Joseph's account conveys this breathless, child-like sense of ex-citement and joy, especially when she is not isolated, and this is enhanced by the use of the present-tense. In no other account is the confining space transformed so easily by the language of domestic normality, and although she tells us that time passes more quickly under the new conditions the book as a whole seldom carries the immense burden of time that weighs upon so many other accounts. The grammatical sleight-of-hand of the pre-sent obscures the gap that in fact exists between the moment of writing and the moment of experienced time: when exactly is the "now," the point, or the passage, of passing time that Joseph seeks to convey? It is impossible to say, nor does Joseph's language attempt in any way to make palpable such passing time – the almost unbearable "eating head" that is so much part of Herman Charles Bosman's narrative in *Cold Stone Jug*.[7] Time dur-ing the trial is measured by the progress of the case, in prison by diary-like entries which briefly record significant events. Only once does Joseph ask the question on behalf of the reader "How does time pass?" The answer is brief, almost cursory:

> I read, I do crossword puzzles, walk up and down the cell, or lie on the bed. I can add to the diet if I wish, but beyond a few biscuits and some jam, I really don't have much interest in the food. How long will this go on? Who knows? It's very quiet without the African women in the other cells and I miss my daily walks with Lillian – but on Tuesday I shall see her! And after that? I wish I knew. (88-89)

Again, Joseph does not seek to *represent* the passing of what we might call "prison time." She states, fleetingly, what she does to pass it, quite unlike Albie Sachs, for example, who devotes much of his *Jail Diary* to recreat-ing for the reader the intricate processes of forcing time on, of getting

---

[7] Herman Charles Bosman, *Cold Stone Jug*, Cape Town, 1969.

through each moment of the day.[8] There are indeed fleeting glimpses of this above, as Joseph's narrative, still in the present tense, alternates between imitating her own interior speech during the experience of "prison time" and answering the anterior question ("How does the time pass?") that belongs entirely to a later time, the time of writing, directed at a reader on behalf of whom the question is posed.

In this extract we can briefly see two different chronotopes, by which time is "materialized" in two different kinds of "event": the actions of reading, doing crossword puzzles, standing up or lying down, and the psychological processes of the interior monologue. Of course, the first two actions are themselves essentially psychological, which should alert us to the intense interaction of time and space in prison. Restrictions in space mean that there is very little to *do* to assist the passage of time, and this places an immense burden on the psychological means for achieving this. Each process makes use of different linguistic conventions, made available at very different points in literary history. One is tempted to say that Joseph's relatively cursory treatment of the passage of time as a problem of representation indicates a very different overall evaluation of the experience of incarceration from most other prison narratives: she has recourse to books, puzzles, a bed, a varied diet, other people, even flowers, within a prison regime that allows her not only some freedom of choice but also to speak of the space of imprisonment as something she can variously appropriate as her *own*:

> The trial is adjourned again for a week, to April 26th, but we don't mind so much now, for we have met each other again, and the week ahead seems nothing by comparison. Back to the gaol again at lunch time and even the forbidding gate has lost its horror. I feel quite in touch with the world after my visit to the great outside and to the Court. Hannah has also given me some red gladioli and red carnations for my cell and it looks quite cheerful. I have even become used to the gaol food and eat it all up with jam and sweets and biscuits to help out. (96)

The grounds of the prison remind Joseph of her own garden (87), and even the jailers are represented as well-meaning, kindly, almost motherly: "The little wardress Mrs Wessels, who is in charge of us, is delicate and considerate […] she is gentle and kind and wants to be comforting" (85). But however cozy her own relationship with warders and fellow white prisoners might be, her awareness of the different and differentiating treatment

---

[8] Albie Sachs, *The Jail Diary of Albie Sachs*, London, 1990.

of black prisoners complicates and fractures the sense of community that Joseph is able to establish. Her friend and fellow detainee, Lillian Ngoyi, is separated from her and given the meager and unpalatable diet reserved for African prisoners, although unusually, she is kept in the same section of the prison and Joseph is able to see her regularly. This contact intensifies Ngoyi's bitterness and Joseph's sense of guilt at her own superior levels of comfort:

> I feel so ashamed that I have a bed and get meat with my food, while Lillian has only a mat and blankets and gets mealie pap and boiled mealies. It is really terrible to be right in the midst of these African women and to be better off. She says too, that when she goes to have a bath it is in an "open place" with a stable door. I am not quite sure what she means, but it certainly is far worse than the ablution block where I go, despite its open toilets and half-door bathrooms. There are baths, even sometimes with plugs – and the little wardress Mrs Wessels, who is in charge of us, is delicate and considerate and waits outside the block until I am finished. (84-85)

Significantly, this guilty reflection comes immediately after Joseph's account of her gifts of flowers, "a stupendous parcel of tinned meats, chocolates, biscuits, liver sausage, spaghetti and heaven knows what," and the Colonel's birthday wishes (84). She is prompted for a moment to rue the fact that she is not permitted to share these birthday treats with Lillian Ngoyi, but ultimately her sense of etiquette towards the white wardress overwhelms her political or even personal obligations to her black friend:

> The only difficulty is that I am not allowed to share any of this with Lillian and this makes me feel embarrassed and even unwilling to take any of it myself. But Mrs Wessels, our kind-hearted little wardress, insisted that I have some liver sausage and brought it to me with such pleasure that I could not refuse. (84)

Her professed inability to refuse is a very different kind of compulsion from that felt by subsequent prisoners, or even Joseph's black contemporaries: Joseph experiences not the indignation or anger at differential treatment that we see in Makhoere, but an uneasy conflict between different sources of embarrassment which, for a moment at least, puts her on the side of her "kind-hearted little wardress."

The ideological space which Joseph describes above, in which neither gaoler nor cell is experienced as alienating or threatening, stands in stark contrast with not only her account of Lillian's complaints, but with the verbatim accounts, by Nelson Mandela and others, of brutal, inhuman treatment at the hands of the same system, from which Joseph quotes freely and at length in *If This Be Treason*. "We know the conditions of the Newlands non-European cells and are anxious about our friends" (64), Joseph writes, but there is no ready passage between her own present-tense accounts of her treatment and the perfect-tense reportage of Nelson Mandela, for example (68-72). In purely grammatical terms, Joseph's immersion in the moment of present experience does not allow her the moral and political distance in terms of which to weigh up her conflicting senses of embarrassment, which might have allowed her to move beyond such a symptomatic emotion to broader considerations of resistance or self-exploration. The toilet and ablution facilities of black prisoners are literally beyond her imagination, the racist symbolism of their diet erased by her own ample choice of foodstuffs, their brutal and dehumanizing treatment by warders hardly mentioned.

While it celebrates in often exhilarating ways camaraderie and commitment of non-racial resistance to apartheid, and is especially valuable for its dissemination of the voices of those charged and imprisoned with her, the chronotopes of Joseph's narrative bear all the marks of an essentially racist, bourgeois world. This is both a product of Joseph's own sensibility, her ingrained responses to a world in which white women share a social purview from which black women are essentially excluded, and to the particular regime in 1960, before 90-day detention, solitary confinement, deprivation of everything that renders existence human, and brutal interrogation and torture. Three years later, in 1963, things were very different.

The very title of Ruth First's prison memoir, *117 Days*, attests to an intense preoccupation with time. And it is clear, from the opening sentence, that in this narrative prison time and prison space are experienced together as peculiarly determinative and constricting. "For the first fifty-six days of my detention in solitary," First writes, "I changed from a mainly vertical to a mainly horizontal creature. A black iron bedstead became my world."[9] This is not an experiencing self presented *in medias res*, but the product of considerable later reflection on the ways in which the narrator was, from the beginning, a "creature" of time and space, one transformed in both material and psychological ways by a space that is experienced as cramped, claustrophobic, dirty, uncomfortable, cold, comfortless, and foul-smelling. Given First's lifestyle outside the police cell it is a world not only severely constricted, but also turned upside-down. The window, barred and meshed, is "a closing, not an opening," the "naked

---

[9] Ruth First, *117 Days*, 9.

electric bulb" burns as a "single yellow eye," the "gray prison blankets were as heavy as tarpaulins, and smelt of moldy potatoes"(9). In contrast to Joseph's domesticated "room with a view," First's description transforms the potentially domestic in the objects and spaces into the alienating and the oppressive. Yet, even in this opening description we learn of the powers of adaptation and transformation, even control and self-possession, on the most meager of terrains. First "learned to ignore the smell and to wriggle round the lumps on the mattress," and although she "feared to become one of those colorless insects that slither under a world of flat, gray stones," feeling that the iron bedstead was "like being closed inside a matchbox" (9), that shrunken world is soon transformed into a kind of "room of one's own" by her withdrawal into an interior space which is in effect the real space of *117 Days*:

> Yet the bed was my privacy, my retreat, and could be my secret life. On the bed I felt in control of the cell. I did not need to survey it; I could ignore it, and concentrate on making myself comfortable. I could sleep, as a long as I liked, without fear of interruption. I could think, without diversion, I could wait to see what happened, from the comfort of my bed. (9)

The world constituted by the "black iron bedstead" is essentially an inner world, in which the horizontal passivity of the body is balanced by the untrammeled activity of the mind. First almost seems to welcome the opportunity to be free of people and their impositions: she can think "without diversion," "concentrate on making myself comfortable," and, with the sense of control over her life that is the very antithesis of most detainees' experiences, sleep "without fear of interruption" while choosing to ignore everything that constitutes the physical or material space around her in a new-found "retreat" or "secret life." Fear, the quintessential emotion of the detainee, is reduced by the platitude to the irritation of being imposed upon; comfort, hardly likely on a lumpy mattress smelling of moldy potatoes, becomes a state of mind. As she reflects explicitly later on, the prison cell is a projection of First's fantasies beyond its walls of escaping from the uncomfortable and irritating pressures of other people, including her family: "for as long as I could, I would draw satisfaction from the time I had, at last, to think! Uninterruptedly, undistracted by the demands of daily living and working" (18).

Of all the books under discussion, First offers the most highly developed representation of an interior self, one which is not only able to withdraw from a threatening world, but which is also determined to present itself to that world (in the shape of the reader) as someone utterly disciplined and controlled. More than anyone else, she attempts to represent the process of that interior existence, often reproducing the passage of time as a stream of consciousness and self-consciously reflecting on the difficulty, not only of passing time, but of conveying its achingly slow progress. It is not surprising that First should have access to a chronotope that has become synonymous with modernism. She is well-read and highly educated, with a highly developed sense of the literary. When she is detained, she has Stendahl's *The Charterhouse of Parma* at hand to take with her (along with such unlikely, but characteristic, items as silk underwear, makeup, eyebrow tweezers, a mirror), and it is precisely this sense of the conventionality of prison behavior that allows her some ironic distance on her own thoughts: "Yet, not an hour after I was lodged in the cell, I found myself forced to do what storybook prisoners do: pace the length and breadth of the cell" (9-10). The abiding problem of detainees, the struggle with empty time, tests the apparent equanimity of the opening pages, which significantly acknowledge the inescapability of self-deceit: "It was too cold to sit, so I lay extended on the bed, trying to measure the hours, the days and weeks, yet pretending to myself that I was not" (9). Such pretence is like trying to play poker against oneself, and it raises a central problem of representation in the prison narrative. As First remarks, not a little disingenuously, "someone might ask me one day – when? – the size of my cell," and she would be able to give a clear answer. The interjected question about time, however, raises far greater difficulties. In the absence of events, actions, or characters in terms of which time may be materialized, it is exceptionally difficult to convey what is in essence the burden of the detainee's experience. The problem is different for the prisoner who is not in isolation, for although time might pass heavily for a convicted prisoner living communally, isolation strips both the self and the narrative of the basic means of continuity and coherence.

Confident at first that isolation will provide a much desired retreat from the public world, First soon realizes that "isolation and privacy" are "not the same thing by any means" (29), chiefly because her solitary confinement renders her totally dependent on her gaolers (her "enemies") for everything: "I had to shout or bang on the door when I wanted to use the lavatory. The wardress stood by while I washed. The daily programme, whatever I pretended, was not mine but theirs" (30). Both the sense of control that she projected from her "secret retreat" in the opening page and her claimed relief from external interference are recognized as self-deceptive, and by the time she is transferred to Pretoria Central Prison – "like being sealed in a sterile tank of glass in a defunct aquarium" – both the lack of human contact and the peculiar sterility of the new prison space begin to change radically her representation of time and self. Describing her imprisonment as an "abandonment in protracted time," First begins an extended description of the results of such a systematic and alienating "dissociation from humanity": "I was suspended in limbo, unknowing, unreached" (71). This sense of being in limbo, which is as much a product of the new space in which she finds herself as the lack of human contact, drives the narrative inwards, into the interior spaces of reading (the Bible), day-dreaming, and self-reflection. Her early project of self-sustained and self-sustaining thought ("I [...] tried to shake myself into disciplined thinking") is now rendered much more difficult, and First turns, like her contemporary detainees Sachs and Hugh Lewin, to the imagined world of an imagined novel to give a different shape to her situation, the fictional chronotopes providing a relief from the relentless burden of immediate "prison time":

> I devised a plot for a novel. The characters were me and my friends, all cast in heroic mould. We planned and organized in opposition to the Government, called for strikes and acts of civil disobedience, were harassed and chivvied by the police, banned, arrested. Then we were locked in prison cells and here I was again, grappling with life in a cell. I did better than that. I spent hours getting behind the political declarations of my characters, dissecting their private inclinations, scrutinizing their love affairs and marriages, their disillusionments and idle talk. When my imagination faltered I turned again to the Bible. I was ravenous for reading matter. (71)

Initially the novel offers First the chance to rewrite her life and those of her companions, but even her imaginary world is soon reduced to the constricting realities of her immediate condition. More significantly, however, First's novel, like her memoir, turns inward, becoming a means for "getting behind" her characters, for exploring and "dissecting" the very "secret retreat" that First celebrated on her opening page.

Just as the plot of her novel cannot escape her present condition, so one suspects that the "private inclinations," "love affairs and marriages" and "disillusionments and idle talk" of her characters are projections of her own life and concerns, and thus offer little escape from her immediate condition. That is why, when the imagination inevitably fails, it is reading matter from a source other than herself that First craves, even if it is no more than the scraps of newspaper wrapped around her sugar ration. Whether these are bits of advertisement, a paragraph or two from the Salvation Army newspaper, or merely a discarded prison identity card, First scans each one eagerly to "devour the words" (72). Tony Holiday has suggested privately to me that he and his companions in Pretoria Central and on Robben Island smuggled newspapers at great personal risk because, as politically aware people they needed to know what was happening outside. I am sure that that is true, but it ignores the almost ontological need that prisoners generally experience for language that does not originate from themselves. As First puts it, "perhaps a dozen words in all" on the identity card – semantically almost totally empty – "were like an archaeological find, proof that some people in this society recognized the value of written language and were able to use it" (72).

In his own prison memoir, Albie Sachs, detained at the same time and under similar conditions, records how he, like First, decided to "write a book" as a "way of fighting back."[10] But for him the problem of the chronotope – of finding adequate ways of not only representing but rendering material the imbrication of the particular qualities of prison space and time – is insurmountable. Written language, for First the archetypical signs of humanity and society, is for Sachs in detention an inadequate measure of his condition. He decides that only the three-dimensional materiality of the theatre will do:

> Yet a book is too flat, too controlled, too wordy and abstract. It requires pencil and paper and calm surroundings. In a book the material of life is rolled flat and sliced up into two-dimensional pages. I want something better, more immediate, with live people standing up and voices sounding [...] My present world has too much shape and volume to be compressed into a book; it needs air and height. The cells are too sturdy and real to be crushed into the flatness of words [...] I will write a play. (93)

Of course, Sachs never does write his play; he writes a book which reflects on the problems of representing prison space and time. He tells us not only about his play, but about his struggle to force himself to "think about the play, the play, the play" (94) in order to represent his attempts to force the passage of time. The three-dimensionality of Sachs' stage and audience ("I crave a response, a communication with live people" [92-93]) is, as his chapter title indicates, a fantasy, an attempt to free himself of a space and time denuded of the social by moving outward rather than inward in his imagination. First finds the movement into interiority and memory, not liberating and stabilizing, but increasingly disorienting:

---

[10] Albie Sachs, *The Jail Diary of Albie Sachs*, 92.

> I put myself through a concentrated self-scrutiny but in a scattered, disor-
> ganized fashion and I found myself not with clearer insight into myself in
> this abnormal situation, but with a diffused world of the past diverting me
> from the poverty of the present. I was appalled at the absence of my inven-
> tive and imaginative powers. (72-73)

Jean Middleton, writing her account some thirty-five years after her
incarceration, is able to account for such mental weakness by invoking
later psychological studies of the effects of solitary confinement, explaining personal passages of aimlessness and disorientation, which must have
been debilitating and terrifying at the time, as the loss of concentration that
comes with all solitary detention. Her distance from the moment of imprisonment, her subsequent understanding of its psychological processes,
and her focus on her imprisonment with other women mean that she devotes much less attention to the problem of coping with empty time or
time as such, itself a function of solitariness and inaction. First writes that
"minutes, hours, days, weeks are measurements of time for normal living.
For the prisoner in idle isolation, hours and days go by too slowly for them
to be acceptable measurements of time" (74). Time is thus not so much
measured in prison as manufactured, made, acted upon by a protesting but
also passive consciousness:

> I still had my watch. I glued my eyes to the small hand and tried to *see* the
> passage of time [...] I riveted my eyes to the window trying to make time
> pass in the activities of others, but I was conscious all the while of what I
> was trying to do and time, I now learned, did not move while you watched
> it. Like sand dribbling through an hour-glass the passage of time became a
> physical act dribbling through my consciousness. It seemed I had to push
> time on for it to move at all, for in my cell it had lost its own momentum.
> (74)

Time as a "physical act" "dribbling" through her consciousness shows that
under these conditions the mind's relation to time is both active and passive, or perhaps neither, lying between agency and helplessness. It is only
by engaging in small, Sysiphusian acts like folding and refolding her
clothes, packing and repacking her suitcase, dusting and polishing "everything in sight," filing her nails "painstakingly," plucking her eyebrows and
legs "one hair at a time," and stitching and restitching an improvised cal-
endar and the hems and seams of her çlothes and bedclothes, that First
gives herself "the impression that [she] was pushing time on, creating
days, weeks, and even months" (74).

These activities are, of course, highly gender-specific, as if the weight
of empty time forces consciousness back into mechanical, cultural stereo-

types, but they are complicated by peculiarly colonial factors of class and race. First remarks pointedly at the beginning of her detention of the ways in which the prison system as a whole perpetuates such stereotypes by continuing to privilege her as a white "Madam," above the menial tasks of domestic chores: "I, a prisoner held under top security conditions, was forbidden books, visitors, contact with any other prisoner; but like any white South African Madam I sat in bed each morning, and Africans did the cleaning for the 'missus'" (37). Notwithstanding First's ironizing of herself as "missus" in prison, it was, of course, a role that she played quite readily in her domestic and political life. Indeed, as her daughter, Gillian, points out, it was only through the labor of domestic servants who kept house, cooked, and cared for her children that First was able to sustain the political and social lives that she pursued with equal intensity, and the lack of freely available domestic labor in London put a strain on First and Slovo's relationship.[11] Furthermore, unlike her fellow black prisoners, who are stripped of all personal possessions, First is permitted to keep everything that allows her to preserve her identity as one of the "well-dressed Madams" in the gaol. Her representation of the behavior of black female prisoners who were performing exactly the same services for her as they would have in her own home is distanced and alienating. Even her admiration for the subtle acts of resistance in the form of these women's mimicry of the wardresses and her amusement at their polishing routine betrays her distance from them. She comments on their ignorance of their rights as awaiting-trial prisoners without intervening in any way, and even when she subjects herself ironically to their scrutiny by representing herself as she must seem to them, there is no sense that this perspective might forge some kind of solidarity between herself and them. If anything, it confirms their (and her) entrapment in mutually alienating worlds: "The cleaning session was a chance to get out of the cooped-up communal African cells on the other side of the building, and an opportunity to check on the police station talk that in the women's cells were sitting well-dressed Madams equipped with suitcases, pillows and thermos flasks, as though they had fallen on bad days" (38). If anything, First is quite happy both to cultivate and to project the image of a fastidious, well-dressed middle-class woman, both in terms of her own sense of identity and as a way of subtly negotiating differential treatment. As someone who considered her silk underwear

---

[11] Gillian Slovo, *Every Secret Thing: My Family, My Country*, London, 1997, 43, 102, and 112.

as important a comfort in detention as a Stendahl novel, First consciously projects herself as the very antithesis of the white prostitutes or black domestic servants who share the police cells with her to her gaolers, even if she does maintain a welcome ironical distance between the writing and the represented selves. Of her transfer to Pretoria Central Prison, she writes:

> I minced in my high heels and thrust my bosom out firmly, free to impress them, I thought, while I was still outside a cell. I was so preoccupied with making a dignified exit that I dropped the biscuit tin I was carrying and had to get down on my hands and knees to scoop up the biscuit pieces. (61)

The picture may be wryly self-deprecating, but there are other areas in which her middle-class fastidiousness is both asserted unselfconsciously and accepted by her gaolers. Her refusal to use the "po" – the sanitary bucket in the cell – and to bathe later in the day are not countered by the matron, and throughout her account of her admittedly excruciating isolation in the prison, First maintains her detachment with regard to the other prisoners, especially black women, although she does signal her differential treatment through her subtle indication of her own fastidious elevation above the noisy, crowded, communal discomfort of prisoners whose imprisonment by class and race preclude any choice or sympathetic concession: "But the noise did not last long and the stretch of the night slid into quiet and loneliness for me, and overcrowding in the fetid stench of downstairs cells for the African women who slept beside open sanitary buckets during the night" (71). This comment prompts the question whether for First there is any position between "loneliness" and "overcrowding," whether the communality that doubtlessly exists among the black prisoners and even the white prostitutes and drunks in the cells in Marshall Square is possible for her.

In First's view, to find herself falling back into the habits of the housewife or black servant as a means of making or pushing time means not only that she has succumbed to the inevitable pressure of solitary confinement, but that she has allowed intrinsic personal weaknesses to get the better of her:

> Life in suspension was a perfect trap for a meandering mind like mine. Daydreams replaced activity and purposeful thinking. Partly it was confinement in a vacuum that was doing this to me, but partly it was a succumbing to my own nature and to the difficulty, which I felt acutely, of thinking and composing systematically without the aid of pencil and paper. (73)

The need to think clearly and systematically, is a special mark of her memoir, although her guilty sense that imprisonment reduces her to the weaknesses of her "nature" is in fact the central aim of that whole system of incarceration that Michel Foucault ascribes to the rise of the modern prison, which, in its relentless modes of surveillance, aims precisely to turn the isolated prisoner inwards upon herself in a process of relentless self-examination and transformation. That First's need to preserve herself through her capacity to think conforms to the aim of her incarceration is made plain by an off-hand remark by one of her interrogators when she complains of having nothing to read: "If you have something to read you will not think about my questions, Mrs Slovo" (83). The studied formality and politeness of this remark furthermore confirms First's further entrapment even in prison within the identity of a white, respected middle-class woman. It is unthinkable that a black woman would have been spoken to in this way. More important, First is encouraged, no doubt both as part of the interrogative technique and because of her own undoubted sexual attractiveness, into an obviously sexually charged relationship with one of her interrogators that marks her essential ideological difference from a black woman in her position. "It was the romantic coup of the decade," First's daughter was later to write, "a gaoler who had fallen in love with a beautiful communist – and Viktor did nothing to subdue it. His eyes shining, he admitted he'd fallen for her."[12] Although there is nothing in First's account that suggests her own attraction to him, as Viktor later claimed, it is clear that their encounters were erotically charged. At her weakest after being moved to the "sterile aquarium" of Pretoria Central Prison, and after the horrible psychological blow of being released at the end of her 90-day period of detention, only to be re-arrested immediately, First responds to a policeman with above-average charm and intelligence out of a desperate need for human company and conversation: "I had not been aware that solitude was giving me a craving for conversation, any conversation, even with a detective" (83).

This is not at all unusual; indeed, it is a systematic feature of solitary confinement, clearly, as the remark by Nel confirms, part of the calculated process of getting information from detainees. Even Emma Mashinini records that she looked forward to her interrogation sessions:

> These outings – to the doctor, to the interrogation, to my visitors – served a very good purpose, because it was going out to meet people, to see other

---

[12] *Ibid.*, 84.

> things and most of all to see people. Even interrogation I looked forward to.
> And if they didn't call me for interrogation, I really wanted to remind them,
> because interrogation was better than to be isolated and all by myself for
> months. (85)

First's sessions with Viktor are, however, different, as they mark an unusual affinity between interrogator and prisoner which is ideologically and
historically determined. Many of the conversations that First records with
Viktor occur in the relatively relaxed and informal space of the car journeys on which she was being transported between prisons and interrogation sessions:

> There was conversation during the drive back – unlike the drive to Pretoria
> when Nel and Van Rensburg had ignored me after the start of the journey
> and after a few of their barbed comments had gone home. But between Vik-
> tor and me there was an atmosphere of bristling animosity. He was provoca-
> tive; I was waspish. And felt all the better for it. (88)

They speak of brandy, Viktor noting a brand that First recommends, he
brings her a bottle of eau de cologne in her cell, remarks on the fact when
she fails to put on lipstick and make-up, asks whether she had been wearing a nightie or shorty pajamas when he walks into her cell unexpectedly
while she is in bed, and when she asks provocatively whether he, in a flash
of anger at a remark from her, would hit her, his answer is explicitly
erotic: "'You've got a twisted mind,' he snarled. When his fist clenched I
tilted my chin upwards in mock acceptance of the blow. He had regained
complete control. 'I'd rather kiss it,' he said" (140).

One of the most remarkable achievements of *117 Days* is its acknowledgement of sexuality, even though it is quite clear that First as narrator is
attempting to reconstruct the contradictions of the relationship. One of the
contradictions is her own admittedly ambivalent erotic response: in the
Beatrice-like waspishness, in the provocative and inviting tilt of her chin,
in her guilty readiness to see him even when she is determined, like a lover
wishing to break up a painful affair, not to see him again. It is difficult,
however, to determine whether her knowing comments about Viktor as
part of a cynical interrogative system are constructions or interpretations
made from a later vantage-point: "He was exerting every muscle to prove
that he was different, susceptible to me, so that I would prove susceptible
to him" (141). Whatever the case, the erotic element of First's relationship
with Viktor is from the beginning also a process of surveillance. In First's
very first description of Viktor he turns in the front passenger seat of the
car "to watch me during the journey as we set off in the direction of Jo-

hannesburg," combining the scrutiny of the gaoler with an underlying sexual gaze. As their relationship develops he speaks to her as a knowing, indulgent, and paternalistic lover: "'I will never lose my temper with you,' Viktor told me repeatedly," and, more ominously, "I know you better after a month than people who have known you your whole life" (137) and "If you tell me anything it must be the truth, or I will know" (141). Of this dependency on her interrogator, First writes, "I loathed myself but it seemed I could not resist taking part in this exchange with another human being, talking, responding, proving I was not a caricature, a prototype, but a person" (140). She believes at first that "he was becoming a fascinating case study," but soon realizes that, despite his affable chatter about himself and expressions of concern for her, the power of the gaze belonged to him, not to her. She is especially exposed and vulnerable when Viktor begins to sit in on her visits from family and children, and her anxiety at his continuous presence, made all the worse for being apparently considerate and sympathetic, culminates in her inability to read a thriller with the forbidding title, *The Night of the Thousand Eyes*: "for the first time in my life I was afraid of a book, because the thousand eyes of the title were the force of telepathy and I felt the eerie presence of Viktor's scrutiny at the back of my neck" (142). Her attempted suicide is provoked by her sense of helpless entanglement after she begins to make a statement and realizes with horror that she has no hope of controlling the process: "I was breaking down my own resistance. It was madness for me to think I could protect myself in a session like this, in any session with them [...]. I was open to emotional blackmail, and the black mailer was myself" (122, and 127). Her intense scrutiny of herself at this point, and her discovery that a perfectly interior life is not sustainable, leads at the same time to an at least implied feeling of guilt at having succumbed to the relationship offered by Viktor. This is at the same time an acknowledgement of the depth of self-deception, signaled unintentionally by her description of one of her strategies for evading their interrogation: "I decided to play the fluffy-minded frightened girl in a spot, given to inconsequential comment, with an inflexible inability to concentrate and grasp the essence of a problem" (128).

No doubt First did put on such an act, conforming to a stereotype of female helplessness and fuzzy-mindedness that she assumes of her gaolers, but it is significantly a view which she repeatedly projects of herself in her interior struggles to cope with her imprisonment. If she pointedly tries to put aside thoughts of herself as a mother, First nonetheless is prepared – in the smallest details of passing time by plucking her eyebrows and wearing make-up to her interrogation sessions, in the only half-ironic projection of herself as an extravagant bourgeois housewife to her inquisitors and a "white madam" in her tiny cell to her readers, in the core conceptions of her interior "self" – to conform to conceptions of gender that have recently been subjected to critical scrutiny. Her daughter suggests that her relationship with Viktor especially "had hurt"; that "it was Viktor's treating her like a woman that had almost allowed him in" (92). In one sense, of course, her gaolers and inquisitors had always treated her "like a woman," a fact that First acknowledges through the inclusion in her memoir of other voices and stories which tell of the horrific brutality meted out by the same people who detained her to people who did not share her gender, class, or race. Certainly, both Slovo and First suggest that it was precisely because she was a woman that she was not charged in the Rivonia trial. What counts as "being treated like a woman" in South Africa is of course determined by immense ideological and historical factors. By the time that they "came again" (144), in the barbaric form of a letter bomb in 1982, Colonel Klimdt's claim that "we still have respect for women in our country [...] still have some feeling for women" (122) was, literally, history. But both Klimdt and Slovo might, with greater accuracy, have talked of being treated like a *white* woman, a difference of which Joseph, through the presence of Lillian Ngoyi, is at least self-consciously aware.

Jean Middleton, the last white woman in this study, was imprisoned at the same time as Ruth First, but her conditions of incarceration, and her representation of the experience, are significantly different from those of her fellow member of the South African Communist Party. Although Middleton did not occupy anything like as senior a position as First, unlike First she was indeed charged, and sentenced to three years' imprisonment in the notorious Barberton gaol. Middleton spent fifty-three days in detention, most of it in solitary, followed by an awaiting trial period with her fellow accused in the Johannesburg Fort. Her account of her experiences differs from First in three significant ways: it lacks the intensity of First's first-person interiority; it is much more self-consciously concerned with gender politics, both inside and outside prison, and it focuses on the problems of community, especially in Barberton.

If First was able to live an active, perhaps even hectic, social life through her political activities before her banning order, Middleton's political activism is precisely what alienates her from ordinary white South Africans in her daily life. She records that "underground work had the effect of imposing a sad isolation" (9), preventing her from making new friendships and even from maintaining old ones. In prison, too, Middleton is especially concerned with the tension, so characteristic of prison life, between "overcrowding" and "isolation." At first delighted to be put into an "unexpectedly large and pleasant cell" which "overlooked the prison grounds" and came replete with a "wicker chair," Middleton records that, despite the envy of her fellow detainees who are contained in "very small cells, with black walls some without windows [...] and with ceilings of chicken wire" (32), she is isolated from them, unable to take part in their relatively easy chatter. When she and her companions are split up and sent to different police stations in order to counteract their solidarity, she records the usual fears of prisoners subjected to solitary confinement, including the debilitating fear of self-betrayal recorded by First: "alone in my new cell, I felt acutely anxious, terrified, panic-stricken, almost beyond control [...] afraid of what I might do in a state of emotional disintegration" (36).

Unlike First or Joseph, Middleton's apprehension is fuelled not only by the fact that she is left on her own for four weeks to "think [...] before they came to interrogate me again" (37), but by feelings of extreme anxiety and vulnerability at the possibility of physical torture. Like First, however, Middleton retreats into a habitual gender role as a form of self-protection:

> I was very careful about my appearance, afraid that, if they took me by surprise and found me looking untidy, it would hurt my vanity and therefore put me at a disadvantage. I made up my face, went on dyeing my eyebrows and eyelashes every week, and wore the shabby trousers and sweater only at weekends, when I believed I was likely to be left in peace. (37)

In part, of course, this routine is a way for Middleton to exert some limited control over her life, and to maintain some semblance of "normal" behavior beyond the prison, including a greater degree of casualness over weekends. But the "vanity" of which she speaks is not lost on her interrogators, who characteristically play the "good cop, bad cop" routine by alternately complimenting her on her appearance and screaming at her that she is "filthy."

Throughout her account, Middleton is acutely aware of her "privileged" treatment as a "white woman," from the relative courtesy of her gaolers, to the home-made food cooked by a policeman's wife and her right to a bed and sheets, in contrast to the black men who were restricted to "one mat and one blanket each." She is, however, scathing about the ways in which women are excluded and disempowered within the libera-

tion movement, and the extent to which their contributions and their suffering was either downplayed or ignored after liberation in the 1990s. During their trial, their lawyers failed to consult properly with the women,
with the result that the men and women adopted conflicting defense strategies: "We should all have taken part in deciding our own defense; but we
had committed ourselves, and the line of defense was being decided at the
meetings in the men's gaol" (76). For the first time Middleton qualifies her
use of the first person plural, indicating that only the women in the group
fall within the collective "we." The men believed that the women were be-
having too militantly, especially in their insistence on singing in the van on
the way to and from the court, and in their outspoken defense of their political positions. Some of the men chose to downplay their involvement in
the Communist Party, even denigrating those who were members, a line
which worked directly against the women's decision to admit and defend
their membership. As Middleton puts it:

> for those of us who hadn't gone into the witness box, this was to be our only
> opportunity of speaking our minds in open court, the only chance we were
> going to get, of putting our point of view. We wanted the statements to be as
> strong and impressive as we could make them [...]. They were furious con-
> demnations of the unjust and racist structures of South African society. They
> were defiant. They expressed no regrets. (77-78)

Such defiance extended to the clothes they decided to wear to court, carefully planned to make an ideological statement about the "normality" of
communists:

> we felt that, in the media and in popular mythology, communists figured as
> maladjusted, unreasonable and dangerous, different from ordinary, decent
> people. Looking presentable in public was a matter of pride. We were going
> to wear high-heeled shoes, sheer stockings, our most elegant dresses and ap-
> propriate jewellery. (62)

These women, generally marginalized both outside and inside their political organizations, including the trial which was overshadowed by its most
famous accused, Bram Fisher, chose to speak forcefully both in terms that
are socially acceptable (dress) and in areas where they were generally silenced.[13] More significant, however, is Middleton's complaint of the ways
in which women political prisoners continued to be marginalized, even after liberation: "Though times had changed, the notion remained, that men

---

[13] The trial, as Middleton puts it, "became known as the trial of Bram Fischer and
fourteen others," 62.

were at the cutting edge of imprisonment, and women inhabited some ladylike and comfortable world" (117). She recounts a SABC radio programme on former political prisoners in which not only were all exprisoners interviewed men, but one of the men spoke on behalf of women prisoners, "mentioning what he called the 'general impression' of women's gaols, as being 'softer'" (118).

Middleton claims, on the contrary, that women suffered *more* hardship because they were more easily isolated, and therefore deprived of the companionship and solidarity that is crucial to the survival of political prisoners especially. "The smaller the group," Middleton writes, "the more intense is the social impoverishment of each individual prisoner" (118). First demonstrates the debilitating effects of such social impoverishment in the case of someone held in solitary confinement, and although Middleton spends some time rehearsing similar experiences during her fifty-three days of solitary, it is her unusual reflections on the tensions of communal imprisonment that makes her account singular. Very few memoirs by political prisoners in South Africa, male or female, black or white, speak of the burdens of community. For understandable political and historical reasons, most present a rosy picture of solidarity that, one suspects, resides more in ideological correctness than in consummation. This is not to say that community is not vital, nor that prisoners do not support each other. However, in a narrative in which the communal "we" predominates over the solitary "I," Middleton reflects on the fractured and fracturing nature of a small, confined, unchanging community of women in which emotional and physical deprivation systematically undermined the possibility of warmth, friendship, and support: "There is no doubt that we supported and saved each other, and that without each other we would all have been lost, but our relationships very nearly destroyed us too" (102). Habitual attitudes to others are turned by confinement into relentless aggression, "bitchiness," and a heightened emotional vulnerability exacerbated by the "misery and rage" of those surrounding one. Under these conditions of spiritual "aridity" a lesbian relationship seems to promise longed-for warmth, companionship, and support: "None of us were lesbians, and we sometimes remarked to each other that, if we had been, there would have been more softness, more tenderness, and certainly more enjoyment, in our lives" (101). This tentative speculation, in which sexuality is seen as the passage to humanity,[14] is starkly contrasted with male accounts of sex in

---

[14] See, for example, Middleton's account of their suggestion that a love affair

prison, where it is generally a preoccupation either with the excruciating absence of women or, more terribly, as a form of systematic violence in the form of rape, brutal subjugation, or underlying threat.[15] It is also tellingly undermined by the way in which she chooses to exemplify the relentless misery of their social and physical entrapment: "We wanted kindness and friendliness, but couldn't achieve it. It was like an unhappy marriage that those concerned couldn't escape from" (102). Menstruation, a constant but generally underplayed source of discomfort and humiliation for female prisoners, becomes for Middleton an important reminder of her own sexuality, so that when she stops menstruating the severance of this aspect of a fuller humanity overrides the convenience of the loss, which her male doctor can see in only practical terms:

> He was astonished that I thought it a serious problem. "This prison is full of women who aren't menstruating," he said, and added, "Do you really want to menstruate?" It was a sensible reply. Outside prison I had regarded menstruation as most women regard it, that is, as an unmitigated nuisance [...]. In prison, I regarded it differently; I suppose I felt it was one of the few remaining links with my sexuality (101).

Middleton's book is remarkable for the way in which it negotiates the difficult path between "solitariness" and "overcrowding." It sets out to tell the story of a group of people, in a sense on behalf of that group. It acknowledges from the outset the limitations of experience and perspective to which it is subject. But even when the narrative is most narrowly preoccupied with the suffering and experiencing "I" it places that self in relation to an outside world, to other people. Unlike many who claim that prison is either a reflection of life outside, or that it is only in prison that one's "real self" is revealed, Middleton insists that prison existence is essentially abnormal, distorting, and damaging, and that the "real self" is what one is "outside, in the real world" (102). Of course, that "real world" (in which, on one of her visits to the dentist, Middleton is reminded "how pleasantly people spoke to each other, how they smiled"), is a construct determined by the construction of the prison itself, its removed and desired spontaneity and friendliness perhaps overly heightened by the constrictions of incarceration, its similarity to certain structural features of

would make a particularly fierce wardress "better-tempered," 89.

[15] See Hugh Lewin, *Bandiet,* Cape Town, 1989; Herman Charles Bosman, *Cold Stone Jug,* Cape Town, 1969; and especially Moses Dlamini, *Robben Island Hell-Hole,* Trenton, N.J., n.d. For a discussion of attitudes to sexuality in male prison writing, see David Schalkwyk, "The Rules of Physiognomy: Reading the Convict in South African Prison Writing," *Pretexts* 7:1 (July 1998), 81-96.

carceration, its similarity to certain structural features of the penitentiary, especially in apartheid South Africa if one is a black woman, overlooked.

Anyone who reads Emma Mashinini's *Strikes Have Followed Me All My Life*, a biography not restricted to her incarceration, but the story of her general struggle as a black woman in which the sexism of black men is almost as oppressive as the racism of apartheid or the economic exploita- tion of capitalism, will be struck by the ways in which the structures into which Mashinini's life is forced systematically resemble those of the peni- tentiary. It is not as if Mashinini's "real self" lies between the four walls of the prison cell, but rather that the self is continuously shaped by forces that are not essentially different from those of the prison, confirming a deep personal sense, never conveyed by the white women discussed above, that apartheid South Africa was structured as a prison for black women. This is not to say that black women are deprived of all agency. Mashinini is a per- tinent case of a black woman who not only took control of her life as a trade unionist, but who also, unusually, writes self-consciously and criti- cally about her struggle against those shaping forces.

Black women are not a major focus of the narratives of Joseph, First, and Middleton, who are themselves confined by the structural separations of apartheid which are merely reconfirmed in gaol. Joseph's friendship with Lillian Ngoyi is strained by her own relatively privileged treatment, and she sees in the warders a gentle concern that would certainly not have been experienced by her black companion. Middleton openly acknowl- edges her distance from black women, encountering them only marginally or fleetingly as voices at the end of a corridor, or as the poor condemned woman who exists for them only as a plate of food that they dish up three times a day, the food itself a reminder of their difference from her: "Three times a day, we remembered the regulation white prison meals, which we so disliked and despised, were to be a privilege for her, till the last morn- ing of her life" (99). First, as I have suggested, is not only distanced from black prisoners by her satirical eye and her merely ironical description of herself as a white "madam," but, more significantly, by her quasi-erotic re- lationship with her interrogator. If black people are structurally absent from these narratives, Mashinini on the other hand experiences the over- whelming presence of whites as an unbearable intensification of her im- prisonment and suffering:

> But I was so glad – oh my God, I was so glad to see a black person, even a black police person. I was so sick of seeing those white people. To see al- ways white people, white people pushing your food to you through the door,

> white people pushing you and telling you "Come" and "Go" and what to do
> – it was making me ill. Because if you are black you have a need for people
> of your own colour. And with my envy of white people, now to be sur-
> rounded by them made me realize again how stupid that was, to envy their
> skin or hair. It was no privilege to be among them. It was a misery and a
> deprivation. (73)

In a narrative marked by its restraint this is remarkable for its intensity of
feeling, marked not only by the expletive, but by syntactical pressures of
repetition and parallelism. The repetition of "pushing" renders her as an
object, like the food propelled with such inhumane coarseness into her
cell, while "those whites" and "their" and "them" introduces a sudden split
in Mashinini's relationship to her readers. To be confined to contact with
whites only is for Mashinini as debilitating as general sensory deprivation
for other prisoners, and it is paralleled by her unusually painful response to
the blinding whiteness of the exercise space: "The first day I actually fell
to my knees, trembling to stand up, because this light was so bright and I'd
been so cold. It was blinding, blinding, this hot sun" (69).

Bearing in mind Dorothy Driver's acute observations on the ways in
which Mashinini negotiates a passage between the liberating philosophy of
Black Consciousness, which marks her mature rejection of white standards, and the critical necessity to "complicate and renegotiate the simple
reversals implied by Black Consciousness,"[16] we should not take this page
as an example of reverse racism. Rather, it is the product of isolation more
total than anything experienced by Mashinini's white counterparts of the
1960s, and intensified by the ingrained racial asymmetry of Mashinini's
incarceration and her difficulty in working through that isolation in narrative terms. Since her isolation was total, she has none of the communal resources available to Middleton and Joseph; the possibilities of her relationship with her gaolers and interrogators are totally different from First; nor
has she any of the narrative resources of self-consciousness and interiority
that are available to the more widely read and educated white woman.
Where First is able to reproduce narratively the strategies she used both to
push prison time, making it her own in a sense, and to explore alternative
constructions of selfhood, personal history and present defense against her
gaolers through a highly developed sense of interiority, Mashinini can only
gesture towards these aspects of prison experience. But that is not to say

---

[16] Dorothy Driver, "Imagined Selves (Un)imagined Marginalities," *Journal of
Southern African Studies* 17:2 (June 1991), 337-54 (p. 347).

that Mashinini's grasp of the forces at work in her incarceration and the country as a whole is defective.

Mashinini's narrative contains from the beginning an acute sense of an historically changing self, one in which earlier beliefs, attitudes, and experiences are represented and re-appraised by a later, narrating self, and her account of her incarceration is informed throughout by a grasp, presumably acquired after her release, of the strategies employed by her gaolers to wear down prisoners through isolation and deprivation:

> This is how they work. They put you in a room, and confine you there so that you must think you are the only person who is arrested and detained. They don't want you to be exposed to the knowledge that there are other people detained as well. (54)

This contrasts with First, who finds the knowledge that others were detained with her "selfishly reassuring" (26). Whatever is reassuring about Mashinini's understanding of the *modus operandi* of the detention system is, however, a later construction, incapable of assuaging the terror of the moment. Even from her perspective after her release, Mashinini can record her bewilderment, humiliation, and disorientation immediately after her arrest:

> "You're a fat, Kaffir meid," one said to me [...]. I was shocked, and all by myself, and it seemed everyone had an insult for me, that everyone who walked past had a word of insult to say to me. I was just in the center of a mess [...].
>
> My mind was concentrating on the journey, and inside I had a picture of my husband, and a picture of my neighborhood, and I was thinking that in fourteen days I'd be back.
>
> I don't know where we went. They took me many different ways, just to cause me more confusion, and they were insulting me all the time.
>
> But then we stopped, and I saw we were in Pretoria.
>
> I think it was then I realized I was really in trouble. I was taken to the offices and put into a cell. And I thought then, now I am under arrest. Now I am detained.
>
> Because to me, Pretoria Central Prison was a place for people who have been sentenced to death.[17]

Amid the confusion and disorientation of her external world, Mashinini turns "inside," not in the freely discursive and speculative modes of a fully developed self-consciousness, but in relatively static forms: the retained "pictures" of the well-known and the intimate that have been left behind,

---

[17] *Strikes Have Followed Me All My Life*, 53-54. Contrast this with Viktor and Van der Merwe's remark of First that "She's a nice girl," in Ruth First, *117 Days*, 128.

and in the truncated thoughts of arrest and detention. Once inside the prison "for people who have been sentenced to death," Mashinini experiences another kind of death as she is stripped, like all detainees, of everything that links her to a shared humanity with life outside. This stripping, usually described in some detail, but here conveyed through the emotional significance of a gold chain given to her by her daughters and her rings, leaves Mashinini, as she puts it, "just with myself. The bare me" (61).

Unlike First, Mashinini makes no attempt to represent the weight of empty time – the "physical act dribbling through my consciousness" – but merely records that she was able to record the passing days by "my meals and by dark and light, by how many nights, how many getting ups" (61). After the passage of two weeks, represented in no more than a half a dozen sentences, she dispassionately records the endurance of a self that has had nothing to sustain it, but which is now distanced, rendered as an alienated object, by the third-person pronoun: "And it was still Emma. I was still sane. I was myself" (62). Hovering between "it" and "I," Mashinini conveys the tenuousness of her grasp on her incarcerated self. As the dead time of isolation proceeds – broken only by the uneaten food, the offer of a bath after two weeks, the debilitating information that she has been converted from a Section 22 to Section 6 detainee – she records an increasing listlessness, a drifting from her early, active self into total passivity: "All my trade union experience of demanding to see and not being refused just fell aside. Even going to bed was an effort. I was just a lump" (63).

It is clear that for Mashinini isolation was an especially devastating experience, especially unremitting, a slow dribbling away of the self in the form of memory loss and paranoia, apathy and despair. This is especially marked by the terrible experience of forgetting her daughter's name:

> One day, thinking about my own children [...] thinking about their faces, and putting names to them, I could see my youngest daughter's face and I wanted to call her by her name. I struggled to call out the name, the name I always called her, and I just could not recall what the name was. I struggled and struggled. I would fall down and actually weep with the effort of remembering the name of my daughter. I'd try and sleep on it, wake up. I'd go without eating, because this pain of not being able to remember the name of my own daughter was the greatest I've ever had. And then, on the day when I actually did come across the name – this simple name Dudu, or "Love" – I immediately fell asleep, because it was such a great relief. But that was after days of killing myself to remember my own child's name. (86)

No novelist could have invented a scene more symbolically apt than this one. The self which is still reassuringly present after the first two weeks of empty waiting here dissolves in the very process of attempting to retain and re-enact the small rituals of normal community and intimacy. If Mashinini consoles herself on the initial journey to Pretoria through the inner picturing of her husband and neighborhood, here she goes beyond mere picturing, or even merely correlating names and faces: she wishes to maintain intimate contact by "*calling* her by her name" and her struggle is not merely to re-call but to "call out the name" aloud, as if to render her daughter present to herself. This crucial loss of memory is both a kind of death and a cause for the most intense self-affliction – "killing myself to remember my own child's name." We see in this passage the almost magical import of names for human beings, far more significant than a mere label. The "simple" name, when it comes, is actually a very complex phenomenon. Its very simplicity signals everything that is contrary to the brutal conditions of her incarceration, both through its meaning, "Love," and its signification of Mashinini's most intimate membership of human society, denied so systematically by the conditions of detention.

It is clear, then, that in her almost total deprivation of human company, Mashinini attempts to represent a sense of an enduring self, even if it is only to convey its deathly experiences. Absence, emptiness, nothingness constitute the core of that experience to the extent that it is reflected as an interior space, even during the momentary (and paradoxical) relief of interrogation, when the police attempt to wrest the "truth" from her: "Always they wanted the truth, when I had no more truth to tell. I don't think they ever understood that in fact there was nothing to give away. But they always tried to find it, this nothing" (75). Few statements could capture so succinctly the curious, frightening relationship between interrogation and "truth": not a manifold of real events waiting to be released into the present, but a fiction, a projection of interrogation itself upon the emptiness of the interrogated. If First experiences the process of writing in interrogation as vertiginous loss of self and an inevitable slippage into betrayal, Mashinini sees this writing as a way of escaping the constant bullying control of her gaolers, of regaining command over herself:

> I would sit and write, and write. And this was better for me. Maybe it was a way of being able to think what to say without for once anyone pushing me and going on – "Come on, come on, now. Speak." And being rough about it. (76)

What Mashinini writes about, in these written "confessions," is "my trade union matters" (75), supporting J. U. Jacobs' suggestion that the "confession" of autobiography is in its form a mimicry of interrogation.[18] But such mimicry is not uniform. Unlike First, Mashinini uses writing to externalize rather than internalize the self, thereby forging some sort of respite from interrogation from within it. This need to reflect the self off the world outside is conveyed in the following passage, in which she reflects on the sudden emptiness caused by the abrupt cessation of her interrogation sessions:

> That was it – bang. No word. Nothing about why. And I missed them. I thought once again I was going to be sitting in that room all by myself. I didn't think I knew myself any longer. *There was no mirror.* It's odd what happens to you when you don't see yourself in a mirror for such a long time. You don't recognize yourself. You think, who am I? All I had to recognize was a jersey which was sent to me by a friend. It was her jersey and I could recognize it. But I didn't know any longer how to recognize myself (87; my emphasis).

In its poignant simplicity, this is beautifully put, the other side of her terrible loss of her daughter's name. In the balanced images of mirror and jersey, Mashinini touches on the social as the foundation of the self, crystallized in her native proverb, *Motho ke motho ka batho babang.*[19] Without a mirror, in effect, without other people, self-consciousness cannot be sustained. What does sustain Mashinini's sense of herself "inside" are fragments from "outside": her daughter's name; the chain from her daughters and her rings taken away when she is arrested; images of her husband and neighborhood; writing of her trade union activities; and the jersey that negotiates a passage between these two "spaces": hers and not hers, inside and outside, a token of friendship and support from beyond the walls.

Her need for a "mirror" to reflect the continuing self is in turn reflected in her unusual refusal, bordering on paranoia, to respond in any way to the admittedly merely formal solicitations of her gaolers. In contrast to detainees who fought for, and eagerly accepted, the right to books, newspapers, and other personal comforts, Mashinini resolutely refuses to request anything from, or make any complaints to, the magistrate who makes his fortnightly visits. Those who fought for some kind of judicial control or monitoring – however compromised – of detainees could hardly have imagined the degree to which prisoners like Mashinini would see them merely as an extension of the system of detention:

---

[18] J. U. Jacobs, "The Discourses of Detention," *Current Writing* 3 (1991), 193-99.

[19] "A person is a person because of other people." This is the title of one of Jeremy Cronin's prison poems in *Inside*, Johannesburg, 1983.

> But I thought after all that, here is somebody who comes in as though he is a friend to ask me what I really need, and he says he will provide me with whatever I want. And all I said was that I didn't want anything. I mean, they can take you, isolate you, kick you, and then all of a sudden they find you a friend, as they seemed now to have. But I never made a request [...]. And when he said, "Any complaints?" I never made a complaint. It would not serve any purpose (64).

The whole system here is seen as totally "other," the formal, administrative roles of inspector and magistrate domesticated, so that an official request for complaints is read as the approach of a devious, hypocritical "friend." That Mashinini does not understand at least the theoretical separation of magistrate or judge and gaoler is shown by her claim that "they knew. They had their little window [...]. So they knew all was not well with me. They did not need to ask what was wrong" (64). On the other hand, in the light of other prisoners' claims of the mere formality of such visits, and the general complicity of gaoler and judiciary that has since emerged, Mashinini is absolutely right: "They knew." In part, this omniscience is experienced as the most acute sense of the panoptic pressures of the penitentiary celebrated by Bentham and acutely anatomized by Foucault:

> It was a very frightful thing, that window. Whilst I was sitting on my only sitting place – there was no chair, I had to use the bed to sit, to sleep, to do everything – I was always sitting opposite that window, which was sealed. But when I was on the bed, trying to sleep, not expecting anybody, I would just see two eyes piercing at me. All I could see was their eyes. It was very, very frightful. I couldn't get used to it. I thought, it's like an animal, to see those two eyes, and I'm in a cage. It was frightening.[20]

The quintessential asymmetry of the panopticon is astutely reproduced here: the prisoner unable to see out, unable to move out of the line of vision, incapable of exercising the body in any different space or form, unable to exercise the mind in any way that will alleviate the weight of space and time, constant suspense at being "pierced" by the eyes, disembodied, inhuman, "frightful." Initially different from First's opening claim to be able to control her cell from the "privacy" of her bed, it is finally matched by First's similar sense that the window is a "closing, not an opening" (16), her description of the "single yellow eye" of the "naked light bulb" (9), and her own intense discomfort at the peephole in her cell-door (29).

---

[20] Michel Foucault, *Discipline and Punish: The Birth of the Prison*, Harmondsworth, 1991, 64.

This is a torture, targeted as it is upon the "soul," as bad as anything wrought upon the body. As Mashinini puts it, gesturing towards the torment of that "soul" which in Foucault's view is the invention of the penitentiary: "These people gave fine ways of torturing you. They let you torture yourself" (65).

One of Mashinini's initial causes of bewilderment is the total lack in detention of the forms of courtesy and civility that frame ordinary human intercourse, and in a sense constitutes ordinary humanity. We have seen Middleton bewailing precisely the inability of her group to maintain such often overlooked modes of contact and support. The inhumanity of her gaolers is utterly confounding: in their abruptness, their rudeness, their insults, their failure to explain themselves or even to say why her interrogation would end, and it is signaled especially strongly in her refusal of the better quality food until it is explained to her, by the person who shows her the "first act of kindness," that everyone gets the same food, and that there are others, like her, in detention.[21] That act of kindness, together with the knowledge that she is not alone, signals a kind of regeneration of spirit in her, displayed by her sudden wish to clean her cell, to wash away all vestiges of criminality from it: "Why must I be sitting in a cell of rapists and people who stole cars and who were selling liquor? So I washed the walls as far as I could, and my toilet was nice and clean, and again and again I'd pour the disinfectant into it" (80). This is a telling rehearsal of Mashinini's earlier claim, before her incarceration, that a meticulous attention to housework was the only source of pride for black women as a whole: "We believed in cleaning those houses. They were our pride. What else did we have to show pride in? Only our little rooms were our pride" (17).

In a sense, Mashinini's newly discovered activity is a result of her rediscovery of community, and it is especially ironical that, despite the "most royal treatment one could expect" (91), her treatment in a Danish clinic for the sufferers of torture and detention should replicate the conditions of her incarceration in South Africa: in the loneliness, the loss of identity through having to adopt another name, the interviews themselves in which she is told to "dig and dig and speak about everything" (92), in her being told over again that she must learn to be selfish, in her fear of betrayal, and in the overwhelming whiteness that, as it did in her cell in South Africa, surrounds her. It was, as Mashinini herself says, "yet another

---

[21] A young white South African who has chosen to do his National Service in the police force, rather than in the Defence Force.

detention" (91), her release only "a kind of freedom."[22] Her return to public life brings her face to face with sexism and male domination in the
trade union movement that she had had to struggle against in every aspect
of her life, and the terror of continuous surveillance haunts her in the form
of her fear of speaking about her detention. But the ultimate imprisonment
comes after her return from Denmark, in South Africa, with the murder of
her son-in-law who seeks to intervene in a necklacing, and in the literally
unspeakable death of her daughter, Penny, which she cannot bring herself
to describe in the book. The book itself, however, offers a kind of release,
something that, like her writing about her "trade union matters" under interrogation, she has control over herself, in its personal history offering a
passage to another, different generation that was becoming increasingly
militant and intolerant of the weakness of its elders and parents: "This
book [...] is an opportunity for me to speak to my children" (110).

Caesarena Kona Makhoere's *No Child's Play: In Prison Under
Apartheid* is the voice of that different generation, proclaiming in its title
not only the harshness of imprisonment, but the putting aside, by one of
the "children of Soweto," of childish things. Makhoere was detained on 25
October 1976, after her father, a policeman, had revealed her hiding place
to the security police. She was interrogated, assaulted, tried and sentenced
to five years' imprisonment on 27 October 1977, after a year in detention.
This year – 367 days, 250 days longer than First's detention – is represented in six pages. The rest of the book, just over a hundred pages, is devoted to the five years she spent first in the women's section of the Kroonstad Gaol, then in Pretoria Central and Klerksdorp Prison. Although Makhoere spent long periods of her time as a convicted prisoner either in isolation or in solitary confinement, her detention, like that of others, was entirely solitary. After her conviction she did have the company of fellow
prisoners in both Kroonstad and Klerksdorp.

I emphasize this because it is indicative of the focus of her narrative,
in which an interior self is almost entirely absent. Certainly Makhoere
makes no attempt to convey the pressure of prison time through language;
time, the very substance of the isolated and detained consciousness in
other memoirs, is virtually absent in *No Child's Play*, which confines itself
to the description of action, event, and the unselfconscious expression of
emotions and attitudes like anger, indignation, condemnation, and self-
assurance. If Mashinini seeks a stable, recognizable self without at times

---

[22] This is the title of the chapter that records Mashinini's release and treatment.

being assured of it, the issue does not arise for Makhoere, who simply acknowledges the limits of her ability to convey weakness and humiliation: "The ordeal I went though still hurts today. Other people have described how helpless you feel, how at some point you no longer know you're human; that's how I felt" (8). Forced to try to describe the experience of confinement, Makhoere offers a perfunctory account, a mere catalogue of relatively abstract actions and mental states, time being counted by the very measures which First pronounces too crude to catch the slowness of its passing:

> There was nothing. Nothing. No bible. No reading material at all. I was there on my own. Twenty-three hours 30 minutes went by like this. I was taken for a bath. After the bath, exercise. Back in the cell. For the next 23 hours 30 minutes, speaking to myself, singing, laughing, growing paranoid, hallucinating. You think of all things.
> I got depressed. The anger, the hatred was building.
> It affected my mind. At about eight o'clock in the evening I would hear footsteps, and think, "These people are coming to kill me." It worked into my mind. (73)

At this most intense moment of solitariness, in which bodily stimulus and action are reduced absolutely, Makhoere uses the word "mind" to donate some kind of interior locus of this torture, but is unable to sustain a properly developed representation of self-consciousness. The "mind" of which she writes is removed, abstracted, a mere word, one might say, just as the second-person pronoun in "you think of all things" renders the "thinking" denoted even more general and impersonal.

One grasps well enough what she wants to convey about solitary detention, but there is neither an attempt to relive the experience nor the movement into self-exploration that this condition induces in First or Sachs or Lewin. In a very perceptive review essay, Dorothy Driver has remarked on the absence of what she calls "self-doubt" in Makhoere's writing: "In Makhoere's account generally, narrating and experiencing selves are rarely split, leaving no space for self-criticism or character development that autobiography and other first-person narration typically invite, and that Benson and Mashinini, to different degrees, employ."[23] Driver goes on to say that Makhoere's exclusion of any space for an inquiry into the constructions of the self in her writing means that "she remains 'in prison under apartheid' [...] even when she is apparently free" (353). It is difficult not to share Driver's unease with the relentlessly com-

---

[23] Dorothy Driver, "Imagined Selves (Un)imagined Marginalities," 352.

bative mode of *No Child's Play*, with its incorrigible presentation of a self given to total resistance, to "say[ing] No at every turn" (349). Gitahi Gititi has suggested, following Es'kia Mphahlele, that this stance is in itself an "aesthetic," although she, too, takes Makhoere to task for "political sloganeering."[24]

To speak of such writing as an *aesthetic* is, however, to review the notion that first-person narrative necessarily provokes self-criticism or character-development, or that a first-person narrative without these qualities is intrinsically defective. What Makhoere's narrative displays is a finely nuanced grasp of the protocols and conventions of ordinary social intercourse, the absence of which is so disturbing to Mashinini. By refusing to make any complaints, register any requests, or eat the food thrust at her, Mashinini refuses to acknowledge the people who treat her with systematic contempt as human beings, she refuses to share her humanity with them. This is a kind of resistance, although in Mashinini's case it leads to a loss of self, a collapse of a tenuous kind of interiority into the emptiness of the absent mirror or the fragile possession of a borrowed jersey. Makhoere makes this resistance her own, working through the public forms of language and behavior that the historical development of the first-person narrative has taught us to see as mere outward signs of an inner condition. When Makhoere insists that the warders begin their own sentence with her, she is insisting on the fact that they are incorrigibly tied to her and her companions through a complicated web of social connections. Underlying this sense is an unshakeable conception of a moral order: of the imperative of mutual respect and equal treatment. Makhoere's strategy is never to allow her gaolers to use these connections as a way of maintaining power over the prisoners: to insist that these connections be mutual, and that can only operate under certain conditions:

> Captain Callitz and this fool Du Plessis began to take the line that: "You people are never satisfied. When we give you this you want something more. Every day. I've never heard you saying thank you." And then we would ask them, "What is there to thank you for? To thank you for imprisoning us? Then you must be joking." (36)

A gaoler who expects thanks opens himself or herself up to the humanity of the other, to being rebuked by the withholding of thanks. This is what

---

[24] Gitahi Gititi, "Self and Society in Testimonial Literature: Caesarina Kona Makhoere's *No Child's Play: In Prison Under Apartheid*," *Current Writing* 3 (1991), 42-49 (p. 43).

especially upsets Mashinini in prison: the complete lack of common courtesy, of the conditions which make it possible, and it is in part what causes
her debilitating withdrawal into herself. It is in the logic of thanks as a
speech act that it cannot be demanded, and this Makhoere understands perfectly well, turning it into a devastating source of moral power over her
captors. When she refuses to stand at attention for inspection in the morn-
ings it is because she is expected to smile a greeting during that inspection,
and she balks, more than anything else, at the lack of mutuality in the
greeting: "That parading was disgusting, humiliating – how could they expect you to be polite to them while they continued to control your life, to
control your everything?" (54). When Makhoere and her companions in-
vent the "dis" – to disregard the person speaking, as if they did not exist –
as a weapon, they are collectively adopting Mashinini's refusal to treat
verbal transactions with gaolers as proper conversations, as interactions
between human beings.[25] The "dis" is so powerful because it denies the
humanity of the other, severing the contact that makes the exercise of
power possible:

> Now we took a resolution that we were not going speak to them: they knew
> our position. They would come and we would ignore them. We called it
> "dis," for "disregard" – you "dis," you give them "dis." That one weapon
> completely frustrated them, they became flustered. They did not know how
> to handle that. (52)

Makhoere's delight in this "weapon" arises not only from its effectiveness,
but also from the pleasure of their inventiveness, a creativity forged together and encapsulated in the relish with which she shows off the coined
word. This relish, born of a communal self-consciousness, is denied
Mashinini, who is unable to use the same strategy as a weapon precisely
because her solitariness prevents such self-consciousness.

For all the crassness of Makhoere's sloganeering, for all her uncritical
insistence on the unshakeable solidarity of her prison community (in stark
contrast to Middleton), and for all her unwillingness or incapacity to investigate through the first person the social construction and contradiction of
the self, she is able to pinpoint so precisely both the moral emptiness of the
penitentiary and its stupidity and to demonstrate modes of resisting it. A

---

[25] For an argument that the interactions between European colonizers and the original inhabitants of the Cape were mere "verbal transactions" and could not be said to
be conversations, see Anthony Holiday, "Conversations in a Colony: Natural Language and Primitive Interchange," *Pretexts* 4:2 (Summer 1993), 3-19.

great deal of that resistance lies in refusing to be compromised by the very framework of relationships between prisoner and gaoler that Joseph, Middleton, and First, in varying degrees, accept. There are of course precise historical and social reasons for the difference, although the peculiar quality of Makhoere as a person cannot be discounted. I want to suggest, in conclusion, that it is also connected to the nature of representation itself, to the different qualities of the "I" that writes these narratives, and to the historical and structural complicity of the narrative of self-conscious interiority with the very nature of incarceration since the eighteenth century.

In its extensive concern with interiority, and through First's own considerable command over the representational conventions of time and space as processes of an essentially *inner* consciousness, *117 Days* conforms through its representational form and modes to the very "technology of representation" upon which Foucault claims the modern art of punishment rests (104). This perhaps startling claim about the isomorphic relationship between First's representational strategies and the aims of the modern penitentiary is supported by John Bender's argument that "novelistic representation, which restructured the chaotic (though once culturally functional) experience inside old prisons implied a new kind of confinement – the penitentiary – conceived narratively on the lines of the realistic, *consciousness-centered* novel."[26] It may thus be that the narratively more sophisticated accounts of incarceration such as First's do not represent a superior and more commandingly distanced and self-reflexive grasp of the processes of detention, but rather reflect in very determined ways an economy whose purpose is precisely to render docile a body (and mind) that may be "subjected, used, transformed, and improved."[27] The "invention of the soul," which Foucault attributes to the birth of the modern prison, is reflected in relatively recent representational conventions by which "the penitentiary is imagined as the meeting point of the individual mind and material causes."[28] Unshaped by the sense of the soul that Foucault attributes to the penitentiary, and which Bender argues is similarly constitutive of the rise of the first-person narrative as Driver describes it above, the "I" of Makhoere's narrative is a different signified from the "I" of First's. Each "I" brings different rewards, explores different terrains, is able to withstand different pressures, and is liable to

---

[26] John Bender, *Imagining the Penitentiary: Fiction and the Architecture of the Mind in Eighteenth-Century England*, Chicago, 1987, 11 (my emphasis).
[27] Foucault, *Discipline and Punish*, 137.
[28] Bender, *Imagining the Penitentiary*, 43.

withstand different pressures, and is liable to be complicit with very different structures.

ON THE EDGE OF EXISTENCE:
ALEX LA GUMA'S *AND A THREEFOLD CORD*

Nahem Yousaf

Alex La Guma's *And a Threefold Cord*, originally published in 1964, can be seen as his first attempt at writing a novel rather than a "long story," as was the case with *A Walk in the Night*. In *And a Threefold Cord* La Guma focuses on dual protagonists: the unemployed colored Charlie Pauls and the unremitting rain which permeates every aspect of his protagonists' lives in a manner that is redolent of apartheid itself. Indeed, Brian Bunting described *And a Threefold Cord* as "drenched in the wet and misery of the Cape winter, whose dreary tones Alex La Guma has captured in a series of graphic prose-etchings."[1] La Guma has himself stated that he wished to "correct" the holiday-brochure impression that an overseas readership might hold about South Africa: "I am contesting the official propaganda of South Africa's natural beauty and trying to show the world that the tourist poster world of wonderful beaches and beautiful golf links is not the total picture."[2] From this one may conclude that La Guma's intention was to re-write the popular preconceptions that a non-South African might hold about South Africa and concomitantly to re-insert, into literature, the daily reality of those who did not form a part of the privileged white minority. Furthermore, the rain functions as a metaphor for the regime's relentless incursions into the lives of those it oppresses. La Guma was not unaware of the role played by capitalism in the racist ideology that forced certain sections of the South African population into squalor and degradation. Writing in *Sechaba* he asserts that:

> in the face of increasing forms of apartheid and racial discrimination in politics and economics, it is not surprising that the physical and social life of the Colored community is deteriorating at an alarming degree [...] Social prob-

---

[1] Brian Bunting, "Preface" to Alex La Guma, *And a Threefold Cord*, London, 1988, viii.
[2] Cecil A. Abrahams, *Alex La Guma*, Boston, 1985, 72.

lems which might exist under "normal" capitalist conditions are aggravated seriously by racial discrimination.[3]

On first reading, *And a Threefold Cord* appears to be a simple story following Charlie Pauls' attempts to maintain the shack that functions as home for Ma and the dying Pa Pauls and their sons Charlie, Ronald and Jorny. But whilst this might initially appear to be a reasonable summary, it is also somewhat reductive in that the Pauls represent only one family in a community that encompasses Africans as well as other colored inhabitants whose plights are shown to be markedly similar. The idea of community is of central ideological importance in this text as it functions to elucidate the proposition that group action is far more effective than the random acts of individuals. Indeed, the title of the book is taken from Ecclesiastes IV: 9-12 to indicate this position:

> Two are better than one; because they have a good reward for their labor. For if they fall, the one will lift up his fellow: but woe to him that is alone when he falleth; for he hath not another to help him up. Again, if two lie together, then they have heat, but how can one be alone? And if one prevail against him, two shall withstand him; and a threefold cord is not quickly broken.

La Guma stated in an interview that he intended to show that "while people have got their own problems, or what they believe to be their own problems, these problems are not actually entirely their own but they are shared by other people."[4] The issue of solidarity is an ideologically salient one, and the novel incorporates a number of incidents and sequences which speak directly to this feature of La Guma's efforts to raise awareness of context and consciousness. We are informed that in an effort to find better housing, the Pauls moved from the country to Windermere – the ironically named settlement, when one remembers the Wordsworthian pastoral of the lakes. It is to be assumed that this was also an effort to increase their opportunities in the job market, since in the years preceding the 1960s, the Western Cape was one of the biggest industrial areas in South Africa. Housing shortages in the area and rapidly expanding urbanization led to what has been described as "a mushrooming of squatter settlements in the Peninsula, especially at Windermere and Retreat."[5] These

---

[3] Alex La Guma, "The Time Has Come," *Sechaba* 1:III (1967), 14.

[4] Abrahams, *op. cit.,* 71.

[5] Yvonne Muthien, *State and Resistance in South Africa*, 1939-1965, Aldershot, 1994, 17.

in turn led to the development of disenfranchised communities in which groups were forced to live in appalling conditions with little support from white authorities but a great deal of hindrance, since the apartheid state's insistence on separate development demanded that Africans and coloreds live separately. It is in one of these communities that the Pauls find themselves, with Pa Pauls renting a piece of land on which to build his *pondokkie*, the description of which bears quoting:

> Dad and Charlie had scavenged, begged and, on dark nights, stolen the materials for the house. They had dragged for miles sheets of rusty corrugated iron, planks, pieces of cardboard, and all the astonishing miscellany that had gone into building the house. There were flattened fuel cans advertising a brand of oil on its sides, tins of rusty nails which Charlie had pulled from the gathered flotsam and jetsam and straightened with a hammer on a stone; rags for stuffing cracks and holes, strips of baling wire and waterproof paper, cartons, old pieces of metal and strands of wire, sides of packing-cases, and a pair of railway sleepers. (17)

The effort of accumulating the materials belies Charlie's efforts to maintain the "upkeep" of the shack. In the rainy season it takes all his energy to prevent the place from flooding or being swept away in the high winds. In fact, H. Britten in his *Report of the Commission of Enquiry into Conditions Existing on the Cape Flats and Similarly Affected Areas in the Cape Division*, was prompted to conclude in 1943 that the pondokkie "owes nought to any school of architecture." Its design, the report states "is determined entirely by the scraps of material which go into its structure" in the way La Guma describes, and, "piece by piece, scrap material is bought, begged or filched and added to make room for a growing family. There are no windows, ceilings, and very often no door. Sanitation is non-existent. Many of these hovels would do a disservice to animals."[6] Most significantly the *pondokkies* are considered unfit for animals, yet the racist system that relegates blacks to the status of animals prevents them from earning adequate wages that would allow them to rent the only slightly improved council accommodation. We are informed that Alfy, Caroline Pauls' husband, works hard, yet he is unlikely to qualify for, or be in a position to afford, council housing, despite the fact that he and his pregnant wife live in an old "packing-case." To compound matters, research into the context La Guma describes, uncovers that

---

[6] H. Britten, *Report of the Commission of Enquiry into Conditions Existing on the Cape Flats and Similarly Affected Areas in the Cape Division* (1943), 14. The quotation comes from Muthien, 38.

the cost of living in Cape Town was consistently higher than in other industrial areas. Despite the higher wage rates in the Peninsula, conditions of living in the squatter camps nevertheless reveal serious poverty and squalor.
Socio-economic surveys reveal that between 50-70 per cent of all African
households in the Cape Peninsula lived below the poverty datum line (PDL)
between the 1940s and 1960s.[7]

The backdrop La Guma creates in this novel is tied carefully and consciously into a reality that he had left behind; hidden from the tourist, it
preoccupies the writer in exile.

In the South Africa of the 1950s the colored community are either unable to participate in wage labor or are forced to accept a meagre return on
their labor power. In *And a Threefold Cord* we discover that of Ma Pauls'
four children only Ronny works and, on closer examination, only three
other characters in the novel – Alfy, Freda and Uncle Ben – are in employment. Of these characters Alfy is in regular employment, the nature of
which is not specified, whilst Ben's employment as a painter is reliant
upon the weather, and Freda is in poorly-paid work as a maid to a white
family. Yvonne Muthien has analyzed the coordinating factors that contributed to the vast majority of colored people being unemployed. She explains that employers preferred African to colored labor, believing Africans to be physically stronger and more reliable when compared to their
colored counterparts whom they stereotyped as unwilling, even alcoholic,
absentees, prone to be generally inefficient.[8] The predominance of this
level of stereotypical thinking underscores the paradoxical nature of apartheid: on the one hand it is a capitalist system that relies on cheap black
(African) labor in order to function, yet on the other it constructs strategies
to prevent the fair employment of – in this context – the doubly marginalized coloreds. To this end, the coloreds depicted in *And a Threefold Cord*
are forced to live below the poverty datum line, which results in their existence as an underclass. Free from the measures of the pass system, they are
nevertheless restricted in their movements in economic terms and in specific relation to the Group Areas Acts. This last point is somewhat lost on
Ursula A. Barnett who mistakenly argues that in La Guma's fiction characters may support a Marxist cause but that class struggle is relegated to
background. In emphasizing white victimization of blacks, she asserts:
"Although La Guma does not believe in thinking in color, he makes it

---

[7] *Ibid.*, 28.
[8] *Ibid.*, 75.

clear in his fiction that the conflict is not identical with the class struggle."[9] Whilst it is true to say that some of La Guma's characters support a Marxist cause, Barnett is grossly oversimplifying her discussion of capitalists as a reading of *And a Threefold Cord* makes clear. The white regime represents capitalist interests and to this end the police are also representative of capitalist orthodoxy, despite the fact that they may dress their activities in the guise of protection from and security against subversive elements.[10] In the South African context, the workers' struggle was part of the popular struggle and as trade unionist Joe Forster, for example, has pointed out, an "important effect of this development was that capital could hide behind the curtains of apartheid and racism."[11] South African apartheid and capitalism operate as interchangeable practices. The long-term effects of the process ensure that apartheid "nestled into a pragmatic accommodation with capitalism," to borrow Muthien's phrase. For Muthien the empirical confirmation is the formation of a black working class who were treated inequitably in a system where capitalists did not need to pay labor at the cost of reproduction.[12] The question that one should ask is whether that black population is aware of its exploitation and, if so, what it intends to do about it? In *And a Threefold Cord,* La Guma points quite explicitly to the concomitant relationship between wage labor and living conditions: the two are reflected in the regime's less than equal treatment of blacks both inside and outside the workplace. The desire for equal rights is not voiced in this text in an overtly theorized manner but, as I will show, the germination of consciousness, away from the fatalistic trope displayed by certain characters, is nevertheless present in the character of Charlie Pauls.

The limited choices open to those forced to inhabit the area are clear. Either they follow the communitarian line and become active agents in an effort to maintain community, despite the obstacles of unemployment and harassment at the hands of the security forces, or they become pseudo-capitalists and attempt to maintain a livelihood at the expense of their neighbors. La Guma juxtaposes these two options in the preparations for Pa Pauls' funeral. We are presented with Missus Nzuba who is willing to

[9] Ursula A. Barnett, *A Vision of Order*, London, 1983, 132.

[10] See Karl Marx, "On the Jewish Question," in *The Early Writings*, Harmondsworth, 1992, 230.

[11] Joe Forster, "The Workers' Struggle — Where Does FOSATU Stand?" quoted in Michael Vaughan, "Literature and Populism in South Africa: Reflections on the Ideology of *Staffrider*," in *Marxism and African Literature*, ed. Georg M. Gugelberger, Trenton, New Jersey, 1986, 195-220.

[12] Muthien, *op. cit.,* 31.

let Ma Pauls have water in order to wash the dead body before burial and in so doing represents what La Guma sees as a vital element in any resistance to apartheid: a communitarian spirit, and a desire to support one another intra-communally. La Guma underlines this feature of extra-familial support by making Missus Nzuba an African who, therefore, may be understood to be in a much worse position in relation to apartheid law than her (colored) neighbors. In contrast to this woman, he presents an unnamed man whose racial background is unspecified and who actually profits from the sale of water to the community. The torrentially heavy rainfall, and the problems that ensue for the settlement dwellers who struggle to combat its deleterious effects in their fragile homes, functions as a metaphor for the oppressive elements of apartheid rule. But La Guma adds another dimension to the life-sustaining function of water, namely its use in capitalist enterprise:

> Water is profit. In order to make this profit, the one who sells the water must also use it to wash his soul clear of compassion. He must rinse his heart of pity, and with the bristles of enterprise, scrub his being sterile of sympathy. He must have the heart of a stop-cock and the brain of a cistern, intestines of lead pipes. (72)

Kathleen Balutansky sees these two episodes – Missus Nzuba's offer of water for the washing of the dead body and the unnamed man's selling of water – as reflective of La Guma's desire to show how the devastating effects of poverty divide the community, "preventing it from achieving the togetherness necessary for its survival."[13] I would argue that his intention is actually much more strategically posed than this abstraction implies. La Guma in juxtaposing these two episodes, is attempting to demonstrate that capitalism has no strategic place in a community that is voiceless and marginalized. The first incremental steps towards opposing apartheid lie within the practices of the community itself, not outside of it, and certainly not in emulating white capitalist practices. In this last point, I concur rather with JanMohamed who writes that "the merging of the man and the product does perfect justice to the moral transformation necessitated by the economic exploitation of others."[14] The man is a man no more; he has in effect become the product – the heartless water pump – which is of more

---

[13] Kathleen Balutansky, *The Novels of Alex La Guma: The Representation of a Political Conflict*, Colorado, 1990, 36.

[14] Abdul JanMohamed, *Manichean Aesthetics: The Politics of Literature in Colonial Africa*, Amherst, 1983, 240.

value to him than the needs of the community. JanMohamed believes that in the limited community of *And a Threefold Cord* individuals are at best partially aware of their victimized status and are, consequently, self-pitying.[15]

But we also need to bear in mind that La Guma's nascent community is itself in a state of flux and change. In the context of the novel, apartheid regulations do not allow Africans, coloreds and Indians to live together, and the reader cannot fail to be aware that it was only a matter of time before the law would separate this mixed community. I would argue that rather than indulging in self-pity, La Guma's characters are actually, on the whole, distrusting of one another and that it is this that prevents them from uniting. To compound matters, the security forces are in such an unassailable position of power that the community can neither escape them nor stand up to them. In a Fanonian sense the "the settler-native relationship is a mass relationship":

> The settler pits brute force against the weight of numbers. His preoccupation with security makes him remind the native out loud that there he alone is master. The settler keeps alive in the native an anger which he deprives of outlet; the native is trapped in the tight links of the chains of colonialism.[16]

In *And a Threefold Cord* the unannounced security and police raids that the community is subjected to are exemplificatory of the dialectic Fanon describes. The rule of surveillance promotes what Fanon calls "auto-destruction,"[17] where "the settler or the policeman has the right live-long day to strike the native, to insult him and to make him crawl to them." In his turn the native is capable of "reaching for his knife at the slightest hostile or aggressive glance cast on him by another native; for the last resort of the native is to defend his personality vis-à-vis his brother." So, by "throwing himself with all force into the vendetta, the native tries to persuade himself that colonialism does not exist," and Fanon concludes that "on the level of communal organizations we clearly discern the well-known behavior patterns of avoidance."[18] This is most clearly the case with Roman who in his efforts to assert his masculinity – an attribute that is inherently undermined by apartheid – finds that the most convenient victim for his violent rage is his wife. Fanon's paradigm does not, however,

---

[15] *Ibid.*, 243.
[16] Frantz Fanon, *The Wretched of the Earth*, London, 1990, 42.
[17] *Ibid.*, 42.
[18] *Ibid.*, 42.

apply to Charlie. Charlie does not avoid the immediate problem of apartheid, and this is best exemplified through his growing political consciousness and his awareness of the helpless plight of those around him, most particularly Freda and Ronny. In defending Ronny against Roman, Charlie is simply fulfilling a familial obligation that is indicative of his realization that two are indeed better than one.

A number of criticisms have been leveled against *And a Threefold Cord*. For example, Abdul JanMohamed believes that, if we judge the novel purely on the basis of its plot, it is "a weak and paltry affair," only lifted out of such a negative reading by the strength of the descriptive passages which, in his view, are more important than the narrative itself.[19] In a similar vein, Vernie February suggests that a "concentration on external forces occurs at the expense of individual characterization."[20] What these critics fail to acknowledge is that La Guma is not necessarily intent on providing a mimetic representation of characters. The characters are not intended to act as his mouthpiece, but as autonomous individuals who act according to their own motives and principles, that are inevitably shaped by the overarching impact of apartheid on their lives. In my reading, once Charlie Pauls is established as the novel's hero, for the hero to function as such there must exist the conditions for his self-consciousness to be expressed outside of the authorial function. For Bakhtin self-consciousness is salient in breaking down "the monologic unity of an artistic world." In the world of the novel this only comes about when the hero as "self-consciousness" is

> represented and not merely expressed, that is, does not fuse with the author, does not become the mouthpiece for his voice; only on condition, consequently, that accents of the hero's self-consciousness are really objectified and that the work itself observes a distance between the hero and the author. If the umbilical cord uniting the hero to his creator is not cut, then what we have is not a work of art but a personal document.[21]

Charlie Pauls functions as a hero in the Bakhtinian sense precisely because La Guma does not interfere in his coming to consciousness. Even though the exploiter of the community – the water seller – functions as an example of the lack of community spirit, Charlie does not see him or comment

---

[19] JanMohamed, *op. cit.,* 239.
[20] Vernie February, *Mind Your Colour: The "Coloured" Stereotype in South African Literature*, London, 1981, 154-55.
[21] Mikhail Bakhtin, *Problems of Dostoevsky's Poetics*, trans. Caryl Emerson, Manchester, 1984, 51.

on him in the way that the reader might.[22] Rather, Charlie needs the memory of a conversation that took place outside of the community to spur him towards a critique of his own and his neighbors' living conditions. Charlie has advanced from the position held by Michael Adonis in *A Walk in the Night*, to become a more developed example of an individual whose perspective echoes that of Franky Lorenzo from that novel.

In the essay "Culture and Liberation" La Guma argues that "life is the stimulation of artistic endeavor" and "man's struggle to reach higher levels of civilization." For La Guma art should address "the central questions that involve life."[23] His ideas encompass the need for art to reflect life experiences ideologically rather than mimetically. In my context, his politicized aesthetic coincides with Medvedev's assertion that "all the products of ideological creation" are material, "having significance, meaning, inner value. But these meanings and values are embodied in material things and actions. They cannot be realized outside of some developed material."[24] *And a Threefold Cord* is that "developed material." In this novel La Guma deliberately draws attention to the inequities that exist between his black and white characters in order to demonstrate that the prevailing material conditions are responsible for creating a totally disenfranchised underclass. Consequently, Medvedev's assertions as to the realization of an ideological reality are played out in this text, "realized in words, actions, clothing, manners, and organizations of people and things – in a word: in some definite semiotic material."[25] In this way social criticism and political belief are enmeshed in La Guma's organized attempt to place his nascent community in a position of understanding, rather than passive acceptance, of its lived condition. Charlie Pauls is his primary semiotic material.

---

[22] This point is lost on Gerald Moore who argues, in a contradictory manner, that "La Guma has sought to show in Charlie the dawnings of an ideological consciousness, but he has weakened this by making it only a recollection of some half-understood words spoken by a 'slim rooker' with whom he once worked." Moore goes on to say that "La Guma could equally well have shown Charlie as coming to certain decisions by himself (as in his striking of the policeman and his taking in of Freda), without the aid of these rather adventitious appeals to the rooker and his opinions." See Gerald Moore, *Twelve African Writers*, London, 1980, 112.

[23] La Guma, "Culture and Liberation," *World Literature Written in English* 18 (1979), 27.

[24] P. N. Medvedev, *The Formal Method in Literary Scholarship: A Critical Introduction to Sociological Poetics*, trans. Albert J. Wehrle, Baltimore and London, 1978, 7.

[25] *Ibid.*, 7.

Charlie Pauls is surrounded by people who exist in a condition of helplessness and ignorance, apparently devoid of the desire to resist their allocated status. For example, Ma Pauls and Uncle Ben are both drowning in the quagmire of their religious beliefs, advocating the view that their subordinate position is not a result of apartheid at all. Ma Pauls, in talking about life with her husband, opines:

> He worked for his family and when he couldn't work no more, he lay down and waited for the Lord Jesus to take him away. Now he's gone away to the Lord and he's away from sickness and hunger and gone to rest from his work. He carried his cross, too, like Our Lord Jesus, and now the burden is taken from off his shoulders. (67)

This kind of stoical resignation is also present in Uncle Ben with his "We got to trust in the Lord" (49). It is arguably such abject reliance on an otherworldly power, with resignation bordering on defeat, that prompts Charlie to recall the words of a pipe-laying workmate he met whilst working away in Calvinia:

> Always reading newspapers and things. He said to us, the poor don't have to be poor [...] This burg say, if the poor people all got together and took everything in the whole blerry world, there wouldn't be poor no more. Funny kind of talk, but it sounded awright [...] Further, this rooker say if all the stuff in the world was shared out among everybody, all would have enough to live nice. He reckoned people got to stick together to get this stuff. (49-50)

Although it is easy for Uncle Ben to dismiss this as "communis' things. Talking against the govverment" (50), Charlie cannot finally dismiss the words which are symptomatic of the growing consciousness that has taken root in him. The pipe-layer functions to initiate Charlie's politicization. Volosinov articulates this in terms of a linguistic exchange:

> I give myself verbal shape from another's point of view, ultimately, from the point of view of the community to which I belong. A word is a bridge thrown between myself and another. If one end of the bridge depends on me, then the other depends on my addressee. A word is territory shared by both addresser and addressee, by the speaker and his interlocutor.[26]

In participating in the conversation about the pipe-layer's words, Ben unconsciously allows Charlie the opportunity to address an essential issue, namely the question raised earlier in this chapter, why are blacks marginal-

---

[26] V. N. Volosinov, *Marxism and the Philosophy of Language*, trans. Ladislav Matejka and I. R. Titunik, Cambridge, MA, and London, 1973, 86.

ized under apartheid, and what can they do to ease their oppression? In this act of dialogue, Charlie reaches a new understanding of his poverty-ridden situation. For Charlie it cannot simply be that the good Lord deems it so; it is rather that whites will not allow blacks equality of opportunity and equal rights. Charlie considers the *burg*'s comments and concludes that they "sounded awright," which is indicative of the fact that he has not yet fully assimilated the meaning behind the words of his interlocutor. However, he has reached a level of understanding that Bakhtin describes as "active," whereby the word is assimilated into "its own conceptual system filled with specific objects and emotional expressions, and is indissolubly merged with the response, with a motivated agreement or disagreement." In this way, "primacy belongs to the response, as the activating principle: it creates the ground for understanding, it prepares the ground for an active and engaged understanding. Understanding comes to fruition only in the response. Understanding and response are dialectically merged and mutually condition each other; one is impossible without the other."[27] To this I would add that the word is not finalized at the point of utterance, but has the potential to live in the memory of its intended recipient, the ability to be recalled at another, opportune moment. Charlie recalls and reworks the words he heard uttered at Calvinia, as an initial stage in his approaching understanding of his condition and context.

La Guma shows that a gradual cumulative understanding of one's environment is possible, but that it will be a slow process if it is left in the hands of one individual rather than in the hands of the community. Marx's statement that liberation is an "historical and not mental act," brought about by "historical conditions, the development of industry, commerce, agriculture" but most importantly by "the conditions of intercourse" is given resonance in this context.[28] In the first instance the marginalized community is denied equal access to labor, and is therefore victim to the ideas of the ruling class that are "at the same time its ruling intellectual force." This entails a recognition that the class that controls material production also controls mental production so that "the ideas of those who lack the means of mental production are subject to it."[29] La Guma identifies the victims of this ideological brainwashing as ordinary people like Ma Pauls and Uncle Ben. Religious indoctrination acts as the ideology

---

[27] Mikhail Bakhtin, *The Dialogic Imagination*, trans. C. Emerson and M. Holquist, Austin, 1981, 282.
[28] Karl Marx and Frederick Engels, *The German Ideology,* London, 1989, 61.
[29] *Ibid.*, 64.

controlling the ordinary people, the people who cannot or will not contemplate political action as a means of altering their lived conditions. Those who privilege the teachings of the church above all else also place their trust outside of the political community that has the potential to help them in concrete ways. Scepticism about political action is quite clearly present in the notion that community, in this case predicated on Christianity, is "better" than individualism which is misunderstood as politics. Charlie's idea that the poor people should form a union is dismissed by Uncle Ben with, "Sound almost like a sin, that. Bible say you mustn't covet other people's things" (50). Ben's mindset is as rigid and unbending – and as unworldly – as a missionary-education statement:

> It is our belief that with the spread of better understanding in Church and college circles the future of South Africa is one we can contemplate with a fair degree of optimism in the hope that Christian influences will dispel illusions, transcend the mistaken political expedients of pseudo-segregationists and usher in a South Africa of racial peace and goodwill.[30]

Uncle Ben and Ma Pauls firmly represent the type of thinking characterized by one Christian spokesperson in the belief that communism should be rejected because it "stood for violence" and a "crass, materialistic [...] outlook on life which rejects all religious and moral idealism."[31] But La Guma is not suggesting that religion and politics are not commensurate with each other, and this is best exemplified through Charlie's response to Ben: "Bible say love your neighbor, too" (50). La Guma's point is simply that one should use any means necessary to educate the masses into understanding the ramifications of the oppressive conditions they endure. Whilst it is true that Charlie Pauls will not follow his parents' lead and trust in the Lord, he is capable of understanding that unity is an essential element in mass resistance, and can discern that the Church might have a role to play, even if, at this stage, it is aimed at the older generation who need to be educated out of their current monologic mindset.

Marx's oft-quoted idea that "the mode of production of material life conditions the social, political, and intellectual life process" and that it is the social that determines the population's consciousness, has a significant

---

[30] From D. D. T. Jabavu, *The Segregation Fallacy and Other Papers*, Alice (1928) quoted in Gail M. Gerhart, *Black Power in South Africa: The Evolution of an Ideology*, Berkeley, 1978, 24.
[31] R. Philips "Communism or Christianity: The Present Day Question for Native Youth," *South African Outlook*, 1st August 1929, 148, quoted in Gerhart, 38.

impact on the unemployed Charlie.[32] He is gradually coming to the realization that, in order to maintain its hegemonic position, the regime "strives to impart a supraclass, external character to the ideological sign, to extinguish or drive inward the struggle between social value judgments which occurs within it, to make the sign unaccentual."[33] This is the process of silencing the majority, and beating it into submission. It is a process of reinforcing the monologic nature of apartheid. The war that Charlie initially has to wage is centered within his community; he has to demonstrate that the real enemy is the white apartheid regime, and that it is the regime that is responsible for characters like the drunken Ria, the prostitute Susie, and the bully Roman. By denying these characters subjectivity, the apartheid structure devalues their self-worth and self-esteem, leaving them locked in the petty lives they lead, without the option to escape its ever-tightening grasp.

Charlie's growing political awareness functions to exemplify the fact that, in order to break free of the manicheanism that is the lot of the majority population, individual antagonisms need to be left to one side and a degree of solidarity is required to smash the regime. In recalling the words of his pipe-laying mate, Charlie understands that mobilization of the people at events other than funerals and celebrations is not only necessary, but essential if things are to change for the better. The ruling ideology curtails individual thinking and prevents La Guma's characters from realizing that there is another way of life, a way of living that is not predicated on the laws of apartheid. Medvedev's statement that "the ideological environment is the realized, materialized, externally expressed social consciousness of a given collective" is particularly pertinent in the apartheid context where the epistemic violence that *is* apartheid has taken root in the minds of the community. Medvedev bases his analysis in the belief that the ideological environment is determined by political and economic pressures that constrain individual consciousness. These are the decisive factors in the articulation of collective consciousness.[34] Curtailed in this way, Charlie finds himself pitting his wits against his community, precisely because he has come to the specific realization that black people are not inferior to whites. The introverted violence in which blacks turn their anger against each other is sanctioned by the regime precisely because it deflects attention from the regime's oppressive constraints on all blacks. This is a point

---

[32] Karl Marx, *Selected Writings*, Oxford, 1990, 389.
[33] Volosinov, *op. cit.,* 23.
[34] Medvedev, *op. cit.,* 14.

that I will return to in my discussion of the border metaphor in *And a Threefold Cord.*

The highway that cuts across the South African landscape in this novel encapsulates the division between the whites who enjoy all the social benefits and the blacks who are forced to inhabit the squalor of the shanty towns dotted around the Cape. The physical presence of the border marks off those who are economically, socially and politically powerless. The border is more than a physical presence in that it functions as a powerful metaphor for the South African apartheid situation. In the case of George Mostert, whose garage nestles just on the right side of the highway, the border functions to signify a division between purity and impurity: in his thinking and that of his two white customers, crossing the border into the shanty town will result in inevitable pollution and contamination. The narrator glosses this situation with indications that Mostert is "trapped in his glass office by his own loneliness and a wretched pride in a false racial superiority" (38). Conversely, the blacks who inhabit the shanty town are forced to trek across the highway in search of discarded materials in order to maintain their *pondokkies*. Charlie Pauls' crossing the highway is likened to a cockroach crossing the floor, indicating the belittling humility he feels in his honest task. Once in the presence of Mostert, Charlie is forced to play the role of the subservient other:

> "I say, Mister George, I must ask you another pleasure. Other time you give me some scrap to fix up the house. Now the blerry roof is leaking. Rain coming into the blerry house. Well, I reckon, you *mos* give me that stuff last time – "
>
> George Mostert sensed the praise and he cut in, "You want some more scrap?" (39)

This occurs despite the fact that Mostert appears to look forward to the visits from the shanty dwellers; they sporadically alleviate his loneliness while also serving to re-establish his superior position. The point that La Guma makes here is interesting: Mostert is not ill-judged; he is presented as a simple man, living a simple life, yet the subject position that Charlie adopts is called into question. Why, for example, does he feel the need to present a humble and groveling demeanor? The reason seems obvious: the colored man has been conditioned into thinking that this is the appropriate way to address whites. It is only after Charlie recalls his conversation in Calvinia and later hits out at the police officer that his attitude towards whites changes and, consequently, his awareness is heightened as to the effects such debilitating role-playing and border crossings wreak on his internal coherence.

Kathleen Balutansky equates the shanty town and Mostert's garage, believing each of them to be victims of progress left to rot in the face of the highway that passes them by. She believes the descriptions of each "make a clear statement about their similarity in status: they are both wretchedly poor and they are both left behind by the fast developing wealth of the city." In her view, the highway "may separate Mostert's garage from the shantytown, but it passes them both as its smooth asphalt leads the shining cars and loaded trucks to the prosperous bustle of Cape Town."[35] I would argue that these two physical locations are, in fact, antithetical: Windermere faces Mostert's garage across the highway which acts as the border. La Guma describes the setting in this way:

> The highway from the city unreeled like dark, wet adhesive, pasted like a strip across the country, curving in places where it seemed to have come unstuck from the moist surface of the land. The Service Station and Garage stood just off one of these curves in the road where it navigated a bulge of gum, green portjackson wood and wattle, as it by-passed a string of suburbs.
>
> Like a lone blockhouse on a frontier, it stood against the dark-green background of trees, with an air of neglect surrounding it, as if deserted by its garrison and left to crumble on the edge of hostile territory. (36)

The border/frontier metaphor is most appropriate when one considers issues of transgression and punishment; the white George Mostert can leave whereas the coloreds cannot. This last point is made in opposition to Barnett who unthinkingly reproduces apartheid-speak by stating that "George Mostert [...] is as much a victim of poverty as the *brown* and *black* people in the shanty-town around him."[36] This is precisely the equation that La Guma erects in order to refute; Mostert's false pride in his superiority might make him a victim but, as a white man, he is neither inescapably marginalized nor voiceless like the blacks around him. In this context, Medvedev's assertion that "ideological creation and its comprehension only take place in the process of social intercourse" has particular resonance.[37] The ideology that underpins apartheid is reinforced for George Mostert in his connection to the white world, particularly through his conversation with the white customer who stops for petrol:

---

[35] Balutansky, *op. cit.,* 40.
[36] Barnett, *op. cit.,* 132. Emphasis added.
[37] Medvedev, *op. cit.,* 7.

> He [...] gazed across the road. Beyond the opposite edge and the growth of brushwood, the roofs of the shantytown were scattered like gray and brown rocks along a coastline. A cloud of smoke was dwindling in the white-gray air above it.
>
> "What's that?" he asked George Mostert [...]
>
> "That?" George Mostert said, [...] "Oh, jus' one of those slum places."
>
> "Christ, I bet it's mucky as hell. Wonder why the authorities don't clear the bloody lot out. Just brings disease and things." He stared out across the road. "If I had any say, I'd pull down the wholly bally lot and clear 'em out." He shook his head and the wisps of hair, like straw, fluttered. "I don't know what we poor buggers pay taxes for." (106-107)

At a simplistic level this conversation may appear one-sided, with the white, possibly English, customer doing all the talking and instigating the negative comments. But, George Mostert is complicit in such racist thinking by virtue of his silence, which is further compounded when one re-members that an earlier conversation with Charlie evolved into one which was predicated on an almost equal footing. One also notes the fear that the customer expresses towards the shanty community, seeing the men and women as the harbingers of diseases, which aligns his thinking with the fear of "miscegenation" that lurks in the mind of George Mostert. Charlie extends an invitation to Mostert to have a "wake up time" with the inhabi-tants of the settlement and this familiarity prompts Mostert's initial re-sponse of "I don't want any trouble," before he succumbs with the thought that "Nobody would see." He is most concerned that no *white person* should see him fraternizing with the *pondokkie* inhabitants. But, when Charlie continues – "I tell you, I was in Egypt with the war. Had me a French goose in Alexandria. *She* didn't min' what color men she took in. All the blerry same to *her*" – the reaction is aversion: "George Mostert looked a little shocked and ashamed at hearing a white woman talked about in this way" (40).

Charlie's efforts at inclusivity prompt Mostert swiftly to change the subject in order to regain the upper hand, which epitomizes Homi Bhabha's theory that issues of cultural difference emerge at points of so-cial crisis, so that questions of identity are agnostic; "identity is claimed either from a position of marginality or in an attempt at gaining the center: in both senses, ex-centric."[38] It is important for Mostert to demonstrate his *difference* from Charlie, whilst at this stage, Charlie might be seen to rep-

---

[38] Homi Bhabha, *The Location of Culture*, London, 1994, 177.

resent Fanon's notion that the black man has a choice either to turn white or disappear, in that he might be seen to emulate a white man in his action of sleeping with a white woman. Bhabha disagrees with Fanon's assertion that the choice remains restricted to two options when he posits that there is "the more ambivalent, third choice: camouflage, mimicry, black skins / white masks."[39] Bhabha's assertion involves making a *political* choice, and I would argue that Charlie, in choosing to retell this event, is making a partially veiled political point: why shouldn't black and white people live together in some sort of harmony? This is further reinforced by La Guma in his delineation of the shanty town that comprises Africans and coloreds who are prepared to share their limited resources in an effort to instill an egalitarian community spirit.

In discussing the geopolitical environment patterned to include the Susie Meyers, Roman and Ronny Pauls triangle in the novel, Balutansky suggests that La Guma negates hope in their future since they turn their anger on each other and "wallow in their failure and despair."[40] She describes Ronald as a "delinquent adolescent who commits murder out of spite" which risks the implication that blacks inherently translate their emotions into violence and perpetrating acts of violence without logical foundation or motive. More troubling still, she seems to accept and even endorse a belief in inexorable degradation. Balutansky aligns her thinking with Cecil A. Abrahams' equation that the poor living conditions forced upon the *pondokkie* dwellers result in their allegiance to "cheap liquor, prostitution, family quarrels and violence"[41] which betrays a deterministic analysis. Instead, I would argue that La Guma is intent on demonstrating that it is possible to survive *and* to contribute to the community *despite* the living conditions dictated by apartheid ideology. To this end he presents a much more balanced picture of Windermere's inhabitants than previous critics allow. On the night of the police raid the reader is introduced to the feisty Aunty Mina who is not prepared to stand any nonsense from the po-

---

[39] *Ibid.*, 120.

[40] Balutansky, *op. cit.,* 43.

[41] Abrahams, *op. cit.,* 91. From a historical perspective see also, D. Welsh who in "The Growth of Towns" says: "it should be understood that the town is a European area in which there is no place for the redundant Native, who neither works nor serves his or her people but forms the class from which the professional agitators, the slum landlords, the liquor sellers, the prostitutes and other undesirable classes spring." In *The Oxford History of South Africa,* vol. 2, eds Monica Hunter Wilson and Leonard Thompson, quoted in Gerhart, *op. cit.,* 23.

lice officers. This woman, "thick and dark as an oak" stands her ground and uses her anger as a platform for protest:

> "Look here, captain, I'm not giving a damn what you say about it, but what for I'm standing in this rain? You tell me."

> The officer laughed. He was arrogantly cheerful, and thought this fat old aunty was rather fun. He had had altercations with her before. He laughed, "Alright, Mina. We'll give you a nice dry van all to yourself. Then you can have a private cell until you appear before the magistrate."

> Aunt Mina poked the umbrella at him. It had broken in the wind and rain and now consisted of a handle, a flap of cloth, and several frightful spikes, dangerous as some medieval instrument of torture. The officer reared backwards, fearful of his eyes.

> "I'm not frighting for your magistrate, colonel. I paid seven fines awready and I can pay seven more. There! What I'm wanting to know is what for in this rain, hey? You tell me." She possessed the ferocity of an old African buffalo. (90)

Aunty Mina is in trouble not because she does not have a pass, but because she brews and sells beer in order to remain economically independent, an illegal act under a government who refused to promote the selling of alcohol in a community-organized way, preferring the promotion of beer halls that were easier to raid and control.[42] Roman and Ronny's behavior may seem to exemplify a dissipated and disaffected lifestyle, in many ways, but others like Freda and Missus Mbuza and even the irascible Aunty Mina, herself the proprietor of a shebeen, avoid reacting in this way.

In the heterogeneous community he creates, La Guma also demonstrates the hybrid nature of language in the context of black South Africa and illustrates the ways in which such language can be commandeered to resist the dominant apartheid-sanctioned Afrikaans. Vernie A. February in *Mind Your Colour: The "Coloured" Stereotype in South African Literature* argues that La Guma uses "the language of the poor, that peculiar mixture of English and Afrikaans, which I shall refer to as *Englikaans*. This type of language seems to define the oppressive circumstances as well as the tragic-comic position of the poor."[43] Although, of course, English was hardly a non-oppressive language, given British colonization,

---

[42] See, for example, Elizabeth Thaele Rivkin, "The Black Woman in South Africa: An Azanian Profile," in Filomena Steady, *The Black Woman Cross-Culturally*, 215-29, for her discussion of the beer demonstrations of the late 1950s.

[43] February, *op. cit.,* 156.

February's "Englikaans" is more usefully reflective of Bhabha's assertion that the natives challenge "the boundaries of discourse and subtly chang[e] its terms by setting up another specifically colonial space of the negotiations of cultural authority." Since this takes place under the surveillance of the authorities, they "change their conditions of recognition while maintaining their visibility; they introduce a lack that is then represented as a doubling of mimicry."[44] Aunty Mina's refusal to give up her economic freedom and her vociferous resistance to apartheid laws and protocols – such as avoiding eye-contact with the whites – points the way forward for the other inhabitants, most notably Charlie who watches her confront the policeman, in their fight against the regime.

For Balutansky and Abrahams, Ronald is little more than a violent thug who kills Susie out of "spite," but the reality of the event is carefully bound into a representation of the colonized as a tightly wound spring. In Fanon's terms, "the surface of his skin is like an open sore which flinches from the caustic agent; and the psyche shrinks back, obliterates itself and finds outlet in muscular demonstrations which have caused certain very wise men to say that the native is a hysterical type."[45] This is as true of Roman who fights with Charlie and regularly beats his wife as it is of Ronny who, in his blind desire for Susie, unthinkingly murders her and therefore inevitably commits himself to a death sentence. La Guma posits the notion that the political development of certain characters is stunted primarily because of their individualism. For example, Roman is described in the following terms: "Between terms of imprisonment, he took to drinking and blamed all his miseries on his wife. Having no capacity for any sort of advanced thought, he struck at those nearest to himself, and he went for them like a drowning man clawing madly over the heads of other drowning shipwrecks, in order to reach the dubious safety of a drifting oar" (64). Roman's instinct for survival is paramount, regardless of the cost to his family. Indeed, having fathered eleven children, he shows little interest in their welfare or well-being. The implicit aim of *And a Threefold Cord* is the need for community values over individual needs, but La Guma ascertains that these will only be met once self-worth replaces self-loathing. Roman, for all his apparent strength, finds it easier to massage his bruised masculinity by beating up his wife rather than face the reality of his situation, that is his emasculation in the face of the politics of apart-

---

[44] Bhabha, *op. cit.*, 119.
[45] Fanon, *op. cit.*, 44.

heid, a politics that refuses to see black people as better than animals. The respite offered by beating his wife's head "with faggots, or her face with his fists," or whipping the children, is short-lived because, in the longer term, the only way to disentangle himself from the situation he finds himself in is to focus his anger against the regime. Like Roman, Ronny is caught in an economy of individualism where "violence is a cleansing force" which has the potential to "free" him, in Fanon's terms, "from his inferiority complex and from his despair and inaction; it makes him fearless and restores his self-respect."[46] After losing his fight with Charlie Roman "went back to his hovel and bludgeoned her [his wife], as a sort of compensation for his own defeat" (65), and after hearing the friendly taunts from his brother about his relationship with Susie, Ronny is rejected by her. It is disbarment from her house that promotes feelings of hatred: "The blerry bastard bitch, she better not mess me around [...] She better not bogger around with other *jubas* or I'll give her what for. He stumbled away through the oozing muck and strewn bricks, rage and disappointment mingling with the unraveling knots of hatred" (60). The reason these two related incidents are of particular relevance to this reading is, quite simply, that any understanding of the psyche of the ordinary inhabitant of the shanty town must take into account desire; whether it be desire for a relationship or desire for a better life. Desire for equal treatment as an inalienable right is dismissed by apartheid, which, in turn, fuels petty squabbles and promotes intra-racial violence between those who have a little more than those who have nothing. For Susie Meyers, existence is the simple pleasure of escaping the reality of living in poverty in a dilapidated house: "The house had been four-roomed once, long ago, but one side and the back had collapsed, leaving a rambling pile of wet rubble and the gaping interior, like the scene of a bombing. All that was left were a front room and the kitchen," leaving it resembling a "haunted house in a movie picture" (59-60). Through the lyrics of Bing Crosby and others singing of moonlight and roses, she momentarily transcends the house and the limits of her physical existence. Susie is not averse to befriending men in an effort to exploit them for monetary gain and more concrete hopes of escape. This is precisely the relationship she engenders with Roman who can offer her money and drink – ephemeral release – whilst Ronny can offer her nothing but his affection.

---

[46] Fanon, *op. cit.,* 74.

Desire for Susie provokes Ronny into killing her. He is warned by Charlie to avoid Susie but the warning goes unheeded and Ronny is drawn to her like a moth to a flame. Susie understands her power over Ronny and sends him away in order to see Roman, which fires the feelings of anger and humiliation in Ronny. But Ronny realizes that he is not strong enough to fight Roman and overcome his rival: "When unappeased, violence seeks and always finds a surrogate victim. The creature that excited its fury is abruptly replaced by another, chosen only because it is vulnerable and close at hand."[47] The rivalry between Roman and Ronny over Susie can best be expressed as the microcosm of the macrocosm that is Charlie's thinking about the oppressive regime. Indeed, René Girard's assertions in *Violence and the Sacred* are as relevant to black South Africans in crisis as to this love triangle in particular:

> The rival desires the same object as the subject, and to assert the primacy of the rival can lead to only one conclusion. Rivalry does not arise because of the fortuitous convergence of two desires on a single object; rather, the subject desires the object because the rival desires it. In desiring an object the rival alerts the subject to the desirability of the object.[48]

In desiring freedom from objectification, blacks look to what the whites have and demand the same things and the same treatment in society as whites receive. This is the first step that Charlie has taken through repeating the ideas of another. To augment Charlie's dawning politicization, La Guma shows how characters like Freda are only worthy of their employer's cast-offs, but may turn their employment to advantage through stealing odds and ends to supplement their meagre wages. The employment of maids remains common practice in South Africa, and the poor treatment of those in this type of employment under apartheid mirrors the treatment of blacks in general. In an extensive survey, Jacklyn Cock discovered that the majority of white employers believed their maids to be intrinsically inferior, thus mirroring apartheid policy of the superiority of whites. She discovered that white employers did not trust their maids and consequently treated them as little more than ill-paid servants who might undermine the situation at any opportunity. In an effort to counter the problem of low pay, many of Cock's respondents said that they paid their maids with cast-offs and left-over food. Freda finds herself in a position

---

[47] René Girard, *Violence and the Sacred*, trans. Patrick Gregory, Baltimore and London, 1977, 2.
[48] *Ibid.*, 145.

where she needs to work in order to support her children: "domestic servants are most accurately to be viewed as trapped workers. They are trapped in a condition of subjugation and immobility within which they are subject to intensive exploitation."[49] Susie Meyers, on the other hand, is more akin to Willieboy in *A Walk in the Night* since she has no visible means of income and spends much of her time drifting from place to place in order to find chance opportunities for financial support. Her chief interests appear to be music, drink and men. In this sense, she is presented as the "other" to the hard-working and responsible mother, Freda.

The border that is the highway on the edge of Windermere is a dangerous zone for Susie Meyers who is shown to transgress the mores of apartheid by attempting to prostitute herself with George Mostert in order to get a drink of his brandy, and access to his motor car and money. And whilst George is tempted by the thought of a sexual encounter with Susie, the thought is quickly pushed away with "One didn't go with colored girls; it was against the law" (82), reiterating his ingrained belief in his inflexible superiority over the colored girl. It is Susie's desperation for acceptance into a society where her poverty and position are not an issue that finally leads to her death. George Mostert's rejection of Susie makes her bitter and angry, which leads her to taunt Ronny into believing that she slept with George, and he kills her. In a highly ironic and convoluted sense, the white man is implicated in the death of Susie and the eventual death of Ronny for her murder: his alien presence in the locale is implicitly related to the demise of these two unfortunate characters. In contrast to the circumstances surrounding Susie Meyers' death, La Guma shows how poor housing is directly responsible for the death of Freda's children. In an effort to stave off the cold and to dry the shack, Freda is forced to keep the poorly functioning primus stove lit, but in an accident it topples over and sets the *pondokkie* on fire, burning the children. The tragic deaths of the children along with Susie and, subsequently Ronny, might have been avoided had the oppressed been afforded equality of opportunity with whites rather than felt the presence of whites as an infringement.

On the night of Mostert's aborted visit and Susie's death, the shanty town is raided by the security forces searching for dagga and pass law violators. The security police violate the privacy of innocent inhabitants: they disturb Caroline giving birth, label Freda a "whore" and round people up

---

[49] See Jacklyn Cock, *Maids and Madams: A Study in the Politics of Exploitation*, Johannesburg, 1980, 124.

in a superficial show of strength. It is on this night that Charlie hits the police officer:

> "You got any business here, man?"
>
> "Just looking," Charlie said, and feeling suddenly malicious, grinned at the policeman through the wet stubble on his face.
>
> "Move off" the policeman said. "Go home. Eff off."
>
> Something smoldered inside Charlie and now he said stiffly: "I'm just looking. Can't a man watch his own people being effed off to jail?"
>
> "Oh," the constable said, his moustache moving as he spoke. "Oh, a hardcase bastard, *ne*?" His hands started to grope for the handcuffs on his belt while his shadowy eyes watched Charlie.
>
> Charlie said, his voice surly: "Okay, I'm a hardcase. Now what then?"
>
> "Bet you're one of those Communist troublemakers. I'll show you."
>
> Charlie grinned insolently through his surliness. His eyes watched the constable's hands. They were big and red, the colour of wet ham, as they fumbled with the handcuffs. Then the policeman turned his face slightly, to call for assistance, and Charlie hit him suddenly on the exposed jawbone.
>
> It was a hard snapping blow, with all his weight behind it, and the policeman's feet left the ground and his back struck it with a hard, muddy, plopping sound, as if he had been dropped from a great height. Then Charlie was off, past the flaying khaki-clad legs, heading for the darkness. (91)

This is a crucial incident in the narrative as it is the second time that Charlie and his thinking are named "communist." This is especially significant since Charlie now has a name for his burgeoning political thinking and this is exemplified through his inclusive terminology of "our people" rather than the narrower focus on self that is displayed by characters like Roman and Ronny. The individualistic approach of Michael Adonis is replaced by the kind of community affiliation represented by Joe in *A Walk in the Night*. And, in direct contrast to Adonis who was unable to stand up to the police officers he encountered, Charlie takes the step of speaking to the constable as an equal. When this fails he strikes him.

Abrahams argues that *And a Threefold Cord* is "more devastatingly pessimistic" than *A Walk in the Night*, since it does not offer Charlie Pauls "a way out of the nightmare of poverty and terror."[50] Balutansky believes

---

[50] Abrahams, *op. cit.,* 92.

that while Charlie's hitting the police man offers him "a large measure of personal relief [...] it remains clear that its personal political repercussions are still very remote."[51] What critics like Balutansky and Ursula Barnett fail to recognize is that Charlie is now set firmly on the road to understanding that, in order to stand up to the regime, selfish individualism must be replaced by a communitarian ideology in which people help each other in the overthrow of the racist government. [52] Charlie's growing awareness and interest in Marxist politics and their potentially liberatory effects is at the forefront of his mind when he hits the figure of spurious authority. The act of hitting the police-man is not the futile gesture that the murder of Susie proves to be but rather an opportunity for Charlie Pauls to demonstrate his acquisition of what in discussions of resistance has been called "intellectual penetration."[53] Charlie discerns what lies behind the illusion of unassailable authority. Initially displaced into violence on behalf of "our people," the desire for unity overrides the transitory relief in violent ends. It is in a new condition of selflessness that he proposes marriage to Freda after she has been labeled a whore by the security officer on the night of the raid.

In the final analysis, *And a Threefold Cord* represents La Guma's belief that only as a united community of people can the oppressed fight against the apartheid regime. The desire for communitarian politics fulfils an essential need in a narrative that attempts to substantiate a community, and "substantializes cultural difference" and which "constitutes a 'split-and-double' form of group identification [...] through a specifically 'anti-colonialist' contradiction of the public sphere," as Bhabha has it.[54] Only when the oppressed are politically aware will they come to the realization that they are subjects rather than objects.

---

[51] Balutansky, *op. cit.,* 50.

[52] Ursula A. Barnett sees this incident as "a gesture of protest for his own satisfaction," *op. cit.,* 135.

[53] Richard Bjornson in Christopher L. Miller, "Nationalism as Resistance and Resistance to Nationalism in the Literature of Francophone Africa," *Yale French Studies* 82 (1993), 79.

[54] Bhabha, *op. cit.,* 230-31.

POLITICAL FICTION, REPRESENTATION AND THE CANON: THE CASE OF MTUTUZELI MATSHOBA

Kelwyn Sole

By the early 1970s, it was obvious that the crackdown on black political organizations and anti-apartheid groups of the previous decade was under challenge from a combative new ideology which had taken root among young black intellectuals: the ideology of Black Consciousness. In the face of apartheid's divisive racial policies, these young men and women realized that apartheid could only be resisted by a new demeanor among black people, both on an individual and collective level; and a number of organizations relating to political, community self-help, worker and other issues were formed from 1968 onwards. Black Consciousness constructed its appeal on a rejection of assimilation and the gradualist, ameliorative politics of the past. Stressing instead the need for black unity and self-reliance, it promoted the positive attributes of pride, assertion, and the need to formulate black viewpoints and goals to counteract both white racism and the sway white liberal views had held over black political initiatives in the past.

It can readily be seen that the ideological thrust of this new philosophy suggested a necessity for activity on the cultural and psychological fronts as well as the political. Highlighting the necessity for expressions of black identity, experience and viewpoints, Black Consciousness led to a cultural revival among black artists and writers. Forms such as literature could be used to expose social conditions and the true nature of apartheid, allow individuals to express their emotional anger at denigration, and promote the spread of the message of Black Consciousness among a black audience. Writers saw themselves as the spokespeople of the black community, whom they should be prepared at all times to learn from as well as teach. Elitism in art, or notions of "art for art's sake," were vehemently opposed, as black artists sought to "create a new collective consciousness, for which Black Consciousness [...] stands" and to discover a fresh aesthetics which was pertinent to this goal and which was relevant to black people. [1] Consequently the literature that emerged saw its purpose as both normative and transformative, attempting to forge a new conception of subjectivity among black individuals who could thereupon join together with others who similarly perceived the need to combat apartheid on all fronts. Notions of subjecting their literature to, or evaluating it through, pre-existing notions of literary "standards" were rebuffed: Black Consciousness artists wished to discover fresh aesthetic perceptions pertinent to their goals and relevant to black people. In a famous quote from 1980, anthologist Mothobi Mutloatse stressed the need for black artists to "pee, spit and shit on literary convention [...] to experiment and probe and not give a damn what the critics have to say." [2]

Black Consciousness literary expression tended in the beginning to favor those forms which lent themselves to immediate dissemination and audience participation, such as drama and performance poetry. By the end of the 1970s, however, and particularly after the inception of the literary magazine *Staffrider* in 1978, more space was available for fiction writers who supported Black Consciousness to practice their craft. One of the first of these was Mtutuzeli Matshoba. Responding to the 1976 student uprisings with a "berserk" need to "spill some of [his life's] contents" out on paper, and fuelled by his admiration for the new philosophy and his general wish to "reflect through [his] works life on [his] side of the fence, the black side." [3] Matshoba wrote short fiction, which appeared in published form in the weekly newspaper *The Voice* and *Staffrider* from 1978 onwards. In its early days *Staffrider* attracted a large readership, especially in the black townships, and Matshoba was easily the most prominent, and most imitated, of its fiction writers. [4] He was thus, for a time, possibly the most influential fiction writer in South Africa:

---

[1] The words are those of short story writer Mbulelo Mzamane. See M. Mzamane, "The Uses of Traditional Oral Forms in Black South African Literature," in *Literature and Society in South Africa*, eds L. White and T. Couzens, Cape Town, 1984, 159.

[2] "Introduction" to Mutloatse, ed., *Forced Landing*, Johannesburg, 1980, 5.

[3] M. Matshoba, "An Autobiographical Note," in M. Matshoba, *Call Me Not a Man*, Johannesburg, 1979, ix-x. The author's assumption that literature acts mimetically to reflect reality can be seen in his statement that he sees his writing "as a window onto the black way of life." Quoted in E. Vlessing, "Fighting Fire with Fire," *West Africa*, London, 15 September (1986), 1930. More widely, he asserts that literature "enables you to state your case before you act. It is a way of indicting the person against whom one is to act or is acting so that person will understand the 'why' of it," 1931. Both statements show that Matshoba did not address himself only to a black audience.

[4] By 1980 *Staffrider*'s print run was 7,000 copies; it was estimated that each copy that entered the townships passed through the hands of approximately six readers. See

He has [...] become identified with the magazine, and this association is not gratuitous. *Staffrider*, with its revolutionary insistence on allowing the voices of hitherto suppressed and silenced groups to be heard [...] in whichever style they chose, regardless of traditional literary-aesthetic norms, opened up new possibilities for black literary expression in this country.[5]

The intermingling of descriptions of black social conditions, political analyses, calls to action and heartfelt emotional outpourings in these stories align them immediately with the general impetus of the Black Consciousness philosophy Matshoba embraced.

Many of Matshoba's stories were published in book form as the collection *Call Me Not a Man* in 1979, and their reception was initially extremely favorable. Newspaper and academic reviewers spoke in glowing terms of his detailed observation of black experiences under apartheid, and commented on the manner in which the stories tried to marry political concerns with literary skill. Alan Paton judged them the "best South African short stories I have read for a long time," noting that they had a power to "entertain and hold and even enthrall the reader. Much polemical story writing fails this test";[6] the newspaper columnist Doc Bikitsha praised the "detailed observation and compassionate empathy with those areas where apartheid is most deeply felt" and spoke warmly of their "vision of a growing identity, and a growing commitment to a realistic future for blacks in South Africa";[7] while the academic David Maughan-Brown suggested that the whole collection was "a landmark in the development of South African short-story writing."[8]

Commentators recognized from the beginning that Matshoba's stories were stylistically something of a novelty in South African literature. A number commented on their innovative and multi-generic aspect, noting that the "thinness" of the fictional veneer rendered the experience of being black in South Africa both graphic and immediate. Formal idiosyncrasies of his style, such as the interspersing of the more obviously fictional epi-

---

M. Kirkwood, *"Staffrider*: An Informal Discussion," *English in Africa* 7:2 (1980), 26-29.

[5] C. Mackenzie, "To Kill a Student's Pride: Some Observations about the Anthology *To Kill a Man's Pride* and Its Inclusion in the TED Syllabus," *Crux* 24:1 (1990), 30.

[6] A. Paton, "A Black Talent to Watch," *The Argus* (6 November 1979).

[7] D. Bikitsha, "Doc Bikitsha's Art Clinic," *Rand Daily Mail* (3 October 1979).

[8] D. Maughan-Brown, "Social Realism, Fantasy, Political Conscientization," *English Academy Review* 3 (1985), 218.

sodes in the texts with poetry, exegetical statements and philosophical di-
gressions, continued to raise interest and comments for a number of years.[9]

There have been critics who have attempted to define and characterize
the particular nature of Matshoba's stories more fully. Making links between black African and American practice, Jenny Williams suggested
that an admixture of first-person narration and fictionalized autobiography
was central to the aesthetics of black writing from African-America, and
drew attention to Matshoba's similarities to this. His style functions, she
proposed, to make the individual exemplary rather than unique, and enacts
a notion of the self as representative, typical and ordinary.[10] Employing a
Marxist paradigm, Michael Vaughan traced how the stories showed one of
the new directions South African fiction was moving towards in the 1970s;
a direction with different aesthetic and ideological premises to the convention of "liberal realism" which had previously held sway in English-lan-
guage literature. In his opinion Matshoba was a leading exponent of a new
mode of "populist realism," dispensing with a concern for subtle and
elaborate characterization and interiority as well as the personal character
encounters familiar in "liberal realism." Instead, "populist realism" incorporates, but goes further than, detailed description and mimesis; eventually
emerging as a project in political (self) education that reflects a desire for
self-definition *contingent on* the overwhelming necessity for communal
solidarity and effort among the oppressed black majority. Emphasizing the
special texture of literary expression less, this form of realism was realized
as a formal mode by a group of young writers deprived of a conventional
school education in literature as a result of censorship and the Bantu Education system; who were seeking an appropriate aesthetic to define them-

---

[9] See the comments by David Bunn and Daniel Kunene in *Writing from South Africa: Fourteen Writers on Culture, Politics, and Literary Theory and Activity in South
Africa Today,* ed. R. Gibbons, Chicago, 1989, 19, 35; as well as M. Trump, "Black
South African Short Fiction in English Since 1976," *Research in African Literatures*
19:1 (1988), 39-40; M. Chapman, "The Critic in a State of Emergency: Towards a
Theory of Reconstruction (after February 2)," in *On Shifting Sands: New Art and Literature from South Africa,* eds K. Holst Petersen and A. Rutherford, Sydney, 1991, 6.
[10] See the argument in J. Williams, "Can *OUR NIG* help *The Native Who Caused
All theTrouble?* Some Thoughts on a Theory Which Proposes that a Knowledge of
American 'Black' Writing Can Provide Insights Which Are Useful in the Study of
South African 'Black' Writing," *A.U.E.T.S.A. 90 Conference Papers Vol II: South African Autobiographical Writing,* Association of University English Teachers of Southern Africa Conference, University of Stellenbosch (3-7 July 1990), especially 6-7.

selves and serve as a foundation for appealing to a less literary black audience.[11]

Some of the early attempts to distinguish the stylistic particularities of Matshoba's stories suggested that, if anything, he was a new kind of "storyteller" at work within a modernizing environment. Their specific narrative texture feeds the illusion that the author and the first person narrators generally employed in most stories are one and the same; and that they in turn merge into the numerous anonymous figures of the township whom they represent and for whom they speak.[12] The narrator's tendency directly to address readers and comment on the fictional action as it unfolds, when taken together with the confidential tone he employs and his friendly, conversational facade, the employment of exemplary incidents and stereotypical characters, the preponderance of conversation and debate and the stories' overall ethical and didactic intention all point to the oral, folkloric and communal aspects of this style.[13]

That there is a trace of the oral mode present is beyond question: indeed, in some of his stories (such as "To Kill a Man's Pride" and "A Glimpse of Slavery") he goes so far as to introduce song and sound effects into his fiction, or write in the form of a dramatic dialogue. Yet such a "storytelling" designation requires more detailed analysis for, as David Bunn has noted, Matshoba's stories are more properly an interpenetration of individually written short fictional and communal storytelling modes, inhabiting a generic space somewhere between the two.[14] Referring to Walter Benjamin's well-known article on "The Storyteller," Vaughan has spent most time arguing for the storytelling characteristics of Matshoba's work. According to this critic the stories display a number of qualities associated with the oral storyteller, that figure whose presence has been displaced in the twentieth century by the novel and its modernizing impera-

---

[11] For further discussion of these points, see D. Maughan-Brown, *op. cit.*, 217-18; M. Vaughan, "Literature and Politics: Currents in South African Writing in the Seventies," *Journal of Southern African Studies* 9:1 (1982), 118-22, 132-38; M. Vaughan, "*Staffrider* and Directions within Contemporary South African Literature," in White and Couzens, *op. cit.*, 196-97, 204-205.

[12] M. Kirkwood, "Remembering *Staffrider*," in *Ten Years of Staffrider 1978 — 1988,* eds A. Oliphant and I. Vladislavic, Johannesburg, 1988, 1-2.

[13] For further discussion of some of these points, see M. Trump, "Part of the Struggle: Black Writing and the South African Liberation Movement," in *Rendering Things Visible: Essays on South African Literary Culture,* ed. M. Trump, Johannesburg, 1990, 168; Trump (1988) *op. cit.*, 36-39; Chapman, *Southern African Literatures,* Harlow, 1996, 373-74 and Maughan-Brown, *op. cit.*, 217-18.

[14] Bunn in Gibbons, *op. cit.*, 35.

tives. Matshoba's narrators are frequently travelers, who experience life over a wide range of geographical locales and matters of concern and participate directly in the anonymous, communal life of their fellows through the interchange of experience and viewpoints, whilst exhibiting fellow-feeling and giving counsel.[15] Mike Kirkwood, then co-director of Ravan Press, noted a few months after the publication of *Call Me Not a Man*:

> I confess that I find it difficult, as I read Matshoba's stories, not to see him in front of me. It is the polar opposite of James Joyce paring his fingernails behind the complete and self- sufficient artwork. And these aren't "short stories" because the short story suggests deliberate artifice to me, pre-eminently among prose-forms. Neither are they stories in the traditional sense. Yet Matshoba seems to me the story-teller come to life, all the same.[16]

It is noticeable, however, that a strain of uncertainty was visible in some critics' pronouncements as to the formal value of the stories from the beginning. Lionel Abrahams, for instance, interspersed his positive comments with an anxiety that they disregarded "a number of rules for effective fiction" — in particular those regarding lack of narrative economy and the disruption of the illusion of fictionality.[17] Yet despite this, there was a general consensus during the late 1970s and early 1980s among liberal and radical critics, black writers and readers alike that Matshoba was one of the most notable of the fiction writers of his time. However, from 1984 onwards Njabulo Ndebele, recently returned from university studies in England and the United States, subjected Matshoba and other Black Consciousness writers to a wide-ranging and influential series of critiques. He accused them of remaining content to stress the most spectacular and superficial aspects of black South African society. Content to comment moralistically on their oppression, their predilections have resulted in a mimetic, descriptive literature able only to reiterate the Manichaean terms of apartheid, and inadequate to the task of drawing black readers into a process of empathy or allowing them to experience themselves as anything but victims. In the case of Matshoba specifically, he felt that:

---

[15] While this is a constant theme in Vaughan, its most direct expression can be found in M. Vaughan, "The Stories of Mtutuzeli Matshoba — A Critique," *Staffrider,* November 1981, 45-47. For Benjamin's original article, see W. Benjamin, *Illuminations*, Bungay, 1973.

[16] "Introduction" to Mzamane, ed. *Hungry Flames and Other Black South African Short Stories*, Harlow, 1986, xxiii.

[17] L. Abrahams, "Fiction with Flexibility," *Rand Daily Mail* (1 October 1979). He hints at the occasional absence of "subjugation of the material to the form, for integrity of the illusion, and […] objectivity in the presentation of characters."

Matshoba's depiction of social reality in his stories (is) simply too over-whelming. His basic technique has been to accumulate fact after fact of op-pression and suffering, so that we are in the end almost totally grounded in the reality without being offered, at the same time, an opportunity for aes-thetic and critical estrangement.[18]

Taking issue with Vaughan's positive evaluation of Matshoba's emphasis on "situation" rather than individual experience, and his concomitant sug-gestion that a concern with individual subjectivity in character develop-ment inclined writers towards "bourgeois individualism," Ndebele advo-cated a return to full-bodied characters who were more than "mere ideas [...] marshaled this way or that in a moral debate." For Ndebele, good writing should be more concerned with processes of injustice than finished products. Focusing on characters' inner processes of thought and under-standing, even if they were "villains" within their social context, would al-low the audience to see them "condemn themselves through their drama-tized effects."[19] Shortly thereafter, Lewis Nkosi added his voice to this condemnation (in an article which also criticized Ndebele's fiction) when he censured Matshoba's "naïve realism," which he believed owed a great deal to a "frustrated desire to abolish any space between literature and the horrible reality of apartheid"; and subsequently dismissed any possibility that this work could be seen as "an example of ground-breaking innova-tion."[20]

Perhaps the most arresting aspect of Ndebele's rebuttal of the techni-cal proficiency of Matshoba, though, is the fact that he uses the same arti-cle by Benjamin ("The Storyteller") to assist his argument. Praising the "impersonal, communal" aspect of storytelling, Ndebele is also confident in his belief that this mode can downplay authorial intervention and thus leave space for reader participation. Where he appears to differ most from the version of storytelling offered by Vaughan, however, is in his opinion that storytellers place a minimal emphasis on politics, embracing rather the wider social reality of ordinary experience ("the everyday") in their sto-ries, concentrating on individual processes of consciousness rather than

---

[18] N. Ndebele, "Turkish Tales, and Some Thoughts on South African Fiction," *Staffrider* 6:1 (1984), 46.
[19] These remarks can be found in Ndebele, *Ibid.*, 44, and 46-47.
[20] L. Nkosi, "South African Fiction Writers at the Barricades," *Third World Book Review* (1986), 43; and "Postmodernism and Black Writing in South Africa," in *Writing South Africa: Literature, Apartheid, and Democracy, 1970 - 1995*, eds D. Attridge and R. Jolly, Cambridge, 1998, 79.

political exposition and highlighting the stories' entertainment value as a
necessary mediator for their instructive qualities.[21]

Ndebele's 1984 article, plus subsequent interventions, effected an al-
teration in evaluations of the work of not only Matshoba, but also other
black writers who were part of the movement of committed, politically and
socially explicit art that Black Consciousness had pioneered. Despite publishing a play and giving readings from a novel and fictional autobiography (both still unpublished), within a few years of publishing *Call Me Not
a Man* Matshoba was more or less forgotten in literary circles. He has
since shown a facility for script-writing for video and film and, despite
emerging as a (somewhat controversial) spokesperson for the Department
of Arts and Culture of the A.N.C. in the immediate post-1990 period, has
never re-emerged as a literary force within the country.[22] It is more the
vogue now to dismiss the value of his work altogether, in particular for its
lack of formal value: the lack of aspects such as "setting, conflict, credible
characterization, consistent narrative point of view, the complexities of fictional language and time" in his work and that of his Black Consciousness
compeers of the 1970s.[23]

The uncertainties that are discernible in estimations of Matshoba
around the terms and perceptions popularized by Ndebele could be taken
further than opposing evaluations of him based on the criterion of "storytelling": for instance, one could point out that these stories *do* in fact deal
with the "everyday" milieux of black people under apartheid. The stories
act out — constantly, but expressly in the story "Behind the Veil of Complacency" — the fact that individual life for black people under apartheid
could never be interior or private, given the manner in which racist laws
enabled the authorities to intrude on the private lives of individuals at any

---

[21] See in particular Ndebele, *op. cit.*, 25, and 48.

[22] Matshoba did however publish a short story-cum-re-examination of history, "The
Return of Nxele" (reminiscent of the Nongqawuse episode in "Three Days in the Land
of a Dying Illusion") in the A.N.C. journal *Mayibuye* in March 1992. For information
on, and a discussion of, Matshoba's relationship with film and screenwriting, see J.
Williams, "'A New Act of Mediation': The Screenplays of Mtutuzeli Matshoba,"
Current Writing 4:1 (1992). He has subsequently been involved in writing the screen-
play for the TV video and film *Chikin Biz'nis* (1995 and 1998). For some idea of his
involvement in cultural politics as a D.A.C. spokesperson, see K. Williams, "A Letter
to SANTA," *South* (19 December 1992-13 January 1993); M. Matshoba, "Artistic
Liberation, Not Control, is the ANC Objective," *Weekly Mail* (28 May-3 June 1993);
C. Bauer and C. St Leger, "Winnie and Her Boss in Arts Feud," *Sunday Times* (30 October 1994).

[23] Ndebele, *op. cit.*, 46.

time: witness, for instance, the fear and helplessness the narrator feels in "A Pilgrimage to the Isle of Makana" when he hears the voice of a white official who is looking for him in the outer room of his house.[24] This is a world where:

> Nothing particular "happens" [...] or rather everything happens that is central to the daily lives of millions of black urban dwellers, but nothing that will satisfy the formalist concerns with climax of story, denouement of plot and so on.[25]

The difference between Matshoba and Ndebele's understanding of this aspect is that, while the latter sees the everyday lives of black people as a source of succor, cultural expression and resistance, the former believes that it is the very acceptance of the quotidian reality of apartheid by blacks which entrenched and naturalized its rule. As Williams cogently remarks, Ndebele's paean to the "everyday" is simply insufficient in a situation where the "ordinary" and its normal activities have been subjugated to a consistently denigrating power.[26]

Given that Matshoba's short stories now tend to be either downplayed or ignored, it is instructive to look afresh at their taxonomy and achievements. The fact that critics are prepared to furnish radically different estimations of these stories' worth, even as they jointly laud approaches to South African literature based on the "storyteller" model, suggests that there are deeper issues being played out in such debates. In addressing these it is first and foremost crucial to realize, *contra* Nkosi, that Matshoba is not simply an unconscious purveyor of faulty writing: to identify his work as merely an assertion of "naïve realism" resulting from bad schooling ignores evidence that he had thought about, and tried to address, problems relating to the province of the writer in a conflictual milieu, as well as issues of literary quality and standards.[27]

It is also overhasty to view Matshoba's work as unproblematically preferring the collective to the individual. It is more accurate to perceive

---

[24] M. Matshoba (1979), *op. cit.*, 92.

[25] Mackenzie, *op. cit.*, 31. Although Mackenzie is speaking specifically about the story "To Kill a Man's Pride" here, the point can be extended.

[26] See the remarks in Williams 1992 *op. cit.,* 32 and 34. As Matshoba himself states (Vlessing, *op. cit.,* 1930), his depictions of the "ordinary" serve to bring about individual political transformation: "I thought that letting them see themselves as they are would inspire them to regain their dignity."

[27] See, for example, his remarks in M. Matshoba, "Some Points to Ponder... Thoughts on the Disbanding of P.E.N.," *Staffrider* 4:1 (1981), 45.

his work as gesturing constantly towards the *collaborative*. In line with the Black Consciousness anathema to elitist notions of the artist, Matshoba's stories constantly act out the mutual involvement of black people (including the narrator) with each other,[28] through the medium of conversational speech, an approximation of township idiom, and a language generally speaking available to a "less Liberal and less literary" audience.[29]

Commentators have tended to accept the notion that this narrator is simply a reflection of the author. This opinion is strengthened by the strikingly mimetic aspect of the fiction: Matshoba had a brother who was a political prisoner on Robben Island, for instance, as does the narrator in "A Pilgrimage to the Isle of Makana"; both the author and the narrator live in Mzimhlope, Soweto; and no critic can ignore the riposte of an anonymous lawyer to the banning of *Call Me Not a Man* by the Publications Control Board in 1979 on the basis of the "improbability" of its depicted events.[30]

However, while Matshoba's depiction of the black community is rather more complex and diverse than generally allowed for, there are two basic sets of criteria by which this community is defined. The first is with regard to attempts to unify the apartheid-generated racial group definitions of African, "colored" and Indian under the rubric, "black." We see, for instance, that one of the enduring minor themes of "A Pilgrimage to the Isle of Makana" is the acceptance of "coloreds" into a racial unity. It is also noticeable that characters appear over and over again through the prism of Black Consciousness' tripartite designation of people in terms of their attitude towards liberation. Those who embody the majority of vacillating, passive black individuals whom Black Consciousness wished to bring into political awareness and activism, but who remain for the time being "sacrificial lambs" fearful of whites are seen alongside of those positive, active individuals such as Soks, a:

---

[28] M. Trump (1988), *op. cit.*, 40.

[29] Maughan-Brown, *op. cit.*, 217.

[30] In "Another Glimpse of Slavery: A Lawyer's View," *Staffrider* 3:3 (1980) the close resonances of Matshoba's fictionalization of parolee farm labour in his story "A Glimpse of Slavery" with the brutal nature of existing practices is made clear. There is no doubt that much of Matshoba's work was either based on personal experience or on careful research of areas of black experience he did not know. See the interview with the author in J. Munnik and G. Davis, "Getting Back to Writing," in *Voyages and Explorations: Southern African Writing,* ed. G. Davis, Amsterdam, 1994, 124; as well as the discussion by Davis in "Life on the Black Side of the Fence: Forced Removals and the Migrant Labour System in Recent Black South African Literature," in *Current Themes in Contemporary South African Literature,* eds E. Lehmann and E. Rechwitz, Essen, 1989, 153-55.

typical South African urban black youth [who] foresaw Azania, where ability and not the color of a man's skin or his creed would be the criterion, where no laws would prevent any human being from living naturally, from being human.[31]

Both groups are positively viewed, at least in their potential; and are counterposed strongly to the group of "sell-outs" — the black policemen, community councilors and other agents of the apartheid system — who are past redemption.

In addition to this representation of the black community in line with the Black Consciousness viewpoint, there is evidence that mimesis is subordinated to the manner in which the narrator is characterized and positioned in the stories. While it is true that Matshoba is concerned less with characterization than with situation, and while it is true that the exemplary, modeling purpose of the stories result in a degree of stereotyping of people (especially along racial lines), the character of the narrator is nuanced and carefully crafted. He exhibits the (to Black Consciousness) laudable attributes of self-reliance, pride, resourcefulness and assertiveness: but as importantly he is self-deprecating, ironic, humorous and compassionate, with an inquisitive, friendly and apparently open-minded streak. It is easy to forget that this supposed naivety is a fictional construct, which allows Matshoba to establish an attitude of acceptance and trust on the part of the reader.[32] Moreover, the importance of travel in a number of Matshoba's stories — and the narrator's obsessive self-examination and reflection on experience in those stories where he remains in one place — allow the reader simultaneously to reap the benefits of the first-person narration (an emphasis on subjectivity and a process of discovery through interior monologuing and the highlighting of the narrator's thought processes) with the mapping of different types of black experience. The narrator acts as "a co-ordinator, a principle of relationship and unity [...] a co-ordinating consciousness, of critical and reflective estrangement" for black readers usu-

---

[31] Matshoba (1979), *op. cit.*, 15 and 122-23. In other stories, see in particular the characters of Ntate Ali (28) and Martha (73).
[32] The artifice on the author's part is made clear when one notices (for example) the contradictions that emerge around the narrator's constructed naivety. His fear of the "unknown" when travelling to Cape Town is contradicted by a passage in the same story in which he suddenly appears as a seasoned traveller around the "four provinces" of the country; there is a change of the narrator's name in two different stories, one pointing towards mimesis, the other fictionalization (see Matshoba [1979], *op. cit.*, 95, 110, 112, and 146); and there are other discrepancies as well which demonstrate Matshoba's crafting.

ally trapped in the impelled immediacy of localized "normalcy."[33] Even as this fictional agenda of exposing social conditions and urging the need for a black unity that embraces the diversity of different experiences takes hold the author is, through his choice of narrator, ensuring that it happens without a loss of emphasis on the need for subjective self-examination and psychological transformation. The narrator's love of conversation and his preparedness to listen in to other people's debates and problems, offer the resources of collective experience to both the narrator and the individual reader.[34] Thus, while these stories may represent and "speak for a people,"[35] it is more accurate to say that they enact the intertwined process of individual and communal self-fashioning that Black Consciousness suggested for black South Africans. In order that this may be achieved, Matshoba selects and utilizes not only an informing ideology and philosophy, but also a choice of style and focalization that is anything but artless.

Matshoba fashions his stories thematically so that they return again and again to issues of social prejudice, economic disadvantage and political oppression. Given the ambience of apartheid, it is unsurprising that a preponderance of these relate to racial issues. This has led to a number of responses from critics: some white critics in particular have shown unease at what they regard as hints of racism and stereotyping (bordering on caricaturing) of the black "sell-out" and white characters, which appear at odds to the frequently stated narratorial commitment to non-racialism; while others are puzzled at the extent to which "the opinions with which Mtutuzeli Matshoba interlards his narratives are oddly more enlightened than attitudes he reveals in action."[36] Others have in their turn criticized the usage of a strongly moralistic discourse explaining racial attitudes as distortions of "human nature" at the expense of any discussion of economic circumstances, despite the occasional ripostes the narrator delivers to the black middle class.[37]

---

[33] Vaughan, "The Stories of Mtutuzeli Matshoba — A Critique," *op. cit.,* 46.

[34] This point is made in Vaughan, "Literature and Politics: Currents in South African Writing in the Seventies," *op. cit.*, 132.

[35] Bikitsha, *op. cit.*

[36] See, respectively, Chapman (1996), *op. cit.*, 373-74, and Abrahams, *op. cit.*

[37] Such as his perception of himself as a "fly in a milk container" whilst traveling in a friend's Mercedes Benz (Matshoba [1979], *op. cit.*, 186). For a discussion of the lack of economic explanations, see Vaughan, "Literature & Popular Culture: The Case of *Call Me Not a Man,*" unpublished mimeograph delivered to the Inter-Disciplinary Workshop on "Urban Society in 20th Century South Africa: Capital Accumulation and the Struggle for Social and Cultural Space," Durban 26-28 June 1981, 12-13; and

While a close reading of the stories bears out the pertinence of at least some of such assessments, they are in need of qualification and revision. One of the main ideological purposes of Matshoba's project is to extol the need for black unity in order to overcome the apartheid system, and the overwhelming usage of characterization is to measure individuals in terms of their potential for this program. Despite the narrator's claim that a great deal of the inhumanity of white racism is based on the manner in which they typify and caricature blacks,[38] as a result white characters (such as Koos van der Merwe in "A Glimpse of Slavery" and Mister Merwe in "A Son of the First Generation") tend to be caricatured,[39] with black "sell-outs" (such as Bobbejaan in "A Glimpse of Slavery") similarly treated.[40]

Although a number of mitigating factors for the unrelenting nature of this conceptualization could be suggested — racial discrimination is, after all, the principal social experience through which black South Africans lived out their experience of oppression under apartheid,[41] and it can in this case be suggested that a nuancing of characters, racially speaking, is at odds with the ideological goals the author has set himself — no one has explored the effect of the simultaneously ambivalent and ironic attitude the narrator displays to his own social (especially racial) attitudes. Therefore, although much has been said about the communal intentions of the social representations in these stories and their (un)representativeness, little or no commentary has been forthcoming about the manner in which the representation of the narrator tends to work against the oversimplifying and stereotyping rubric of some of the opinions and enactments offered.

A closer examination of Matshoba's pronouncements over the decade of the 1980s makes clear that his attitudes to race vary in response to political circumstances. In 1981, he is arguing strongly against the disbanding of the multiracial P.E.N. branch in South Africa, suggesting that differentiation on the basis of color among those opposed to apartheid leads to an exaggeration of the differences between them; but five years later his demeanor towards whites appears to have hardened considerably.[42]

"Literature and Politics: Currents in South African Writing in the Seventies," *op. cit.*, 135-36.

[38] Matshoba (1979), *op. cit.*, 6, 8.

[39] *Ibid.*, 31, and 75.

[40] *Ibid.*, 35, and 40.

[41] Vaughan, "The Stories of Mtutuzeli Matshoba — A Critique," *op. cit.*, 47.

[42] Compare the remarks in Matshoba (1981), *op. cit.*, 45; and Vlessing, *op. cit.*, 1930-31.

In his fiction, the vacillating nature of the narrator's attitudes to race are not only apparent, but also the fact that it is authorial intention to make this transparent to the reader by devices such as conversation and interior monologuing. In his usual confidential tone, the narrator registers his feelings about race as soon as they arise, thus detailing the indecisive contours of his own emotions. He is achingly aware of the problematic nature of his own utterances: offering, for example, "sincere apologies for labeling people."[43] In a number of situations, he is torn between his own experiences with "sympathetic" whites and his acknowledgment that the overdetermining racism of the system he was socialized into has had its effect on his own conduct; emphasizing through juxtaposition both his prejudices and his attempts to escape them. Human empathy and fellow-feeling are juxtaposed with a more distanced, coldly analytical eye. In "A Pilgrimage to the Isle of Makana" this happens three times in swift succession. As the previously caricatured "penguin" white ticket collector argues with the narrator's companion on the train, the caricature is disturbed by the more objective perception that here are "two workers flinging their frustrations at each other across the color line";[44] the "revelation" of white, "fairy" children looking for their nanny in the black section of the train is offset by the narrator contemplating how "innocent little whites (grow) into guilty big whites";[45] and his loss of "bitterness and [...] discomfort" in Cape Town as he befriends Phil, Rachel and Sally persists, despite his simultaneous awareness of their fathers' "relentless hold on power."[46] Such a split-eye view of the Other is, at times, negotiated through self-irony: the narrator comments on his tendency to view "all people who befriended whites (as) sellouts except myself where Mark [...] was concerned."[47] As a result of foregrounding the "escalator" emotions he experiences when faced with whites, as well as the implied criticism of himself that these emotions generally proceed or follow, the author allows us to inhabit, and muse over, the processes and causes of his attitudes and prejudices in a manner unusual in anti-apartheid South African literature:

> this racism smears all those exposed to it. I have been smeared, for my whole life. My very existence is determined along racial lines. So, normally, if I see a white I see a white and not another human being. [...] My own

---

[43] Matshoba (1979), *op. cit.*, 189.
[44] *Ibid.*, 102.
[45] *Ibid.*, 104.
[46] *Ibid.*, 127-28.
[47] *Ibid.*, 118.

prejudice can be described as reciprocal or reactive prejudice [...] an offensive defensive reaction.[48]

In addition to the questions about race, criticisms as regards Matshoba's analytical and representational procedures have been strengthened by a growing unease at the gender representations in the stories, particularly those pertaining to black women, as well as his perceptions of some of the diverse groupings which make up a putative black unity.[49] The discussions and representations around the question of women's place within the black community and its struggle for liberation are curiously indecisive and even occasionally contradictory. Writing at a time when the phallogocentric tendencies of Black Consciousness are most noticeable, the author's concerns oscillate in and out of accord with such a tendency.[50] It is obvious that a book entitled *Call Me Not a Man* has as its goal the compulsion for a new spirit of resilient manliness among black men psychologically damaged by apartheid. Even if it is conceded that "man" can act as a generic term,[51] it is still noticeable that the author at times longs for the "authoritative manner of true African men" and a social environment where men could settle their racial differences in a manly way if it were not for the intervention of women.[52] Significant too is the way in which the narrator subjects women to his male gaze (the "colored" woman on Kimberley Station is a case to point)[53], and the manner in which female characters at times actively assist their own objectification.[54] From his urbanized

---

[48] *Ibid.*, 119-20.

[49] *Vide* Zoe Wicomb's remark that the new-born "colored" child in "A Son of the First Generation" is "constructed through a narrative of illicit sexuality, female concupiscence and shame," in Z. Wicomb, "Shame and Identity: The Case of the Coloured in South Africa," in Attridge and Jolly, *op. cit.*, 98.

[50] For a discussion of the role of women in Black Consciousness in the 1970s, see M. Ramphele, "The Dynamics of Gender within Black Consciousness Organizations: A Personal View," in B. Pityana *et al.*, *Bounds of Possibility: The Legacy of Steve Biko & Black Consciousness*, Cape Town, 1991.

[51] The female writer Boitumelo Mofokeng asserted at the time: "As Mtutuzeli says, 'For what is suffered by another man in view of my eyes is suffered also by me' [...]. This is a feeling shared universally. It does not refer to men alone but it is also shared by women." See "Women Writers Speak," *Staffrider* 2:4 (1979), 60.

[52] Matshoba (1979), *op. cit.*, 120, and 30-31. In the latter example, the narrator and a white manager are fully prepared to settle their differences by trading insults and blows, until a (white) secretary spoils the fun by phoning the police.

[53] *Ibid.*, 107.

[54] In "A Son of the First Generation," Martha (who feels contempt for white women's willingness to be displayed as "ornaments") accepts her own objectification immediately afterwards: "Now you look like the queen of Sheba. *Abelungu bakho* are

point of view, the narrator is equally prepared to "other" rural woman, in a manner that fluctuates between romantic approbation and denigration.[55]

Yet Matshoba is unusual for the time of writing in that his narrator seems aware of, and registers issues pertaining to, the position of black women. For instance, he allows male and female migrant workers to conduct a lengthy debate about gender problems in rural societies — which the woman, significantly enough, wins — on the bus the narrator shares with them in "Three Days in the Land of a Dying Illusion." Furthermore, a number of his female characters are assertive and intellectually critical of male attitudes, such as the historical figure of Nongqawuse, who is prepared to "slip out of those traditional chains and state her mind"[56] in the Cattle-killing episode in "Three Days in the Land of a Dying Illusion"; Martha, who wishes to "marry when I like, not when someone else decides" in "A Son of the First Generation";[57] and Mapula in "Behind the Veil of Complacency," who urges her boyfriend to have "sound criteria for evaluating other people, not just their sex."[58]

It can be suggested, though, that the final trend is to write the female characters into supporting a racial unity spearheaded by men. Mapula, for example, finds that her duty is to understand and contribute "ideas that reinforced [her boyfriend's] philosophy,"[59] while the woman in the bus ends by chiding the male migrant workers for their lack of masculinity and courage in the face of their (male) chiefs willingness to accept a sham independence for the Transkei.[60]

Thus the reader experiences a curious sense of disorientation at the narrator's uncertainty whether to treat black women as "beautiful things" or "sisters."[61] Even as women — even the powerful ones — seem more often than not obliged to place their talents and insights at the service of a racial agenda directed by men, it is noticeable that Matshoba exhibits a re-

---

going to wish they were black." When she looked into the wardrobe mirror she saw that Busi was not flattering her. She wished she were a model and not a tea-girl" (80).

[55] Witness the manner in which the narrator, shortly after expressing a paean to "African femininity untouched by western standards" on his visit to the Transkei, speaks of "the picturesque traditional remnants — the huts and the women." *Ibid.*, 161 and 183.

[56] *Ibid.*, 173.

[57] *Ibid.*, 76.

[58] *Ibid.*, 192.

[59] *Ibid.*, 191.

[60] *Ibid.*, 156.

[61] *Ibid.*, 107 and 191.

curring anxiety when writing about women. Mapula, it turns out, would (if she were as intelligent as her mate) delineate him with a less than kindly epithet;[62] while the narrator in "Three Days in the Land of a Dying Illusion," along with his tendency to feel unmanned by the presence of "examples of African femininity untainted by western standards" whilst in the Transkei,[63] is endowed with an self-ironic, bemused tone which serves to destabilize the masculinist philosophy that overdetermines the stories as a whole:

> Indomitable Xhosa woman! Small wonder my friend "Terror," Xhosa by birth, vows always never to marry a woman of the same extraction as his. "They always have an argument to put up against men. Our mothers were the last disciplined lot of Xhosa women. My sisters — boy!" — and he ends up by wincing. My answer to him is always that they are all like that from East to West and North to South of this globe, irrespective of ancestry, and that we need to mobilize in time to defend our divine right to make war and reduce the world to rubble.[64]

The stories of Mtutuzeli Matshoba fit comfortably neither their initial approving reception nor their current dismissal. There is no doubt that the emphasis on commitment and didacticism Matshoba's project evinces is at odds with prevailing fashions in South African academic criticism. Moreover, even as it is possible to perceive the significance of these stories in the particular historical moment of the late 1970s, the manner in which they strive to represent and enact a "black viewpoint" in line with Black Consciousness dictates cannot blur the degree to which they contain their own ideological emphases and limitations. As is often the case with fiction that aims to directly promulgate a worldview, there are degrees of counter-mythologizing present in the stories, for instance in the re-telling of the Nongqawuse episode.[65]

It can be pointed out that the belief that the author is consistently a representative black voice, giving voice to community opinions and perceptions, needs to be mitigated by an awareness of the degree to which

---

[62] "He supposed that if she were sophisticated enough she would have labelled him a male chauvinist pig," *ibid.*, 192.

[63] *Ibid.*, 161.

[64] *Ibid.*, 156.

[65] Trump (1990), *op. cit.*, 164, makes, but does not elaborate on, this point. However, Matshoba's understanding of the *mfecane* (see Matshoba [1979] *op. cit.*, 148-50), even if from a "black viewpoint," can be seen to be one shared by more traditional historians, and in need of the kind of revisions begun in *The Mfecane Aftermath*, ed. C. Hamilton, Johannesburg, 1995.

certain types of black social viewpoint are privileged above others.[66] Indeed, while commentators have noticed the problems arising around gender depiction, this has not been matched with any observation of the more notable problems which emerge with the narrator's portrayal of rural life and migrant workers. These are especially stark in the instance of his self-description in "Three Days in the Land of a Dying Illusion" as one "of the third denomination" (i.e. a traveler in third-class carriages) along with the other migrant workers. His avowed affiliations in this story are quickly dissipated by a number of blithe, unconscious pronouncements indicating a belief that rural people are intellectually inferior and easily cowed.[67]

The degree to which (for example) critics who propound the "storyteller" model are prepared to furnish radically different evaluations of Matshoba's short fiction hints at deeper issues being contested than at first are apparent: issues which I would suggest relate to the shifts around sensibility, taste and politico-literary acceptability which have occurred since February 1990. The current fashion for more dialogic, "democratic" forms of fiction in South Africa is at odds with the palpable degree of commandism and narrative closure in Matshoba's style, although they accord with his goal of using his own fiction as a conscientizing tool for Black Consciousness. Matshoba's narrator frequently sums up the incidents and debates dramatized, and lessons set out, in the stories; going so far as to chide and dismiss readers who do not have sufficient self-awareness and sensitivity to understand them and, on one occasion, even explaining the meaning of a symbol he is using.[68] At worst, Vaughan's observation that Matshoba represents popular consciousness as politically passive and fragmented can be adduced in the fact that the author does not appear always to trust the perspicacity of his readers.[69]

The closing of the distance between speaker and audience implied by the usage of an oral storytelling technique is counterbalanced by a demand, registered stylistically, for a degree of distancing from the action by those readers who wish to understand his purpose. For black South Africans, as the narrator observes at the beginning of "Three Days in the Land

---

[66] See, for example, Trump (1990), *op. cit.*, 168; and Mackenzie, *op. cit.*, 29.

[67] Compare the remarks in Matshoba (1979), *op. cit.*, 143-44, 146, and 186 with *ibid.*, 144, 145, and 151. "The country was too dull and therefore mentally unhealthy. How could one develop a keen and creative imagination where the cow set the pace and the silence and loneliness of uninhabited spaces buzzed in one's ears?" (151).

[68] See Matshoba (1979), *op. cit.*, 188 and 53 respectively.

[69] Vaughan, "The Stories of Mtutuzeli Matshoba — A Critique," *op. cit.*, 47.

of a Dying Illusion," the squashed social reality of communal life can in-
hibit necessary processes of individual self-reflection and understanding.
Therefore, even as Matshoba's fiction calls for black self-identification
and emotional empathy, it demands a degree of intellectual work from
readers; a space to muse over (and eventually decide on the ineluctable
truth of) black oppression under apartheid in the manner exemplified by
the examining, comparing, analyzing narrator. Brechtian estrangement
techniques, it may be added, are not especially in vogue in South Africa at
present.[70]

Moreover, the accessibility of these stories is not always promoted
through the register of language used, despite (again in line with Black
Consciousness dictates) the occasional admixture of English, Xhosa and
Afrikaans indicating township patois in recorded speech. Matshoba is fond
of "terms" — verbal quotes and other indicators of knowledge popular
among better-educated township youth — sometimes harnessing Plato and
Shakespeare to enhance his points; but exceeds this in a sporadic display
of sophisticated and difficult language that sits ill with his desire to reach
ordinary black readers. The ease with which words such as "braggadocio"
(*sic*), "*mesdames*" and "*Regina belli*" are employed, contradict the narrator's expressed dislike of the manner in which English is used as a tool of
social power and personal positioning in South Africa.[71]

These criticisms do not imply that Matshoba's short fiction of the late
1970s does not remain a fascinating, and rich, source for literary discussion and debate. However, contemporary commonplaces in the academy
regarding literary standards, aesthetics and the role of literature in society
have served to deny him his rightful place in the history of the country's
literature. As Shane Moran has pointed out in a recent article, there is evidence of a "New Hellenism" at work in South African letters which aims
to transmute culture and art from its previously held combative and so-

---

[70] The point about the "distancing" of author from fictional material is made in
Vaughan, "Literature & Popular Culture," *op. cit.,* 8. For an example of an eschewal
of estrangement (and promotion of reader "entertainment" and "involvement") see
Ndebele (1984), *op. cit.,* 25.

[71] Critics have tended to read off Matshoba's language usage in the work too sim-
plistically (for example J. Williams [1992], *op. cit.,* 25, 28 and Chapman [1996], *op.
cit.,* 374). Of his reviewers only Obed Musi has indicated something of this problem
(see his remarks about the word "Isle" in O. Musi "When a Man Is a Man," *The Voice*
3, 40 (1979). For evidence around this point, compare the remarks about English usage in Matshoba (1979), *op. cit.,* 5, 99, 101, and 110, with the language used in *ibid.,*
4, 67, 76, 95, 128, and 148.

cially responsible priorities into a new posture of containment, principally through a reiteration of the values of artistic merit and individual sensibility.[72] Despite its invocation of the politics of the post-modern, the tolerance of difference and multiple voices in the new South Africa appears to be in the process of being folded into an assumption of an underlying unity in the last instance, inscribed in terms of an aesthetics of harmony coupled with a social agenda of nation-building. Dissonant elements within South African literary history are either being domesticated, or excluded. The latter has been the fate of Matshoba's stories.

Even well-disposed critics from within the academy have generally tempered their appreciation of Matshoba with comments to the effect that his formal innovations might not be aesthetically self-conscious, and that they should be regarded by critics as synchronically and contextually — rather than formally — significant.[73] Such an inclination shows a patronizing proclivity which is unfortunate. Rather, it seems opportune to stress once again the importance of Matshoba's work as a marginal, anti-canonical expression of black experience, attuned to more than simply the "temporal demands of black experience in the 1970s," as one critic would have it.[74] Even today his stories remain a reading experience which raises many questions about issues pertaining to the role of politics in fiction, writer commitment, narrative focalization, and other crucial concerns. One can but hope that a new generation of critics will begin to raise these issues anew, and remember this prior example.

---

[72] S. Moran, "The New Hellenism," in *Rethinking South African Literary History,* eds J. Smit, J. van Wyk, and J.-P. Wade, Durban, 1996.
[73] See, for example, Chapman (1991), *op. cit.,* 6; Maughan-Brown, *op. cit.,* 218; Vaughan, "Literature and Politics: Currents in South African Writing in the Seventies," *op. cit.,* 133.
[74] Chapman (1996), *op. cit.,* 375.

HISTORY AND MEMORY: WRITING BY INDIAN AUTHORS

Vasu Reddy

Jorge Luis Borges' short story "The Witness" may on first assessment have little, if anything, in common with writing by Indian authors.[1] Yet a second interrogative reading shows some crucial commonalities with some of the texts produced by Indian authors writing in the period 1948-1994. What is significant in the narrative by Borges is a detached, playful awareness of the absurdity of the human condition and central to its theme is a reference to a "universal memory"[2] as a necessary precondition which will perhaps consolidate and possibly "continue" or render "inextinguishable" the "deeds" of its subject who at a stage "populate(d) the dimensions of space."[3] In another sense this narrative, in charting a brief history of a specified, yet anonymous subject turns in on itself towards the end by metonymically invoking a universal aesthetic. If "deed" is translatable as "event" as the narrative suggests, then it stands to reason that all "deeds" are indeed traceable by invoking the trope of a universal memory, which could operate as a tracking device. To "trace" therefore in the Derridean sense would entail "expressing," "representing," "recalling" and "rendering present" as it were by summoning the signs of the past.[4] To this end, the meditative voice that contemplates at the end, "what will die with me when I die, what pathetic or fragile form will the world lose?"[5] seems to be a plea for an act of remembrance, an echo resonant of the Proustian narrative *Remembrance of Things Past.* Inasmuch as this may be read as an appeal for the denial of forgetfulness, the Borgesian statement could also be read as a call for a "presence," one in which erasure of the historicized

---

[1] Jorge Luis Borges, *Labyrinths: Selected Stories and Other Writings*, Harmondsworth, 1970.
[2] *Ibid.*, 278.
[3] *Ibid.*, 278.
[4] Jacques Derrida, "Signature Event Context," *Glyph* 1 (1977), 178.
[5] Borges, *Labyrinths: Selected Stories and Other Writings*, 278.

subject is disavowed and where, in its place "memory" is installed as a device which sutures significant aspects of the past and present.

In investigating the location and production of Indian authors in the apartheid trajectory, it is no coincidence that the writing by this ethnic group is also shaped by questions of history, memory and politics, all of which cluster around apartheid as trope. That the conditions under which some authors happen to be named and contextualized suggests that their narratives and all their attendant signifiers reveal as Linda Hutcheon would have it, an "extroverted, indeed paradigmatic, phenomenon."[6] To claim therefore that the writing by, for example, Indian authors is a "paradigmatic phenomenon" is to acknowledge that the fictional translation of the memory of historicized events operates at a symbolic level which would mean that as reader-witness we constantly negotiate our reading of the witness account as fictionalized "truth." This ostensibly would imply that "history" as a master trope is deployed in a variety of ways to foreground the totalizing logic of apartheid as historical event in South Africa. In turning more specifically to the question of Indian writing it is appropriate to make some initial claims about the Indian in the South African context.

South Africans of Indian origin comprise approximately a million, with almost three quarters living in the province of KwaZulu-Natal, on the east coast. The forebears of the vast majority of Indians came as indentured laborers in the mid-nineteenth and early twentieth centuries when the province of KwaZulu-Natal, known then simply as Natal, was a British colony. South Africans of Indian descent hail from Tamil, Hindi, Telegu, Gujerati and Urdu-speaking heritage. In 1860, the people who came to Natal from India were British citizens because India was a British colony, just as Natal was. It is unfortunate that writers of color have to be named because of their ethnicity (it is not the case that Athol Fugard is known as a white playwright, for example, but simply as Fugard). While this problem is evident, it is also politically necessary to recall the racially designated categories of apartheid in understanding that past. As I write, this is played out in the Equal Opportunity and Affirmative Action Policies of the post-apartheid government. In order to address redress in its transformation of the country, the once polarized nation is forced to reconfront its past by redeploying the same racial categories which once divided it.

---

[6] Linda Hutcheon, *Narcissistic Narrative: The Metafictional Paradox*, London, 1991, 96.

In the case of the South African literary context, it too is divided and this is evident in literary production over the last century. Michael Chapman's *Southern African Literatures* provides valuable insight into some of these divisions in South African writing.[7] While the major focus of this volume is the dynamic relationship between literary culture and political life in countries with contested histories, it circuitously addresses the literary production of writers of Indian descent in the South African context. Like their counterparts, Indian writers have responded in fiction, poetry, drama and other forms (such as journalism) to events circumscribed by the apartheid context. Writings that have secured apartheid as both historical knowledge have largely emphasized the dehumanizing effects of racial oppression. More specifically the vicissitudes of apartheid implied that black South Africans witnessed a more insidious and complex structure of domination that would see some of its literary manifestations in writing that emblematized protest and resistance. Such would be the modality of writing by many writers (both black and white) who sought to bear witness to events of the time by critically interrogating the trauma and pain of systemic violence that characterized the apartheid state.

South Africa has a handful of published authors who could be described as Indian. Apart from Ahmed Essop, short story writer of note, Achmat Dangor (who is cautious to describe himself as an Indian author), Ronnie Govender and Jayaparaga Reddy, the rest appear to be footnotes in a critical history yet to be written. In some cases authors have published one or two books such as Mewa Ramgobin's *Waiting to Live* (1986) and Jay Naidoo's *Coolie Location* (1990). This flippant description may seem insensitive to writers and scholars; yet it should be simultaneously acknowledged that what we know or do not know about writers other than the ones listed above, is also attributed to the lack of a steady and consistent output in their writings. It is also problematic to catalogue writers as Indian when many would resist that labeling. For instance, it is interesting to note that Malvern van Wyk Smith in *Grounds of Contest: A Survey of South African English Literature*, describes Achmat Dangor, Essop Patel and Farouk Asvat as "Colored" writers while Y. G. Reddy groups them as Indian authors.[8] I shall not enter an argument about their identity but will comment briefly on their early poetry.

---

[7] Michael Chapman, *Southern African Literatures*, London and New York, 1996.

[8] See Malvern van Wyk Smith, *Grounds of Contest: A Survey of South African English Literature*, Kenwyn, 1990; and Y. G. Reddy, "Literature," in *The Indian*

The work of these poets, particularly the poetry published in the mid-eighties, is characterized by the interesting use of voice. They engage directly with the violent landscape of apartheid South Africa, displaying an energy which is explosive, and voices that show themselves to be intensely intimate and simultaneously lyrical. History for these poets is violent, and yet, despite the haunting images of an oppressive milieu, there is a positive vision that speaks of a humanity and humanness they see as central, not peripheral, in a post-apartheid world. Dangor, who has written in all three genres could be described as the most productive writer, whose prose work increasingly establishes him as an important figure in South African literature.

In the late eighties, a collection of essays devoted to South African Indians, *The Indian South Africans: A Contemporary Profile* attempted to provide some insight on Indians in order to fill the gap displayed by "the lack of information on this community."[9] In a chapter entitled "Literature," Y. G. Reddy provided a survey of literature produced by members of the Indian community since 1860. Reddy's survey was a second study, a first enquiry took place in 1949 by P. S. Joshi entitled "Literature of South African Indians" in the *Handbook on Race Relations in South Africa*, edited by Ellen Hellman.[10] Joshi acknowledges that even at that stage the task of surveying a limited corpus of texts was "an exhaustive investigation," and besides, his study covered the period 1860 to 1949, a year after the National Party came into power, which saw the rise of the apartheid state. Reddy's study treats the phenomenon of literature as a broad category and he catalogues his analysis into political literature, newspapers, articles, books, booklets, educational and historical literature, theses, creative literature, religio-cultural literature and what he terms miscellaneous literature. While in the eighties the study may have been an appropriate description of developments in the literacy of the South African of Indian descent, the study gave no analysis of development in what could be interrogated as writing with a capital "L." This chapter will offer both a slight survey and analysis by making brief pauses at some texts that call into question history and memory as aspects which define and recall aspects of the struggle against apartheid. These aspects also reinforce the notion of apartheid nar-

---

South Africans: A Contemporary Profile, eds A. J. Arkin, K. P. Magyar, and G. J. Pillay, Pinetown, 1989.
  [9] *The Indian South Africans, op. cit.*, x.
  [10] P. S. Joshi, "Literature of South African Indians," in *Handbook on Race Relations in South Africa*, ed. Ellen Hellman, Cape Town, 1949.

ratives as an ambiguous label. On the one hand it signifies texts which have been written since 1948, and on the other it suggests that these texts confront the consequences of that system. Also included in this chapter are texts that were published after 1994, such as the Ronnie Govender collection. The reason for this is deliberate; though the text is published in 1996, its history is deeply rooted in the period covering 1948 to 1994.

Whatever significance apartheid narratives open up, the defining feature of the texts referred to here, is that their perceptual field invariably signals to a "history" of its subjects. The subject to which we attend is a "person" with a "story" that constantly straddles from and within a history, a point Kristeva explains as:

> the subjective cloud [that] crystallizes into the praxis of a "person" with a story and history, and the text emerges as the work of a subject [...] a work that exceeds life, but whose life shares its structures.[11]

This investigation, while it acknowledges identity as an important variable, will, however, avoid interrogating the notion of "Indian" and what this means in the cultural context of apartheid.

Published writing by Indians in the period 1948 to 1994, the period in which legislative apartheid was the norm, is fairly limited. In the area of theatre and performance there have been numerous productions, particularly since the late 1950s, of important works by Indian playwrights. Many of these works remain unpublished although they are by names such as Ronnie Govender, Kessie Govender, Muthal Naidoo, Ajay Hurbans, Junaid Aman, Dinesh Narandas, Charles Pillai, Farouk Hoosen, Vivien Moodley, Kriben Pillay, Mohamed Alli, Essop Khan, Satchu Annamalai and Pravesh Hurbans. The theatrical corpus of these playwrights, largely performances, have provided interesting explorations of socio-political questions of the apartheid context such as political corruption in the tricameral political system, love across the color line and Indo-Afro relations. All this continues to be important in an attempt to a create a unique voice and identity for Indian theatre.

In the area of poetry, Shabbir Banoobhai (1949), an accountant by training, whose anthologies include *Echoes of My Other Self* (1980) and *Shadows of a Sun-darkened Land* (1984) writes a contemplative poetry that closely resembles the tension between self-awareness and the struggle to transform thoughts into action. The question of race in the broader

---

[11] Julia Kristeva, *Desire in Language: A Semiotic Approach to Literature and Art*, ed. Leon S. Roudiez, New York, 1980, 105.

scheme of restriction and limitation and marginalization is cleverly illustrated in his early poem, "the border" where the border metonymically calls into question the problems of race, distance and alienation. In his work these are concerns that largely typify the tension between the personal and the universal in the context of apartheid.

Ahmed Essop's oeuvre shows close connections to apartheid as the informing context but it is by no means his only point of reference. His debut collection, *The Hajji and Other Stories* (1978; Olive Schreiner Award 1979) was followed by the novels *The Visitation* (1980), *The Emperor* (1984) and two further collections, *Noorjehan and Other Stories* (1990) and *The King of Hearts and Other Stories* (1998). Essop's narrators never operate as autobiographers. Despite this his narratives show experiences that are invariably connected to historical events in the apartheid context. While this fact is perhaps more reflective of his later work, his debut collection, *The Hajji,* is ostensibly characterized by its poignant insight into Indian life, and aspects of Indian culture. The later collections, however, particularly *Noorjehan*, show the Indian in moments of politicization and crises of conscience where questions of identity straddle the divide of the changing African landscape.[12] This collection marks a further development in Essop's work where issues around gender are textualized by highlighting important class divisions in society. These class divisions, while heightened by the apartheid landscape, are inextricably linked to cultural practices and traditions in Essop's work.

An example of one such tradition is the institution of arranged marriages, explored in the title story. Caught in a situation where the tradition is understood to mean respect for culture, Noorjehan capitulates to the wishes of her parents and tradition. Simultaneously, the narrator's observations of this situation are critical, and implicated in it is a moral perspective on the practice of arranged marriages. Again Essop reconfirms his skill as a master craftsmen by revealing the narrator to be an unassuming critical eye on situations:

> I felt sorry for Noorjehan. I could understand her emotional predicament. I had known her to be a girl of precious intelligence and sensitivity. Now, under pressure from her parents and the conventions of their society, she was reduced to the level of a sacrificial victim. Marriage transactions, although wilting under the force of twentieth-century changes, were still conducted, and I had known girls who had been pressured into marriage when they were yet mere slips, hardly ready for its coital demands. (4)

---

[12] Ahmed Essop, *Noorjehan and Other Stories*, Braamfontein, 1990, 4.

The narrator's observations mark an important response to a patriarchal order, and to a culture that has oppressed its women. In Essop's texts, a growing concern has been to locate an understanding of the structure of oppression in relation to culture and patriarchy. Noorjehan's defiance of the father's wishes further corroborates the view that Essop's narratives assess the various cleavages of oppression rather than to simply respond to the dominant ideology of apartheid. By tackling issues of gender and by more specifically portraying strong women protagonists, such as the character of Zenobia Hassen from *The Emperor*, Essop demonstrates cultural facets of women's oppression at a time when writing in South Africa largely concentrated on confronting the apartheid struggle.

Jayapraga Reddy (1948) published *On The Fringe of Dreamtime and Other Stories*, a collection of fourteen short stories written over a period of sixteen years.[13] This collection also contained stories that focused on the Indian caste system and apartheid laws. "A Time to Yield" which was later scripted as "Web of Persuasion," the South African Broadcasting Corporation's first television play with an all-Indian cast, focused on an Indian bride's disillusionment as a result of her arranged marriage. Confined to a wheelchair, Reddy wrote several plays that have been broadcast by BBC and SABC radio.

Less known is the poetry of Deena Padayachee, a writer who grew up in Umhlali, in the North Coast of Natal. *A Voice from the Cauldron* is a collection of thirty nine poems, and each poem is prefaced with an epigram that reads as a pronouncement.[14] The poems in this collection speak to the tyranny of apartheid by expressing contempt and moral indignation at the system. In his poetry there are cries of anger and grief; as well as reflections on the broader struggle for decolonization in countries such as Mozambique, Angola and Zimbabwe. Particularly striking, though not a unique feature of apartheid narratives, is the skilful usage of the lyrical "I" in these poems. Yet again the "I" never shows itself to be an autonomous entity, divorced from the community, but one that speaks with and for the collective oppression of all the marginalized. In Padayachee's poetry history and memory are textualized in the present where waste, confusion and alienation, the underlying themes of the collection, show up yet another subversive voice that attempts to discover its individual identity.

---

[13] Jayapraga Reddy, *On the Fringe of Dreamtime and Other Stories*, Johannesburg, 1987.
[14] Deena Padayachee, *A Voice from the Cauldron*, Domerton, 1986.

Unlike the powerful and impassioned calls to action in Padayachee's poetry, his collection *What's Love Got to Do With It?* reveals him to be a skilled craftsman of the short story form.[15] The collection seems to me to be unique in the perspectives it brings on the experience of living in the Indian community. The title story, "What's Love Got to Do With It?" invoking the Tina Turner hit song of the same title, is a brief piece of personal history that could be traced to Padayachee's medical school training. In the fictional version, the story essentially focuses on the lives of a group of medical students (Indian and African) at Medical School and the role of the apartheid state in attempting to segregate an already segregated medical school. In this story, Padayachee sketches the lives of a group of students while simultaneously foregrounding the dynamics of human interaction in a painful historical period.

In turning to examples of texts by two Indian authors, namely Ronnie Govender's *At the Edge and Other Cato Manor Stories*[16] and *Coolie Doctor: An Autobiography of Dr Goonam*,[17] the latter written in collaboration with academic and activist, Fatima Meer, I would like to show, by closer analysis, how these writings could be typified as narratives that are products of history and memory that testify to real and lived experiences. This is not to suggest that the texts by other Indian authors are less authentic or less "truthful." *Coolie Doctor*, and as the pejorative word in its title illustrates, is a significant document that bears testimony to a generation of Indian activists in the struggle against apartheid. As an offensive mode of address to describe Indians, the word "coolie" was also a symbolic reference to the systematic racism that both the British Government in South Africa and the Afrikaner Nationalist Government would employ against this group.

While it is acceptable practice in literary studies to view autobiography as a theory of life, or as the Greek root terms *auto* (self) + *bios* (life) + *graphe* (to write) would have it signify, "self-life-writing," the text is also a political history of an individual leader. This text is also seminal in its representation of an important generation of Indian activists, and shows the contribution of the Indian community to the struggle. Dr Goonam, a medical doctor, together with other activist friends, Drs. Yusuf Dadoo and

---

[15]   Deena Padayachee, *What's Love Got to Do With It? And Other Stories*, Fordsborg, 1992.
[16]   Ronnie Govender, *At the Edge and Other Cato Manor Stories*, Pretoria, 1996.
[17]   Dr Goonam, *Coolie Doctor: An Autobiography of Dr Goonam,* written in collaboration with Fatima Meer, Durban, 1991.

Monty Naicker, led the 1946 Indian Passive Resistance Campaign against the anti-Indian Land Act and was imprisoned repeatedly. Born in 1906, she was an early suffragette and bent on studying medicine, left for Scotland on 8 March 1928. After qualifying, she returned to South Africa in 1936 and set up her medical practice in the Grey Street complex in Durban, South Africa. Her medical work also took her to India, Britain, Australia and Zimbabwe but as the autobiography suggests, it was largely for her political activity that she is best remembered.

The context of this autobiography, shaped by the effects of history and the precepts of memory, textualize a subject whose ancestors hail from India, and whose father immigrated to South Africa in search of a better life promised by agents of the British Empire. Writing and telling in the case of this autobiography is a privileged practice of the self, where the "I" who is Gonarathnam labors to tell the events of her life:

> I was born in May Street, in Durban, in 1906 on the Southern part of the East African Coast. That made me African, but not quite, for my father had immigrated from South India and my mother from Mauritius. I would be identified as a South African Indian or Indian South African. They named me Gonarathnam. I didn't like my name. It didn't sound feminine enough. I wished it could have been something pretty, ending in an "a" instead of the heavy "m." Later in life, the name suited me because I became strong like it. Since I was the younger of the first two children in the family, they called me "Pappah," "Little One." I never grew to be more than five feet tall. Eventually there were seven of us in the family, three boys and four girls.[18]

In this opening section of her narrative a number of themes are initiated which are important in circumscribing the life of a subject who, from working class roots, and through sheer resilience and determination to become a doctor (a profession that was not appropriate for what was understood as the traditional role for Indian women), comes also to challenge the patriarchal system that would subordinate women. The reference to the non-feminine sound of her name, as well as the implication that the name held a prophetic quality in that it would corroborate her strength of character later in life, all suggest that she had to transgress a number of norms integral to family, community and friends in order to study medicine abroad. The personal struggle to realize a career path also forms an interesting parallel in this text with the struggle she waged for the political liberation of South Africa. In the forties, at a time when legal apartheid was being established in South Africa, she became engaged in the passive resistance

---

[18] *Ibid.*

campaign, a campaign that could be traced back to Mahatma Gandhi's arrival in South Africa at the turn of the century (1906-1909) and a campaign that took on a second phase when legal apartheid was institutionalized when the National Party came to power in 1948. As the phrase suggests, "passive resistance" was understood as a non-violent form of resistance which included peaceful demonstrations, fasting or other forms of non-cooperation that were initiated against the apartheid system. And perhaps the unique feature of Dr Goonam's autobiography, which straddles the generic qualities of both memoir and autobiography, is that the text has more to do with locating her in the trajectory of historical events, than to locate the events in her life history.

The cover illustration of *Coolie Doctor* shows a photograph of a young Dr Goonam, the medical graduate, earnestly gazing into the camera, holding her degree certificate in hand. The photograph of the autobiographical subject therefore foregrounds "self" and "event." The latter in this instance is the life history of a person who, as she notes in her preface, is concerned with the "outmoded traditions of the Indian people, their lifestyle, the social structure with its insurmountable barriers, (and) the evils of apartheid" (9). A further description may be that in the case of this narrative the "self" appears to be the privileged modality. While the photograph, available as the iconic signifier, provides the visual signature that designates the subject of the narrative, it simultaneously signifies that the past to be replayed is to be recast as a "presence," becoming an available sign to be explored, one which does not "memorialize" but opens up a trajectory in which precisely that "lost history" adds to the contextual game of the text. As such the speaking voice in the text situates itself in relation to a historical position. By this I mean that the "I" that recounts the early childhood experiences of growing up in Grey Street, Durban, the development of plans to become a doctor, the voyage to Britain in 1928, the experience in Medical School through to returning to Durban after qualification and the involvement in struggle activism, all signal a history in the project of remembering. It is interesting to note that while the "I" of the first seventy pages of the autobiography is marked by individuality as in a focus on the "self," the "I" from chapter eight becomes a subject of alliance, increasingly associated with collective pronouns such as "we" and "our." It is approximately at this point, at the beginning of World War Two, that Dr Goonam's activism takes shape. And the chapters that follow all hinge on the political events of the time and her place in those series of events. Her narrative is not always prudent about abstracting that which is necessary to the "self" and "event," and often lapses into fairly unnecessary details about the historical facts. However, her descriptions often give an apt description of the political climate and a sense of the oppression of Indians. One such example is her role in a protest march which challenged laws that restricted movement of Indians between provinces:

> My batch consisted of 20 marchers. There were 17 men and three women ·
> with myself. We took the train to Charleston, got off at the station and
> walked on to cross the border. As we entered Volksrust which is a small
> dorp in the Transvaal, we were confronted by a violent demonstration. Local
> whites threw stones at us, spat on us, called us bastards and Coolies and
> threatened to beat us if we didn't step back to our legal boundary. The pres-
> ence of a few white sympathizers incensed them all the more and we had to
> ask them to leave in the interest of our safety. (129)

This passage, with its usage of the possessive pronouns further confirm a politics of inclusion and identification since they frame positions, political configurations and set an agenda which the subject delineates. This politics of identification was one bent on dismantling the apartheid system. In this example, the ethnic and racist demarcations created by the apartheid regime are externalized in the pejorative labels used by the whites such as "bastards" and "coolies" to misrecognize the protestors. Unsurprisingly the racist attack was a physical manifestation of what was being concretized on a legal level that gave the oppressor the recourse to demarcate, curtail and limit the freedom of black citizens.

The scene above shows not simply an event in history that is recalled, but the concrete action taken by the historical subject to transgress the physical boundaries created by the apartheid government. Equally so, the politics of transgression is yet another feature of this text, a feature that could be extended to other narratives that represent apartheid. The statement preceding the quoted paragraph which reads "we organized to deliberately breech this law and court imprisonment" (129) could be read as an act of defiance, a public contestation of the artificial boundaries created to divide people. In many respects the concept of transgression and narratives of apartheid seem to have an uncanny relationship. In the case of Dr Goonam the protest march brings her in direct confrontation with the law. Despite a defense that emphasized the peaceful nature of the protest, and the significance of *Satyagraha* (Gandhi's philosophy of non-violent resistance), the judge's decision was predictable under the circumstances: "It is a violation of the law of the country [...] she is sentenced to six months hard labor, with two months suspended on good behavior" (130).

Transgression, like truth and knowledge, is brought about by the permeation of power in the institutions under control by the state. In order for apartheid to be effective, it had to be externalized in various institutional structures, and the law was integral to its operation. Dreyfus and Rabinow cogently articulate some characteristics: "Power is domination. All it can do is forbid, and all it can command is disobedience. Power, ultimately, is repression; repression, ultimately, is the imposition of the law; the law, ultimately, demands submission."[19] This would be defined as the "juridico-discursive" power, a negative, as it produces limits. Equally important then is that power is accompanied by resistance which takes the form of transgression; resistance is therefore located in the exploitative grounds of the production of power. In the case of Dr Goonam, resistance to different forms of power could be seen in her participation in the passive resistance campaign, her personal struggle to become a doctor despite the conventions of her time, and her resistance to the racism of family and friends. All of this shows that to transgress is to signal an "action." Furthermore, transgression could be read as the pushing to the limits in order to radically challenge hierarchies of power, and this is what opens up new types of subjective experience. Where "power" of the apartheid state imposes limits, Dr Goonam, the autobiographical subject who transgresses, shows in her narrative that she also resists erasure. So where transgression defines the "experience" of a subject operating at the margins of the social, a process characterized by struggle and contestation, such a trajectory allows us to identify the conditions, the defining moments if possible of the autobiography. Therefore it is not co-incidental that *Coolie Doctor* has more to do with explaining the conditions that existed in the life of Doctor Goonam that would determine (and problematize) her becoming a doctor and her role as a doctor turned activist in the struggle for liberation, than it has to do with the way in which racism had shaped her experience. In stating this I am aware that this may be a simplistic explanation for the text. Equally so, throughout the autobiography, the reader is confronted with a text that tells the tale of a relentless woman who saw her role as a calling ("Africa called me" [171]) and this meant that the events of her life were ultimately about one destiny: "And now I await, with all freedom loving South Africans, for negotiations to proceed, the violence to end, and the new non-racial, non-sexist democracy to be born" (173). Limits arise out of a restrictive economy, and if transgression is an effect of a restraining

---

[19] H. L. Dreyfus and Paul Rabinow, *Michel Foucault: Beyond Structuralism and Hermeneutics*, Brighton, 1982, 130.

and aggressive power then it could be claimed that *Coolie Doctor* constructs for us transgressive moments of Dr Goonam's life which operate in the internalized image of memory.[20]

Similarly, in a related yet different narrative genre, Ronnie Govender's *At the Edge and Other Cato Manor Stories* is to be read against the background of the notorious Group Areas. These were residential and business areas set aside for the exclusive occupation by particular "race" groups in terms of the Group Areas Act of 1950. Though published in 1996, the stories in this collection were written over the period of three decades since the sixties. By turns amusing, anecdotal, quirky, lyrical and impassioned, they abound with descriptions of a vibrant community now lost only to memory. The title story, "At the Edge" and "1949," further established Govender in the nineties as an important playwright. His play, *The Lahnee's Pleasure* received critical acclaim in the seventies and survives as one of his few published works.[21] This text, set in a pub in Mount Edgecombe, a town on the North Coast of Durban, is a play that examines class concerns, capitalist exploitation, and racism, by using the physical realities of the pub, divided as it is by a partition into black and white sections. Another unique feature of this play is Govender's experimentation with working class speech patterns, rhythms and accents, which apart from the humor that the patois evokes, also succeeds in highlighting deep-seated class conflicts in the Indian community. This further confirms the view that this is no monolithic community but one shaped by a variety of differences. Over the years he has also written and directed plays such as *Swami, Offside, Inside, Blossoms from the Bough, The Great R31 million Robbery*. These plays, with the exception of *Swami* (published in an anthology in 1986) and *The Lahnee's Pleasure*, are undoubtedly technically and literarily less accomplished, when compared to the collection of stories on Cato Manor. Though focusing on the ethnic, in this case, the Indian experience, the substance of Govender's narratives are ideological rather than ethnic. The plays, as is the case with the stories, concern the broader questions of oppression in the Indian community. While the point of reference is invariably the culture and context of the Indian community, the broader point of reference is always the effects of apartheid in the context

---

[20] See Clare O'Farrell, *Foucault: Historian or Philosopher?*, London, 1989, where she argues "if limits restrict our freedom, the transgression of limits is an expression of our freedom" (40).

[21] Ronnie Govender, *The Lahnee's Pleasure*, Braamfontein, 1974.

of personal experience. As a result (and this is a point Govender acknowledges), his work clearly has an autobiographical thrust.

In turning to *At the Edge and Other Cato Manor Stories* the socio-
political contexts of the late forties and the sixties form the setting of the
narratives. Like Dr Goonam's autobiography, here too the projection of
the past into the writing is embodied in the memory, that sublime weave of
events, happenings and occurrences which texture and circumscribe the
speaking voice that bears witness in these texts. As a writing and telling
subject it "releases," "inscribes" and "understands" the lived experience.
Govender alludes to this in his preface:

> Although I have taken some poetic license in the telling, these stories are
> based on the lives of the people who lived in Cato Manor and deal with ac-
> tual experiences, such as the 1949 riots and an exorcism performed by my
> grandmother. (12)

Cato Manor, named after George Cato, an early Natal settler and first
mayor of Durban, in the forties and fifties, was primarily an African
shanty town (Umkumbaan) housing largely working class African and Indian people who lived quite harmoniously until the infamous Group Areas
Act was implemented. This suburb was in close proximity to an expanding
white population on the Berea, largely white middle-class people, and
when Cato Manor was declared white, approximately two hundred thousand non-white people were forcibly removed to ethnically designated areas such Chatsworth for the Indians, Kwa Mashu for the Africans, and
Wentworth for Coloreds. Like District Six in the Cape and Sophiatown
near Johannesburg, Cato Manor resembled the forced separation and removal of people into ethnically exclusive residential areas designated by
the apartheid state. Though a poor community economically, there is
something rich about the landscape and its people that is reflected in writings about Cato Manor. In his collection of stories, Govender also offers a
celebration of the human spirit in a nostalgic but unsentimental return to a
community that features here as both memory and history.

Gracing the cover of this collection is the photograph of the Shri
Muthulinganatha Easvar Alyam, a prominent temple in Cato Manor. And
if this visual cue is insufficient, a fairly detailed communal map of the
community of Cato Manor is followed by a Prologue in which the reader is
enticed to listen to the memories of a past, a past that is inextricably communal and private, yet fundamentally also public in the injustices that it
had come to symbolize through systematic racism:

But what Cato Manor did teach me, or rather what my mother, a Cato Manor woman born and bred, taught me, was that God was within me and if I listened carefully to that quiet voice inside and really struggled to heed its advice I wouldn't be trapped by the kind of contradiction that makes people build monuments to culture, civilization and consumerism, and yet wantonly destroy places like Cato Manor. Listen, my friends, listen to the voices of Cato Manor, District Six and Sophiatown as we struggle to fashion a new life — a life free from the contradictions that prevent us from seeing God in Everyman. (16)

There is something to be said about the direct mode of address in the preface of this collection. Calling an audience to "listen to the voices of Cato Manor" is a strategic operation in all stories. If memory is the active signifier in effecting the performance and staging of a self-consciousness, it also signals that there is some truth to be told about the events of this community. Cato Manor, in the context of this collection is not simply the descriptive milieu of the events, it is also a symbol of the triumph of the human spirit over the adversities imposed by the apartheid system. Govender as author is also the "knowable" narrator of this collection, holding together the bits and pieces that constitute a picture of a fragmented community that comes to "life" as an effect of history. Govender attempts to recreate in his narratives a sense of the community by recalling protagonists who also often provide a humorous insight into the life of a community that would soon be torn apart by forced removals. Consider the character of Poobathie, whose name is also the title of a story in the collection. On first reading the story of Poobathie, daughter of Harry, a convert from Hinduism to Christianity, it appears that the story essentially centers around her reluctance to convert to Christianity and the alienation she experiences from members of her family due to factors such as her dark-skinned complexion. However, on closer inspection, the story also raises some pertinent questions about the caste system and the way in which it is still practiced in the Indian community, including the way women are sexually exploited and questions related to pigmentation. In this instance, the prejudicial attitudes of people towards those of darker hue features prominently in the story of Poobathie. While it is correct to assume that apartheid had formalized a theory of race, it is also true to say that racism had other versions such as the way it operated within communities and Govender's story in this instance discloses a critical perspective on some of these issues.

Both "At the Edge" and "1949" capture the essence of living in two very different contexts in a time of upheaval and great political turbulence.

The former story centers around the figure of Vellamma, a woman who left India to settle for a better life in the fishing village of Fynnlands, on the Durban Bay. Living at the edge after the death of two sons and her husband, she is depicted as headstrong and an intimately spiritual and loyal woman. Her strength comes from her understanding of God and it is this sense of spirit and appreciation of spirituality that Govender textualizes in Vellamma, the village elder who was both pillar of strength to her family and spiritual healer to her community. In what must be a perfectly apt description of an exorcism, Vellamma exorcizes the demon from Mrs Munien to the amusement of her grandson, Garana:

> Mrs Munien emitted a sullen sound, like that of a trapped animal. She began to sway, and strange sounds emerged from her throat. Her head began to shake frenziedly and her long hair swirled around her. Vellamma didn't move. Her gaze did not waver and it seemed as if she was growing in physical stature [...]. She took hold of a bunch of syringa leaves and she brushed them around Mrs Munien's face and body. Mrs Munien was now writhing on the ground. Vellamma blew some ash on her face and Mrs Munien suddenly lay still as if she had cast off some heavy load. (64)

The supernatural scene in this particular story is also imbricated in issues concerning mysticism, ritual and religion, issues that inform the tapestry of Govender's writings. Particularly striking about this story is the figure of Vellamma, his grandmother, who represents the history of two continents, Africa and India. She is the archetypal mother figure, the ancestor from India as motherland, and the village elder of Cato Manor. She is also the link with Govender's childhood memories of growing up, and the exorcism ritual, as the narrator remarks, will forever hold onto the memory of Garana, the amused grandson: "What Garana was to witness next he would never, ever forget" (63). And while it is correct that where *Coolie Doctor* explicitly names the "I" as the author of the text, in Govender's stories, the omnipotent narrator compensates for the absence of the autobiographical "I" by constantly disclosing itself as the knowing and knowable subject of the Cato Mano community.

An extended elaboration of some of the major historical events that transpired in the same year is offered in "1949". But first the story takes as its fictional departure the story of Dumisane, a Zulu man who was the tenant of the Manirams. He worked as a petrol attendant at what was known as the Model Garage, owned by Mr Percival Osborne, son of a British settler who became a wealthy wholesale merchant. Second, and weaved into the story of Dumisane, his job, his relationship with his landlord and boss, is the turn of events in 1949 which led to riots between Africans and Indi-

ans when an Indian stallholder, who having caught an African boy stealing, had him punished. Third, 1949 was also the year in which the Durban
Municipality had passed what was known as the Pegging Act, the forerun-
ner of the Group Areas Act. The legislation was intended to "peg the en-
croaching hordes of Indians and Blacks to their boundaries" (113). This
event is textualized in a scene between Osborne and Dumisane, where the
former explains his outrage at discovering that Indian neighbors are to
move into the area opposite his garage:

> The only time Dumi saw him (Osborne) completely lose his temper, his face
> blazing red, nostrils flaring and tiny beads of sweat on his forehead and
> pock-marked nose, was when the Mahomedy family moved into the double-
> storey house opposite the garage on the corner of Gillits and Jan Smuts
> Roads. It was quite an event. Looking at the Mahomedy's move in, right
> next to the garage, Osborne was livid, "Why, in God's name, don't these
> people go and live with the rest in their own areas? Why do they insist on
> living with us?" (113)

In Osborne's tirade it is difficult not to notice the racism, hatred and big-
otry that characterized the period which Govender recalls. This scene also
symbolizes the collective racism of white South Africans, which in 1949
was slowly taking shape in the form of legalized apartheid, and it was a
year earlier when the National Party government had come to power prom-
ising a policy of racial segregation. It seems clear that Govender uses the
historical context and situation of his characters to intersect with — possibly even mirror — the broader political context of the time. In this sense
this story in particular foregrounds a sense of the national identity at the
time, one which was fractured, fragmented and distorted by racial, ethnic
and class divisions. In "Over My Dead Body" the penultimate story in the
collection, the future of Cato Manor as a mixed residential area is discussed in a community hall, as its residents challenge the government's
decision to declare it a white residential area. The emotive title conveys a
sense of personal suffering, political sacrifice, and emphasizes the systemic violence that characterized apartheid. In this collection Govender
uses Cato Manor as the physical context, and in a style characteristic of
documentary realism, he captures the vernacular context, notably in its
lyrical echoes of Indian working-class speech patterns and Zulu idioms, to
show that the conflict of races is ideological and its moral implications are
still a matter of questioning and debate.

It is difficult to pin down a representation of writing in the apartheid
context as uniquely "Indian" because that label resists an understanding of
identity as something that is pre-given, fixed and monolithic. However,

that which I have attempted to situate and explore as "Indian" in this chapter may be applicable to, or consistent with, similar experiences by writers of other ethnic groups in South Africa. If the writing by the writers I have assembled in this chapter under the rubric "Indian" is to be further problematized or set apart from others, then perhaps it could be argued that the "experience" which they testify to in the narratives has more to do with apartheid than it has to do with ethnicity. In addition to the authors convened here, the texts referred to have more to do with apartheid as representation than they have to do with identity. After all, identity, I contend, is something quite new and yet to be explored in the post-apartheid context, something dialogical and to be negotiated, as South Africans move from a logic of difference that was conflictual to the contemporary notion of identity that celebrates difference and diversity that is facilitative and productive.

Indian authors, by no means an organized and representative grouping of writers in South Africa, and depending of course on how they themselves define their identities, have attempted to write from what Nadine Gordimer described in the eighties as the "interregnum," the period in the apartheid police state, symbolized by its institutionalized racism. And while the writings display a multifarious treatment of issues which could be considered ethnic, such as the problematic caste system, arranged marriages, class prejudices in the community, superstition and religious fanaticism, the broader circumstances involve a sense of displacement and a development of the national consciousness in the way apartheid contributes to a crisis of identity. More specifically, the reference points shared by individual authors reflect what I at the outset referred to as a universal memory. In a sense, Indian writers have written themselves into the national text, a point Bjornson cogently articulates:

> To write is not only to speak for one's place in the world. It is also to make one's own place or narrative, to tell the story of oneself, to create an identity.[22]

And if, as Michel Foucault argues in *The Order of Things,* the modern is indeed the age of history, then the discourses generated by it are historically grounded and logically must occupy a privileged position.[23] Conse-

---

[22] Richard Bjornson, *The African Quest for Freedom and Identity: Cameroonian Writing and the National Experience,* Bloomington and Indianapolis, 1991, 10.

[23] Michel Foucault, *The Order of Things: An Archeology of the Human Sciences,* London, 1970.

quently, "to write" or "to speak for one's place in the world" is to create a structure for remembrance through which significant moments of a past tainted by apartheid could free subjectivities. The "universal memory" that Borges referred to in his story, is for many authors the context of apartheid and the boundaries it created to reinforce difference as division. It is this context, that "place in the world" which Dr Goonam, Ronnie Govender and many more writers writing in the period 1948 to 1994 would have chosen to capture.

Nevertheless, while it may be unwise uncritically to reduce the literature by the authors featured here as reflective of a particular consciousness, it is with equal measure to be argued that ethnicity is imbricated in the writings by these authors. Though the brief of this chapter was to show how some Indian authors responded to the crisis of apartheid, perhaps further investigation is needed to articulate the intersection of ethnicity with difference and the way this identification could be understood in a conception of identity. In the work of the authors discussed here, it could be argued that apartheid features as a historical system, as ideology and as administration which is externalized as the conflict of race. Indian authors too, like many of their black and white counterparts who wrote within and against the system, return consistently with ethical questions and considerations that seek to understand some sort of "truth" about a human experience that *was* institutionalized apartheid.

JUMP STARTS: NADINE GORDIMER AFTER APARTHEID

Judie Newman

As apartheid has crumbled, the question which has presented itself repeatedly is whether the South African novelist has lost his or her essential subject. Can the white novelist survive the end of apartheid — or has the artist's inspiration disappeared, together with the tools previously employed? The question betrays an assumption — common, I would argue to both postcolonial and post-apartheid writing — that it can engage only with representational, realistic portrayals of an essentially political subject matter — that without Empire — or, in this particular case, without Afrikaner Nationalism — it has no independent existence of its own. The question of use value as opposed to aesthetic value is therefore a question which lies at the heart of postcolonial writing: South African literature simply presents an example at the sharp end of the spectrum.

Recent debates in South African literary criticism have centered upon the problem of the artist's role in relation to society, specifically in what has become known as the Albie Sachs debate, and in the response to the writings of Njabulo Ndebele. During forty years of opposition to apartheid the avowed aim of literary practitioners was "solidarity criticism," placing a strong emphasis on social realism and the evaluation of writing in relation to its adherence to a materialist dialectic.[1] Writing was seen as a "cultural weapon" and was supposed to concentrate upon expressing collective rather than individual experiences in a mode of popular realism. In 1989 Albie Sachs made a speech, "Preparing Ourselves for Freedom," a paper prepared for an ANC in-house seminar on culture.[2] Sachs (somewhat teas-

---

[1] See Graham Pechey, "Post-apartheid Narratives," in *Colonial Discourse / Postcolonial Theory,* eds Francis Barker, Peter Hulme and Margaret Iverson, Manchester, 1994; Susan Van Zanten Gallagher, "The Backward Glance: History and the Novel in Post-Apartheid South Africa," *Studies in the Novel* 29:3 (Fall 1997), 376-93.
[2] Albie Sachs, "Preparing Ourselves for Freedom," paper prepared for an ANC in-house seminar on culture, in *Spring Is Rebellious: Arguments about Cultural Free-*

ingly) proposed banning the phrase "culture is a weapon of struggle"; he
described solidarity criticism and the instrumental view of culture in general as impoverishing artistic production and as merely a means of appear-
ing politically correct. Above all he argued that the result of solidarity
criticism was simply to ensure that all South African literature was about
the oppressor. In his description of recent South African writing, he la-
mented the narrow range of themes, the closing off of ambiguity and contradiction, and the stereotypical nature of character. For Sachs the power
of art lay in the capacity to expose contradictions and reveal hidden tensions. The concentration on the struggle had closed off whole areas of human activity. "And what about love?" asked Sachs, rhetorically:

> Can it be that when we join the ANC we do not make love any more, that
> when the comrades go to bed they discuss the role of the white working
> class? (21)

Sachs' lighthearted, teasing tone was part of his point; the medium was
also the message. For Sachs the editing out of everything but the political,
the filling up of novels with oppressors, trauma, misery, risked a further
reduction of the individual already threatened by apartheid:

> What are we fighting for, if not the right to express our humanity in all its
> forms, including our sense of fun and capacity for love and tenderness and
> our appreciation of the beauty of the world? (21)

A better strategy was to allow art to bypass, overwhelm and ignore apartheid by establishing its own space. Sachs' paper was punchy, if somewhat
lacking in nuance, and it stirred up a hornet's nest of debate. Doubts were
expressed on the pronouncements of an exile (even such an honored exile
as Sachs), who might be seen as out of touch with South African reality,
and the risks of depoliticization were repeatedly invoked. The specter of a
return to the autonomy of the text, in liberal-formalist terms, was raised.
The implicit suggestion that the Movement saw the freedom of artists as
within its gift, envisaging a donor relation to culture, also rankled. Others
simply saw Sachs' comments as premature. Indeed, one of the debates
concerning Sachs' paper had to be cut suddenly short. The Umlazi participants in the Natal COSAW debate left early "because barricades were already being set up in anticipation of a major attack" (87). The struggle
wasn't exactly over.

---

dom, eds Ingrid de Kok and Karen Press, Cape Town, 1990.

In contrast to Sachs (who was, after all, simply producing a short position paper) Njabulo Ndebele's was a more measured and deeply thought response, expressed in a series of essays collected in *Rediscovery of the Ordinary*. Ndebele highlighted the dangers of a quasi-journalistic literature of indictment characterized by the psychology of the slogan and by intellectual powerlessness. Such literature may inform but cannot transform. Indeed Ndebele cautioned against an over reliance on information, which could itself mirror the tactics of the opposition with its concern with information manipulation. Strongly influenced by listening to African oral storytellers (on trains and buses, on their way to work) he noted that their tales were not at all political: "When they talked politics, they talked politics. When they told stories, they told stories."[3] For him such storytellers were the makers of culture. Even when their stories were not centered on resistance, they had a social purpose. Similarly for Ndebele richness of character was not simply the product of bourgeois escapism into an ethos of individualism. Interiority could be a way in which the individual steps out of the network of exchange relations and values, away from the performance principle and the profit motive and towards passion, imagination, conscience. It is against this background of ongoing debate that Gordimer negotiates her own strategy for post-apartheid writing, a strategy which both recognizes the necessary connection between art and its social or political objectives, and also offers a critique of art as merely a weapon of struggle.

Nadine Gordimer's collection *Jump* spans the period in which apartheid was dismantled, beginning with stories centered on defensive structures, whether external (the destabilization of neighboring states), or internal (portrayals of the laager). Along the way individual stories cast side glances at the 1986 repeal of the Mixed Marriages Act ("The Moment"), detainees ("Spoils," "Home"), the underground ("Safe Houses"), township violence ("Keeping Fit"), the growth of "revolutionary tourism" ("What Were You Dreaming?") until the collection closes with a final tale, "Amnesty" centered on the release of political prisoners, presumably in 1990, when the ANC, PAC, and SACP were unbanned and a general release of prisoners took place. Several stories are based on or allude to news items or real events: the secretion of a terrorist bomb in a pregnant sweetheart's hand luggage, for example, or the conditions on the Mozambique/South

---

[3] Njabulo Ndebele, *South African Literature and Culture: Rediscovery of the Ordinary*, Manchester, 1991, 37.

African border which Gordimer reported on for a television documentary.[4] In its reception, the collection tended to be approached by reviewers in terms of its historicity and representation of the real world, with Gordimer cast firmly in the role of the artist as a political figure dealing with the representational. Although Gordimer was actually on a lecture tour promoting *Jump* when she received news of the award of the Nobel prize for literature, the prize didn't do much for the reviews of the volume. The collection was received as something of a disappointment, more the product perhaps of a "cultural worker" than of a Nobel-winning artist. Reviewers tended to detect an overemphatic tone, an excess of political gesture or humorless parable, and in particular a tendency to unbalance a tale by final sentences which spelled out a moral or added an O. Henry "twist."[5] Firdaus Kanga complained that "Gordimer writes a hectoring sentence, underlines a phrase that unbalances a whole story with its weight."[6] In "The Moment Before the Gun Went Off," for example, the last sentence reveals that the young black accidentally shot by the Afrikaner was not his "boy" but his illicitly-conceived son. James Wood felt that this revelation produced the effect of a sudden bump in the last sentence which grounded and spoiled the story, drawing it into brute statement.[7] "Some Are Born to Sweet Delight" concludes as a terrorist bomb blows a plane, the heroine, and her unborn child to smithereens. "Once Upon a Time" ends as a white child is ripped to shreds on the razor wire designed to safeguard his fairy tale home. Conversely, however, critics noted a reflexive subtext in these apparently too obvious stories — a narrator-as-character, candidly admitting to the invented nature of the tale ("Once Upon a Time," "A Journey") or emphasizing the deceptive nature of the facts presented ("My Father Leaves Home"). The presence of the narrator continually reminds the reader that this is story, as she intervenes to annul the action and send it back into the realm of fiction. In several stories ("A Journey," "The Ultimate Safari") Gordimer herself appears as a gray haired lady, watching on the sidelines.[8] For some readers the multivocal form demonstrated a laud-

---

   [4] Nadine Gordimer, "The Ingot and the Stick, The Ingot and the Gun. Mozambique-South Africa," in *Frontiers*, London, 1990.
   [5] Andrew V. Ettin, *Betrayals of the Body Politic: The Literary Commitments of Nadine Gordimer*, Charlottesville and London, 1993.
   [6] Firdaus Kanga, "Jump and Other Stories," *Times Literary Supplement*, 11 October 1991, 14.
   [7] James Wood, "Lyrical Analyst of a Nation," *The Guardian*, 10 October 1991, 27.
   [8] Karen Lazar, "Nadine Gordimer," in *Between the Lines II,* eds Eva Hunter and Craig Mackenzie, NELM Interview Series 6, Grahamstown, 1993, 21-37.

able attempt to end cultural monopoly by a full representation of the Other in a variety of perspectives and narrators, so that the voice of the white bourgeoisie no longer fills up the artistic space of fiction.[9] For others, however, the volume simply failed to cohere.

Gordimer's critics, however, had missed a vital dimension of the collection — and one which makes it one of the most interesting of Gordimer's formal experiments — the explicit connection between story and bodily action indicated in its title. Reviewers were less in touch with the genre of the short story than the author herself. In *Jump,* Gordimer plays with one particular genre of the folktale — the "jump story." One example will suffice to indicate the major features of the genre. This one is from Tennessee:

> A woman went out on the porch of her lonely farmhouse and cried, "Come on my handsome lover." A deep voice answered from the forest, "I'm coming."
>
> The woman returned to the house. In a few minutes she went out again and called, "Come on, my handsome lover." The deep voice answered from the pasture, "I'm coming." Again she went inside. And again she returned to the porch to call, "Come on, my handsome lover." The deep voice answered from the garden gate, "I'm coming." Finally the woman made her last call and received her answer. "Come on my handsome lover."
>
> "I'm HERE," said the voice — and a big black bear *ate her up.*[10]

The story is designed to make the audience jump, quite literally. It is worth noting that this is a slightly unusual example, since it has an erotic element. More normally jump stories are scary in their subject matter; they are grotesque or involve the supernatural: a dismembered hairy toe seeking revenge upon the child who severed it from a giant, a ghost slowly climb-

---

[9] See, for example, Jeanne Colleran, "Archive of Apartheid: Nadine Gordimer's Short Fiction at the End of the Interregnum," in *The Later Fiction of Nadine Gordimer*, ed. Bruce King, London, 1993, 237-43; Karen Lazar, "*'Jump' and Other Stories*: Gordimer's Leap into the 1990s: Gender and Politics in her Latest Short Fiction," *Journal of Southern African Studies* 18:4 (1992), 783-802.

[10] Olivia Murray Nichols, "'The Handsome Lover': A Romantic Example of the Jump Story," *Tennessee Folklore Society Bulletin*, LXVII:3 (October 1981), 124. On Jump stories I am grateful to my informants Gloria Cronin (Brigham Young University), Hasan El-Shamy (Indiana University), Trudier Harris (University of North Carolina), Andrew Hook (University of Glasgow), J. D. A. Widdowson (National Centre for English Cultural Tradition, University of Sheffield) ; and William A. Wilson. See also E. Martin Pederson, "Folklore in ESL/EFL Curriculum Materials," Paper presented at the Annual Meeting of the Teachers of English to Speakers of Other Languages, Atlanta, Georgia, 13-17 April, 1993.

ing the stairs: "I'm at the bottom of the stairs." "I'm at the landing." "I'm outside the door." "I'm at the foot of the bed." This example usefully highlights the elasticity of the folk form, which depends more on performance, structure and audience, than upon static content. The Florida Public Library Youth Program, for example, promoting oral tale-telling as a route to increased literacy, included several jump stories of a traditional nature in its program, but also suggested the incorporation of various types of community involvement: "Have parachutists explain their equipment and talk about their experiences."[11] (In America, airborne firefighters are smoke-jumpers.) The form is not, of course, limited to one social or national group: it figures in the folk traditions of the Arab world, for example, as well as the African-American.[12] Folklore scholars will recognize it as a Formula tale: Motif Z13.1 ("Tale-teller frightens listener: yells "Boo!" at exciting point").

Typically, however, the tale ends abruptly in physical contact with and consequences for the audience, usually as the storyteller tickles, grabs or pounces upon a listener. "Jump stories" tend to be macabre, orally performed by a storyteller, often in a group situation (hence Gordimer foregrounds the storyteller as deceptive performer, and offers the sense of a multivocal group or collective narration). Today they are probably most easily recognized in animal stories told to children (who are a dominant presence in Gordimer's tales). In group narration the teller often pounces upon the child who looks most scared. "Little Foo-Foo," in which a fairy turns a rabbit into a field mouse, is a common playgroup example, told to the under-fives.[13]

Why tell jump stories? Firstly there is an obvious aggressive element here. That "pounce" is reminiscent of the learning experience of the puppy or kitten, a play device which teaches lessons about the hunt. The story usually involves something or someone slowly creeping up on you, stalking before pouncing, and in selecting the most scared person present, pick-

---

[11] Carolann Palm Abramoff, *Once Upon a Tale*, Tallahassee, 1995. See also Robert S. McCarl, "Jump Story: An Examination of an Occupational Experience Narrative," *Folklore Forum* 11 (1978), 1-17.

[12] See Hasan El-Shamy, *Folk Traditions of the Arab World: A Guide to Motif Classification*, Indiana, 1995. For a discussion of the African American tale, "The Golden Arm," told by Joel Chandler Harris to Mark Twain, who subsequently performed it repeatedly on stage, see Andrew Hook, "Reporting Reality: Mark Twain's Short Stories," in *The Nineteenth Century American Short Story*, ed. A. Robert Lee, London, 1985, 103-19.

[13] Thanks to Mrs Lilian Harris and Class 3, Archibald First School, Gosforth, Newcastle Upon Tyne, 1998.

ing off the weakest member of the group. We experience being the prey —
the pounced upon — but the story also offers a script for predation, and in
some stories (that bear, for example) it is the formerly hunted which
pounces in its turn. The return of a dead animal or person, reclaiming bodily parts, also suggests links to the hunt, and to the guilty conscience of the
hunter, with connections to taboo animals and totems. The story thus emphasizes the interchangeability of predator and prey, with the tables turned
as victimizer becomes victim. It may be "only a game," but it nonetheless
offers a rehearsal of violence and victimization, in a secure context.

That context also calls out for comment. Despite the scariness, it is
arguable that there is an element of reassurance in the telling of the tale (as
opposed to the content) in that it ends in bodily contact with a safe adult.
Imagination leads into physical action in the boldest possible sense — but
it is circumscribed within the frame of a secure situation. The story gives
us a playful enactment of fear and pain, fright and tickle, say, but it is only
play, and the pounce is often also the embrace of the family tale-teller.
Above all, then, the jump story is irremediably physical. It involves the
body, both in performance and often in content. "Cadaver Claims its Can-
nibalized Organs" is a representative Arab example.[14] A Virginian recounts a tale in which a child is asked to retrieve bones from a graveyard,
with the bones returning to frightening effect.[15] Indeed it may not be
stretching it too far to see Gordimer's 1974 novel, *The Conservationist,* as
an extended jump story, involving the return of a dead body to plague the
protagonist, who is actually "jumped" (ambushed) at the close in a hallu-
cinatory moment of horror.[16] Certainly the submerged or repressed body
which comes back to haunt the white imagination is generally recognized
as a common motif in Gordimer's work.[17] One of her earliest published
stories, "Is There Nowhere Else Where We Can Meet?" (1953), in which a
black man pounces upon a white girl, is based on "Little Red Riding
Hood," itself a jump story, though in this case the black man is arguably
more the victim than he is the wolf.[18] The genre, then, offers a demonstration of an artistic creation extending suddenly into the "real" world, with
real physical effects produced on the body of the listener. It is therefore a

---

[14] Hasan El-Shamy, personal communication.
[15] Trudier Harris, personal communication.
[16] Nadine Gordimer, *The Conservationist,* London, 1974.
[17] Judie Newman, *Nadine Gordimer*, New York and London, 1988.
[18] "Is There Nowhere Else Where We Can Meet?" in *The Soft Voice of the Serpent*,
London, 1953.

perfect example of a story written with an eye to functioning as a weapon of struggle. It is a form which we might almost expect to have been adopted by the South African writer. It draws on oral tradition so is "of the people" in a way which more rarefied modernist or postmodernist writing is not. (Gordimer cheerfully published one of these stories, "A Journey," in *Playboy*.) The macabre content allows a satiric purpose — the jump story exposes horrors — and the structure (evident in the overall arrangement of Gordimer's collection as well as within individual stories) dramatizes the post-apartheid reversal of roles from victimizer to victim as the setting of the tales comes steadily closer to home.

It is worth pausing for a moment to establish that the case for seeing the collection as based upon the genre of the jump story depends on more evidence than its title alone. In the tales, the O. Henry twists are often extended into an almost physical pounce, as if the reader were seized and physically inscribed in the action narrated. In this respect it is striking how many of the reviewers speak in terms of a sudden bump or start; of "the moment when the political and the personal connect to deliver a blow to the heart,"[19] or of the endings which "strike at the gut."[20] In broad terms the collection emphasizes predation with its repeated images of the hunt ("Spoils," "Teraloyna") or the sexual chase ("A Find"), of children caught, seized or abducted ("Jump," "Once Upon a Time") or vulnerable to wild beasts. In "The Ultimate Safari" children fleeing a Renamo raid cross the Kruger Park in almost equal terror of white police, bandits, and prowling beasts, huddling together by night in a squirming mass lest a lion *"jump* right into the middle of us."[21] Physical activity is thematically important — trekking to safety, parachute jumps, jogging, journeys — as is the suggestion that children's games have suddenly turned to brutal reality — jogging to desperate flight, parachute jumping for fun leading to military activity, a "safari" to a struggle for survival, a child's toy becomes a cache of plastic explosive. By demonstrating how a story can turn into an event Gordimer implicitly thematizes the connection between fiction and action. Hunters and hunted also cross over at several points. In "My Father Leaves Home," the father as a child of thirteen flees pogroms in Europe only to become a member of an oppressive racist regime in South Africa. The nar-

---

[19] Firdaus Kanga, *op. cit.*
[20] Rita Ciresi, "Review of Nadine Gordimer's *Jump*," *Library Journal* 116 (August 1991), 149.
[21] Nadine Gordimer, *Jump and Other Stories*, London, 1991, 39. Subsequent page references are to this edition.

rator, on a pheasant shoot in her father's original country, recognizes that in his treatment of blacks her Jewish father had turned from prey to predator. Watching the shoot the narrator stands aloof: "only a spectator, only a spectator please" (66) she begs, but the shoot merges with the image of past pogroms, Cossacks on horseback riding down human beings, and her father shouting at his black laborer. As she comments, "I did not know that I would find, here in the wood, the beaters advancing, advancing across the world" (66).

So are these stories essentially propaganda or parable, tales designed to pounce upon the reader to make one point with maximum force? As we might expect, things are a little bit more complicated than that. The dangers of too easy a continuum between fiction and action are dramatized in "Once Upon a Time." The narrator has been asked to contribute to an anthology of stories for children, and refuses, despite the argument made to her that "every writer ought to write at least one story for children" (23). Like Ndebele and Sachs, the unnamed writer declares "I don't accept that I 'ought' to write anything" (23). Awakened in the night by what sound like footsteps stealthily approaching, "moving from room to room, coming up the passage — to my door" (23) the narrator finally recognizes that the sounds are merely the creaking of a house built on undermined ground. Nobody is about to pounce on her. Yet unable to sleep she begins "to tell myself a story; a bedtime story" (25). Satiric in intention, the tale opens with a family "living happily ever after" (25) in an affluent South African suburb, their home surrounded by security devices and razor wire. When the mother reads the young son the tale of Sleeping Beauty, however, the little boy acts it out. He pretends to be the Prince, who braves the thicket of roses, and impales himself upon the shining "razor thorns" of the security fence. The story has impelled the child to action — but with fatal results. The child has been "jumped" not by an outside bogeyman but by the very measures which were designed to protect him. The story which the narrator tells demonstrates the risks of storytelling — as well as its power. In little, the tale dramatizes the central issue of the collection — the extent to which the writer should write certain types of story, the risks of too straightforward a connection between story and action, and conversely the costs of storytelling which is cut off from its social context. It is, of course, the European fairy story of white South Africa which has actually killed the child.

If "Once Upon a Time" engages (perhaps too obviously) with the oral tale and the norms of the jump story, the title story adopts a more complex approach. In "Jump" a "turned" Renamo prisoner, is forced to relate his story again and again to his interrogators.[22] The tale which he tells is a jump story, in several senses. His parents had complained when their son took up parachute jumping, "enjoying yourself frightening us to death" (12), but the real military activities are infinitely more scary and involve the abduction of young children, brought in as rewards for the military. Jumped on and imprisoned by newly independent blacks for taking an illicit photograph, promptly politicized, the man had used his contacts in a parachute club to become a counterrevolutionary mercenary, changing sides only when he saw the fate of black children, abducted and raped. The soldier told his story (going over to the enemy to do so) in order to end this other jump story. One pounce upon him has impelled counterrevolutionary action; the sight of others who have been seized impels him to its opposite. The protagonist is discovered at the start of the tale as in a tracking shot through the hotel lobby, the halls, elevator, corridor, apartment door, the room:

> he is aware of being finally reached within all this as in a film a series of dissolves passes the camera through walls to find a single figure, the hero, the criminal. Himself. (3)

The camera jumps him; he is prey to the press. The tale speaks directly to Ndebele's concern with the lack of ambiguity in South African characters. As a "turned" figure, the protagonist is both hero and villain. In addition he has been previously identified with the documentary (his initial arrest was for taking a photograph) and with the manipulation of information. It is only when he sees an abducted child, however, that he is transformed; he reaches the point where "someone begins really to know. Instead of having intelligence by fax and satellite" (17). Importantly the young man has had to tell his story repeatedly into a tape recorder, and the tale reaches us, as readers, with frequent reminders of this oral performance, from interruptions from his interviewers to asides which comment on the narration: "He would explain to his audience," "at this point in the telling" (8). His story has an obvious use-value, as propaganda for the revolutionary side, and he is, as a result, paraded before the television crews of BBC, CBS, Antenne 2, Zweites Deutsches Fernsehen:

> he told his story. For the first few months he told his story again and again in performance. Everyone has heard it now. (6)

---

[22] The story does not specify his political allegiance, but the source for the tale (*Frontiers*) so describes him.

Now that he has contributed his particular story as a weapon of the struggle he has no further role to play: "Once he's told everything, once he's been displayed, what use is he to them?" (18) In contrast Gordimer's story moves into the contradictions and ambiguities of the young man's role, focusing on interiority. The story extends further, focusing upon the whole person, the person who continues after the propaganda story has been told. At the close, the young man looks forward to one final jump, suicide from his upper storey window:

> Jump. The stunning blow of the earth as it came up to flexed knees, the parachute sinking silken.
> He stands, and then backs into the room.
> Not now; not yet. (20)

No final jump is offered to the reader, to wrap up the events in an easy conclusion. Gordimer's story avoids the spectacular or sensational; the story will go on, into the realm of the ordinary.

The role of the body in these stories also raises larger questions concerning social control and the ideal of the "civil" society. In "What Were You Dreaming?" a black hitchhiker picked up by a revolutionary tourist, doing the rounds of the South African political theme park, caters very carefully for his audience in his tale of woe (eviction, illness, seven fatherless children). This is the story they want to hear — not the real details of drink, assault and grievous bodily harm. The white Liberal, sensitive to questions of delicacy, colludes with him, to obscure the truth from the tourist. When she notices the African's missing front teeth she coyly allows him to see it as merely a fabled sign of sexual attractiveness. In fact, the teeth have been deliberately removed as an advertisement for the African's prowess at male-on-male oral sex. In the interests of telling the right story the woman is unable to pronounce the term "cocksucking." The tourist is allowed to dismiss it as "Just another sexual myth." Myth is what conditions his approach to South Africa, which sidesteps ambiguities and unpleasant realities in a fable of the noble oppressed. The body tells a different story.

Several of the stories are even less coy. "Spoils," another staging of the scene of predation, opens with the narrator commenting on the smell of his meat-eater's wind. On a visit to a private game reserve, he is sickened by his own appetite for meat, and by extension, repelled by his participation in a predatory society. "I want no part of it" (161) he declares, no part of the meat, the hunt, nor the global violence brought to him in the morning news bulletin. In direct contrast a fellow guest figures as his polar opposite — a young man who has been in political detention. The latter shows no squeamishness at the terrorist bombs in streets, cars and super-markets:

> these don't confuse *him*, make carrion of brotherhood. He's brave enough to swallow it. No gagging. (168)

When the group are invited to see lions at a recent zebra kill, however, "Everybody is game" (170), game for the excursion, but also in imagistic terms, part of the cycle of predation. In the truck they become an undifferentiated mass "pressed together, swaying, congealed, breathing in contact" (171). Nobody can opt out of this bodily contact — it would be far too dangerous to leave the vehicle so close to the lions. Later the guests settle down to fresh paw-paw and bacon, boerowors and eggs. Back at the kill the dung beetles are already carrying off the zebra's stomach contents. There seems to be no way out of the prey-predator continuum and its violence. In its metaphors the story draws explicitly on Norbert Elias' account of the development of civil society, as exemplified in the slow development of manners.[23] Meat-eating is a particular focus. Elias argues that whereas in medieval society whole carcasses were carved at table, with knives freely flourished, the threshold of repugnance steadily advances until reminders that the meat dish is connected with the killing of an animal are avoided. The meat is carved elsewhere; strong taboos on the use of knives are developed. More generally the distastefully physical is removed behind the scenes of social life, whether it concerns reminders of the dead animal or of the human animal, in physical processes such as sexual and eliminatory functions, bodily secretions, nakedness or aggressive drives. At the close of the story the guide Siza is spotted with a knife. To the white observer it is "the knife that is everywhere" (178) — on the news, on dark street corners, in the gaols. But Siza carves out only a small, skillfully butchered portion of zebra, just enough for his family, leaving the major part of the slaughtered beast behind:

> The lions, they know I must take a piece for me [...] It's all right. But if I take too much, they know it also. Then they take one of my children. (179)

Ironically it is Siza who fulfills the earlier medieval injunction that a well-bred man should be capable of skillful carving, should give away the best portion of the meat and should keep only a small portion for himself. As

---

[23] Norbert Elias, *The Civilizing Process*, trans. Edmund Jephcott, Oxford, 1994. (First published as *Über den Prozess der Zivilisation*, Basel, 1939.)

opposed to the lack of true civility of his guests, Siza operates in a different cultural economy, in which it is not merely a case of "to the victor the spoils," but in which some degree of sharing, of reciprocity is implied, an ability to take part, to play one's part, without either withdrawing completely (and ineffectually) or swallowing everything whole as one of an unthinking mass. Somewhere between predator (lion) and prey (zebra) Siza negotiates a safe part for himself, a part which relies on the folk lesson of the jump story. The jump story, we will recall, involves both fear and playful pleasure. The return of the animal (bear, lion, social embarrassment) may represent a threat, or a pleasure, in the freedom from bodily repression and from the hegemonial net.

This ambivalence of the body features prominently in "The Moment before the Gun Went Off," another treatment of the disjunction between the public story and the internal story. As reported in the press the story of the Afrikaner farmer, regional Party leader and Commandant of the local security commando, who accidentally shoots one of his black workers, will go all over the world. It is in fact an ordinary story of an accident, "there are accidents with guns every day of the week" (111) but in the South African context it becomes spectacular, sensational, and enormously useful to the opponents of the regime:

> the story [...] will fit exactly their version of South Africa, it's made for them. They'll be able to use it in their boycott and divestment campaigns, it'll be another piece of evidence in their truth about the country. (111)

As Marais realizes, he and the black man will become "those crudely-drawn figures on anti-apartheid banners, units in statistics of white brutality" (111). The moment before the gun went off was actually a moment of childish excitement, sharing features with the jump story. Marais had picked up his twenty year old unacknowledged son Lucas to go hunting, with Lucas riding on the back of the truck, the better to spot the kudu. The farmer had a rifle beside him, and when the truck went over a pothole the sudden jolt fired the rifle, killing Lucas, who was leaning over the cab roof. At first the farmer thought Lucas' fall was a joke, assuming that Lucas had toppled off the cab "in fright." The farmer "was almost laughing with relief, ready to tease" (117) as he opened the door of the cab, but "the young man did not laugh with him at his own fright" (117). This time the joke of "Bam! Gotcha!" has ended in death. To the unwary reader the sudden revelation of Lucas' paternity is one more example of white South African hypocrisy, another plank in a propaganda platform. But what

Gordimer's story also shows us is Marais' reaction after the gun went off, a reaction observed but hushed up by the local police captain. "He sobbed, snot running onto his hands, like a dirty kid. The Captain was ashamed, for him, and walked out" (113). Marais' bodily processes have escaped from his control, as they did when he was a "dirty kid" fathering Lucas. The revelation of bodily closeness and connection here opens up a fragile Utopian possibility implicit in the jump story's physicality, the possibility of communication and connection between black and white in the body, in an era beyond the prohibitions of the apartheid state. The police Captain and his laws define Marais as a "dirty kid" for the physical expression of emotion, sexual in the past, remorseful in the present. Bodily shame is located in the police state, not in the father-son relationship. Gordimer has repeatedly envisaged the body (sensuality) as a potential means to political liberation, looking ahead (to borrow a phrase from J. M. Coetzee) to a future when "bodies are their own signs," as opposed to being caught in the signifying systems of a state which considered the individual to be completely classifiable by bodily features.[24] In a jump story bodies are merged – if only momentarily — in a relationship of danger and reassurance, fear and pleasure. There is an escape from social control. Although inevitably fragile and unrealized, physical contact provides a potentially Utopian element in the jump story. In a nation divided according to the body, physicality is fundamental to resistance against oppression.

If the collection demonstrates the importance of action in the pursuit of justice, it also constitutes a searching inquiry into the ethics — and the aesthetics — of such action. In *Spring Is Rebellious*, Ari Sitas argued that:

> In Natal […] grassroots creators have known how fragile their bodies were and how they got broken in gaol; how they got pierced real easy by spears; […] they knew all along that their only "aesthetic weapons" have been their bodies and what their brains remembered or remade into stories.[25]

Gordimer takes the commentator at his word. In its bodily emphasis, in its foregrounding of the oral tale, in its reminders to us of the primacy of story — and of the risks of story — Gordimer amply fulfils the role of the storyteller as maker of culture and — to return to our opening question — demonstrates that there is plenty of life in white writing, even after apartheid.

---

[24] J. M. Coetzee, *Foe,* Harmondsworth, 1987, 157.
[25] *Spring Is Rebellious*, 94.

BESSIE HEAD'S SOUTH AFRICA

Craig Mackenzie

Bessie Head achieved renown as a writer of novels about Botswana, and the South African aspect of her life and work remained relatively obscure until her death in 1986. Since then there have been several interventions which address this lack. Gillian Stead Eilersen's collection of Head's short prose, *Tales of Tenderness and Power* (1989), contains several pieces written or set in South Africa, including Head's most widely anthologized story, "The Prisoner Who Wore Glasses" (first published in 1973).[1] My own *A Woman Alone: Autobiographical Writings* (1990) gathers together the fragments of her South African life in a dozen pieces she wrote about the country.[2] Then the appearance of *The Cardinals* (1993), edited by Margaret Daymond, meant that her most substantial South African work was made available.[3] And the publication for the first time of several of her early poems (in *English in Africa* in May 1996) completed the process of putting her South African work into print.[4]

Works of a bibliographical and biographical nature also appeared. *Bessie Head: A Bibliography* (1986) coincided with her death, and the second, vastly expanded, edition (1992) took stock of the gathering pace of Head scholarship after her death.[5] Randolph Vigne's edition of her letters, interspersed with illuminating commentary, appeared as *A Gesture of Belonging: Letters from Bessie Head, 1965-1979* (1991) and placed on re-

---

[1] Bessie Head, *Tales of Tenderness and Power*, ed. Gillian Stead Eilersen, Johannesburg, 1989.
[2] Bessie Head, *A Woman Alone: Autobiographical Writings*, ed. Craig Mackenzie, Oxford, 1990.
[3] Bessie Head, *The Cardinals: With Meditations and Stories*, ed. Margaret Daymond, Cape Town, Oxford, 1993.
[4] Bessie Head, "Unpublished Early Poems," *English in Africa* 23:1 (1996), 40-46.
[5] *Bessie Head: A Bibliography*, eds Susan Gardner and Patricia E. Scott, Grahamstown, 1986; and *Bessie Head: A Bibliography*, eds Craig Mackenzie and Catherine Woeber, Grahamstown, 1992.

cord Head's prowess as a letter-writer.[6] The most thorough assessment to date, however, is Eilersen's meticulous biography, *Thunder Behind Her Ears: Bessie Head: Her Life and Writings* (1995), the opening chapters of which shed new light on the South African part of Head's life and work.[7] And Kenneth Birch's memoir, "The Birch Family: An Introduction to the White Antecedents of the Late Bessie Amelia Head" (1995), placed in the public domain for the first time the response of Head's white relatives.[8]

The purpose of this article is to draw together the various aspects of Head's experiences in South Africa and her creative responses to these. I offer an overview of her South African life and look briefly at some of the poems and sketches of this period, before examining the only substantial work of this period, *The Cardinals*, and exploring her desire to "transgress" in this work as a response to the severely alienating experiences of her South African life.

On 6 July 1937, Bessie Amelia Emery gave birth to her third child, an event which took place at the Fort Napier Mental Institution in Pietermaritzburg, South Africa. The joy that is customary at the birth of a child must have been absent from this event, however. Bessie Emery (née Birch, and nicknamed "Toby") had been placed in the institution by her mother after it was discovered that she was pregnant. Worse was to come after the birth: the young girl-child, it was discovered, was "colored." In the South Africa of this period, an extramarital affair between people of different races not only broke one of the most entrenched of social taboos, it was also a punishable offence.

Toby was never to emerge from this institution and died there in September 1943. The identity of the father of the child to which Toby gave birth six years prior to her death and the circumstances of the conception have never been determined.[9] The Birch family assumed at the time that the newest addition would be white, but when she was returned by a white

---

[6] *A Gesture of Belonging: Letters from Bessie Head, 1965-1979*, ed. Randolph Vigne, London and Portsmouth, NH, 1991.

[7] Gillian Stead Eilersen, *Bessie Head: Thunder Behind Her Ears: Her Life and Writing*, Portsmouth, NH, London, and Cape Town, 1995.

[8] Kenneth Stanley Birch, "The Birch Family: An Introduction to the White Antecedents of the Late Bessie Amelia Head," *English in Africa* 22:1 (1995), 1-18.

[9] Kenneth Birch remarks in this regard: "Who the father was is completely unknown, and speculation is a waste of time. The event must have taken place in Johannesburg when Toby was out on parole from the family home; a brief encounter; a misuse of her mental state? Was she waylaid? Was she enticed somewhere? We do not know" (Birch, "The Birch Family," 10).

foster-family after just a few days on account of her "strangeness" the notion that young Bessie was fathered by a man of color slowly dawned. Bessie was then placed in foster-care with the Heathcote family of Pietermaritzburg for the next thirteen years.

In the late 1940s the situation in the Heathcote home deteriorated to the point where the local welfare organization decided to have her placed in an orphanage. So in 1950 the thirteen-year-old Bessie was taken to St Monica's Home, an Anglican mission school for colored girls located in Hillary, on the outskirts of Durban. The environment was austere and disciplined, with regular punishments meted out for misdemeanors. It was here, however, that Bessie was to receive an education and some grounding for the lonely and difficult life that faced her.

In December 1951, just under two years after Bessie began life at St Monica's, she received one of the many severe jolts in her life. She was told that she would not be going "home" for the holidays, and that the person she regarded as her mother was in fact not her real mother. She was later to recall this calamitous event in the following way:

> I was called to the office of the principal, a British missionary, who announced curtly: "You are not going back to that woman. She is not your mother" [...] the missionary opened a large file and looked at me with a wild horror and said: "Your mother was insane. If you're not careful you'll get insane just like your mother. Your mother was a white woman. They had to lock her up as she was having a child by the stable boy who was a native."
>
> The lady seemed completely unaware of the appalling cruelty of her words. But for years and years after that I harbored a terrible and blind hatred for missionaries and the Christianity which they represented, and once I left the mission I never set foot in a Christian church again.[10]

The sense of self that the young Bessie had held onto so tenuously was ripped away from her in this manner. She must for some time have had intuitions that she did not really belong to the foster-family, but now she was left with no illusions at all. Not for the last time, she must have felt truly alone in the world.

That there was also a feeling of liberation buried deep inside the misery of these revelations is reflected in some of the comments Bessie was later to make. In a letter to Randolph Vigne she wrote with bleak honesty: "The best and most enduring love is that of rejection."[11] The most that the

---

[10] Head, *A Woman Alone*, 3-4.
[11] Vigne, *A Gesture of Belonging*, 58.

young Bessie could salvage from the wreckage of her life was a sense of existential freedom — a freedom tempered by loneliness and rejection, but that nevertheless held out the possibility of fashioning some sort of life for herself.

She gained her Junior Certificate in 1953, aged sixteen. At this time the austere principal featured in the reminiscence above was replaced by the more humane and spontaneous Margaret Cadmore, whom Bessie was later to memorialize with warmth and humor in her novel *Maru*. Under Margaret Cadmore's leadership, Bessie flourished. Although her interest in subjects other than English began to wane in the second year of her study for the Natal Teachers' Senior Certificate, a two-year course that qualified her to teach at elementary school level, she gained the qualification in 1957 and went to teach at a primary school for colored children in Clairwood, Durban.

It was during this period that the racial legislation affecting the lives of all South Africans (and those of color in particular) began to be put into effect by the National Party after it had won the fateful general elections of 1948. Emerging from the protected world of a girls-only mission home as an impressionable and sensitive eighteen-year-old, Bessie was soon to feel the effects of the racist social programme being put in place. The Durban municipal library was reserved for the use of whites only, and she had to resort to joining the M. L. Sultan Library, which was set up by an Indian businessman and open to all races. One immediate consequence of this was her exposure to books on the Hindu religion, to which the young Bessie was especially receptive given her desire for knowledge and her negative experiences of Christianity at its austere worst.

Teaching was not Bessie's ideal vocation: she was not temperamentally suited to the dull routine of the school day and the constant need to discipline her young charges. She resigned from her job in June 1958 and shortly afterwards left for Cape Town. She moved into the world of journalism, joining the Cape Town office of the *Golden City Post*, a weekly newspaper catering mainly for a black readership. She persevered as a cub reporter and after a three-month trial period was appointed a staff reporter.

Early in 1959 Bessie decided to make the move to Johannesburg. At this time the Defiance Campaign against racist legislation, and, in particular, the pass laws, began to gain momentum. Although Bessie's new job (on the *Home Post* supplement to the *Golden City Post*) was innocuous enough — managing a newsletter entitled "Dear Gang" and an advice column called "Hiya Teenagers" — her brief sojourn in Johannesburg in 1959 and 1960 was momentous. Her association with the Pan Africanist Congress under Sobukwe, whom she admired and later featured in her story "The Coming of the Christ-Child" (1981), led to her being swept up in the events surrounding Sharpeville in March 1960. Although she was not actually present at the Sharpeville calamity, she did witness Sobukwe's arrest at Orlando police station earlier that day. She was later scooped up in the series of arrests that ensued and earned her freedom only by turning state witness. Eilersen reports that in 1972 she wrote a letter to Sobukwe in which she indirectly apologized for this action.[12]

Most harrowing of all the events that occurred in Johannesburg, however, was her first sexual encounter, which Eilersen describes as "a violent and unwelcome one forced upon her," and which, Eilersen avers, was followed by a suicide attempt.[13] She survived — painfully — lost her job as columnist on *Home Post* and returned to Cape Town. Upon her return she attempted to take up her old reporting job but found that she was unable to and resorted instead to writing and printing a pro-Africanist news-sheet called "The Citizen."

Unemployed, and recovering from her breakdown, she sought friendship in the leftist political circles loosely grouped around the Liberal Party: "The fantastic thing about friendships in South Africa is that one always and only meets one's friends through politics," she later remarked.[14] Randolph Vigne was one of the leading figures of the party in Cape Town and remembers her presence at parties and gatherings vividly: "Bessie was a bright and talkative person, but many found her alarming and feared both her deadly, silent stare of disapproval, and her furious outbursts when her fiercely held Africanist views were offended."[15] In one of her early autobiographical sketches of the period, "Letter from South Africa: For a Friend, 'D. B.,'" Head offers her perspective on these events: "I never joined fund-raising campaigns because I can't ask for money. I never paid at fund-raising parties because I was always broke and yet drank as much wine as I could and talked as loud as I could and quarreled with the whites who were there."[16]

---

[12] Eilersen, *Thunder Behind Her Ears*, 49.
[13] Eilersen argues that Head's first violent sexual encounter "casts much light on Bessie Emery's later attitude to sex" (Eilersen, *Thunder Behind Her Ears*, 49).
[14] Head, *A Woman Alone*, 15.
[15] Vigne, *A Gesture of Belonging*, 2.
[16] Head, *A Woman Alone*, 14.

At this time she met fellow-journalist Harold Head and, somewhat uncharacteristically, it was Bessie who apparently made the first physical advances. Harold recalls that she stripped naked before him in the darkness of the local community center at which he was caretaker.[17] James Matthews's later allusion to Bessie's arrival in Cape Town as "that of a shy mission-reared girl who wrote pastoral poems and wore cardigans tightly buttoned up to her neck"[18] resonates ironically against this later revelation. Emotionally, Head tended to be on a "perpetual roller coaster" (Vigne's apt description), and her initial rapture upon meeting Harold clearly constituted one of the "highs." (It appears that after the breakup of her marriage in late 1963, however, she was never again able to approach sexuality with such forthrightness.)

In September 1961 the couple were married in Simonstown, the small naval town south of Cape Town. Harold secured a job with the liberal news magazine *Contact*, edited by Patrick Duncan, and the pair moved into a rooming house in District Six. In one of her early sketches of this period, Bessie vividly portrayed their circumstances:

> The housing situation being what it is, my husband and I were immensely grateful to obtain a clean large room to ourselves with a bathroom and were prepared to put up with the hazardous and inexplicable behavior of our landlord and landlady. Our landlord was forever threatening us with bodily assault, ably abetted by our landlady who alternately suffered from fits of wild generosity and wild anger. One never knew where one stood in such a storm-filled atmosphere. I myself am not usually very obliging.[19]

The candid last admission is significant: given Bessie's own wild mood-swings, there can be little doubt that at least part of the blame for the household disturbances could be laid at her door. Despite such domestic disturbances, however, Bessie was soon pregnant and Howard was born on 15 May 1962.

During this period Bessie was writing the "pastoral poetry" alluded to by James Matthews, the Cape Town-based poet, in his review in July 1969 of Bessie Head's first published novel, *When Rain Clouds Gather* (1968). In this review Matthews provided some vital information about her early unpublished writing. Remarking that *When Rain Clouds Gather* "could not exactly be called the first novel written by Bessie Head, but [...] her first

---

[17] Eilersen, *Thunder Behind Her Ears*, 52.
[18] James Matthews, "Scores with First Novel," *Cape Times Weekend Magazine* (26 July 1969), 9.
[19] Head, *A Woman Alone*, 18-19.

one published," he went on to allude to her "pastoral poems" and added: "From pastoral poetry she advanced to a short-lived four-page sheet edited by herself" and "wrote a novel while locked up in a hotel room in District Six, living on bread and beer supplied by friends."[20]

The news-sheet, "The Citizen," has already been mentioned. The novel, *The Cardinals*, is the subject of discussion in the second part of this article. The poetry was until recently thought lost and irrecoverable. The only poem Head published in her lifetime was "Things I Don't Like" (1962),[21] and she soon abandoned the genre. "Things I Don't Like" was Head's first venture into print as a creative writer. Declamatory, and full of Black Consciousness posturings, the poem attests to her anger and frustration at the time. Its agonistic and confrontational tone, however, is not only sharply divergent from that employed in her later writings, it also contrasts markedly with the other poems of the period. The rediscovery of her other early poems is thus also important in demonstrating that "Things I Don't Like" is atypical of Head's writing as a whole.

In 1995 five forgotten early poems were rediscovered in Cape Town and donated to the National English Literary Museum in Grahamstown.[22] Written in the second half of 1961 and early 1962, they provide an invaluable insight into the aspirant writer's early creativity. One of the poems, originally titled "When I Am Thinking of You" and later simply "Untitled Now," is significant in that there are distinct traces of phrases that would recur in her later writing, in particular *Maru*: "Each day you wake the love is new and new and new"; and "the companion of the stars and the moon and the wind and the sun and the sky and the earth and the distant horizon."[23] The spring imagery in the poem and the half-articulated yearnings for love strikingly anticipate her early pieces from Botswana — "The Green Tree" (1964) and "For Serowe: A Village in Africa" (1965) in particular.

This is perhaps the most significant aspect of Head's early poetry: its anticipation of her Botswana writings. Her alertness to her natural environment (especially evident in "Untitled Now") clearly did not begin with her arrival in a remote African village. The lines, "The earth is a vast space of brown grass — grass and more grass, sweeping out towards the hori-

---

[20] Matthews, "Scores with First Novel," 9.

[21] Bessie Head, "Things I Don't Like," *New African* 1:7 (1962), 10.

[22] For details see Craig Mackenzie and Paulette Coetzee, "Bessie Head: Rediscovered Early Poems," *English in Africa* 23:1 (1996), 29-39.

[23] Bessie Head, "Untitled Now," *English in Africa* 23:1 (1996), 44-45.

zon" and "The expanse of cold blue sky and the expanse of hard brown earth are brooding in the cold evening gaze," are of a piece with her descriptions of the flat Botswanan landscape in *When Rain Clouds Gather*.[24]

By the early 1960s life in South Africa was becoming untenable on both a personal and a political level. The Group Areas Act of 1950 and its various amendments of the late 1950s and early 1960s were making themselves felt in Cape Town where plans were underway to clear District Six and remove its inhabitants to the desolate Cape Flats (an event that would occur only in 1966, two years after Bessie had left for Botswana). The Treason Trial in early 1961 and the arrest of Nelson Mandela a year later were events that indicated that repression on a national scale had begun in earnest.

An event that touched Bessie personally was the arrest of Dennis Brutus in 1963.[25] In a letter that appeared at the time, published as "Letter from South Africa: For a Friend, 'D.B.,'" Bessie mourned the loss of friends and the end of an era: "One is constantly losing friends these days. Some of the refugees, like my friend, 'D. B.' did not want to leave. Wherever he is now, I know he is unhappy. For those of us who are still here, life becomes lonelier and intensely isolated."[26] That Bessie was already contemplating exile is evident from the tone of this letter, published in November 1963. Such sentiments were no doubt hardened by the downward course of her marriage, and towards the end of the year Bessie left Harold and was on her way to Atteridgeville, a township outside Pretoria, to stay with her mother-in-law.

This situation was not to last: Bessie soon fell out with her mother-in-law and by February 1964 had decided that she would try to leave South Africa for good. Her brief association with the PAC prompted the government to deny her a passport, but with the help of the poet Patrick Cullinan she secured an exit permit — which meant that she could leave the country but never return. She applied for, and gained, a teaching position in Serowe in the Bechuanaland Protectorate, and in March 1964, baby Howard in tow, she was on her journey to a new life beyond the borders of a country which had afforded her a childhood and young adulthood of nothing but hardship.

---

[24] Bessie Head, "Untitled Now," *English in Africa* 23:1 (1996), 43.

[25] Brutus escaped from prison but was re-arrested and incarcerated on Robben Island before leaving South Africa on an exit permit in 1966.

[26] Head, *A Woman Alone*, 13.

The posthumous publication in 1993 of Bessie Head's first extended piece of fiction was an event of some importance in the world of South African English literature. Head had long been considered a pioneer and a source of inspiration both for her fellow black South African woman writers (Miriam Tlali, Ellen Kuzwayo, Lauretta Ngcobo, and others) and for those further a field (Alice Walker, Angela Carter, Nikki Giovanni, Toni Morrison). She achieved this status in the late 1960s and early 1970s with her first three published novels — among the earliest novels published by a black African woman writer. The appearance of *The Cardinals* (completed in 1962) set the dates back some six years and demonstrated just how much of a groundbreaker she was.

Head had established a reputation for herself as a pioneering individualist long before critics became aware of the existence of *The Cardinals*. Her first published novel *When Rain Clouds Gather* (1968) reversed the established "Jim-comes-to-Jo'burg" tradition of the time by tracing the passage of the protagonist not from country to city, but from urban ghetto to rural retreat; the novel also boldly proposed a paradigm of inter-racial harmony and collaboration at a time when the Black Consciousness Movement in South Africa was influencing black South African writers to question the value of ties between the races. *Maru* (1971), her second novel, was similarly audacious in its suggestion that deep traditions of racial hierarchy in Botswana could be broken by a marriage between a man at the pinnacle of a class- and race-stratified society and a woman at the bottom of this society. And, in *A Question of Power* (1973), just when most African writers were subordinating individualism to the group and national interest, Head chose to locate the action of her novel inside the consciousness of her central character, thereby implicitly questioning the arrogation of moral and epistemological value to the collective rather than to the individual.

Eschewing the overt "protest" mode that came to dominate South African writing of the 1970s and 80s, she preferred to locate her moral and creative center in individual people, in "how strange and beautiful people can be — just living," as she put it in her social history, *Serowe: Village of the Rain Wind* (1981).[27] And now that the wheel has turned, so much of what was written in such a strident and urgent way in the 1970s and 80s in South Africa seems dated. The work of Bessie Head has not suffered the same fate.

---

[27] Bessie Head, *Serowe: Village of the Rain Wind*, London, 1981, x.

The audaciousness and non-conformism evident in her "Botswana" novels also permeate her first extended venture into fiction — *The Cardinals*. Indeed, what is fascinating to observe in this, an immature work by an immature writer, is the fact that her bold individualism was not something acquired over time in exile in Botswana, but was present in her from the start.

The themes which *The Cardinals* takes up are recognizable to those familiar with Head's work: the girl protagonist, known successively as Miriam, Charlotte, and Mouse, is abandoned by her mother when her family forces her to give her illegitimate baby to a poor domestic worker. (We discover later that Miriam is the issue of a relationship which crosses class and race boundaries.) Her early life is a blur of shanty-town life, a succession of foster-families and neglect. The sole redeeming feature of this uniformly grim childhood is her lessons in literacy from an old man who is the community letter-writer. The poignant description of the little girl learning to write her name under the old man's guidance provides the novel with a remarkable beginning and an abiding motif: Miriam writes her way into an identity and a means of existence, a process echoed in Head's own life-long struggle to give coherence through her writing to the scattered fragments of an emotionally dislocated life.

Deprived of social welfare support upon reaching sixteen years of age, Charlotte (as she is now known) finds a job with *African Beat*, a scandal sheet posing as a newspaper. Dubbed "Mouse" by her two co-reporters Johnny and James, she enters timidly and yet resolutely into the hard-bitten world of sensationalistic journalism. Despite himself, Johnny becomes more and more attracted to Mouse. He is initially unable to reach her in her state of withdrawal, but finds a way of accessing her through writing.

In a twist in the plot, we learn about Johnny's past. He was once a fisherman, we discover, living rough on the beach, muscular and suntanned. He attracted the attentions of a mysterious young white woman, who seduced him. The woman fell pregnant with the fisherman's child, but had already lost contact with him. Her family persuaded her to give up the child and to marry a young man who had won their approval. In despair she did so, but on the eve of their departure for another town, where they were to marry and start a new life, she committed suicide. The reader now knows what neither Mouse nor Johnny knows: that, with the increasing closeness of their relationship, they are in danger of committing incest.

Johnny persuades Mouse to move in with him by saying that he wants to help her with her writing. Mouse accepts, but then finds that Johnny is soon making demands of her: "There are one or two things I want to get straightened out. I just can't have a woman around who dresses the way you do. Cut two inches off those hems and fix up the slips" (73). He also tells her that she must learn to cook and "do a bit of cleaning up too, and buying things" (73). Mouse responds in a way that has become a defensive reflex: "Dazed by the unexpectedness of events, she preferred not to think or feel" (73-74).

Johnny acts in a confusing blend of self-interest and genuine care for Mouse. His disturbingly sexist attitudes — "Your legs are quite attractive but you haven't given anyone a chance to look at them. Men like to look at women's legs" (75) — are offset by some valuable insights that help Mouse unlock her creative potential:

> I do what I like and I think what I like. That's what I call inner freedom. It's absolutely necessary for anyone who calls himself, or thinks himself, a writer. You won't be able to think straight in that tight bunched-up state you're in now. You've got to break off the bolts that are keeping you locked up. (75)

Once she is accustomed to her new surroundings, Mouse is suffused with a feeling of "indefinable happiness" (77). This feeling becomes mixed with a disturbing sense of unease, however, and here we at last encounter squarely the issue that is at the center of the novel. When Johnny gets into her bed the morning after she has moved in, he explains his feelings for her in a way that touches on the theme of incest:

> You can pretend you're my sister for a bit. Move over. My sister always used to sleep next to me and when I woke in the morning, she'd have her arm tight around me like this. I used to like it. It's a comforting feeling to wake up and find someone with their arm around you. Now that I come to think of it, I must have been a little in love with her too. I used to kiss her, not the way a brother should kiss a sister but the way a man kisses a woman. Like this." (77-78)

This is the second time that Johnny evokes the notion of incest in relation to his feelings for Mouse. Earlier, in a conversation with PK, the editor of *African Beat*, he made remarks about Mouse that suggest a genetic bond between them: "It's the inside part, PK. She's got something inside her that agrees with my system" (65).

That Head is consciously working on the theme of incest is illustrated by an exchange between Johnny and Mouse that follows immediately after his allusion to his relationship with his sister:

> He looked at her with the amused gleam in his eyes. "Do you think there was anything incestuous in that?"
>
> "No," she said.
>
> "I think so. Society would think so too. It would condemn me as unspeakable filth for making love to my own sister. A man like that, it would say, would stop at nothing. He'd even make love to his own daughter. All I can say to society is that it's just as well I have no daughter. I'd probably make love to her too." (78)

All of this suggests that the author is attempting to play on the many ironies inherent in the situation. There is a more important issue here, however: to what extent is Johnny aware that his relationship with Mouse might be an incestuous one? And another, even more serious, issue lies beyond this: to what extent is Head attempting to make a case for the redemptive power of an incestuous relationship in an abnormal society like the South African one of the 1950s and 60s?

In *The Cardinals* Head constructs a variant of the Oedipus Rex myth in which an unwitting father–daughter (rather than mother–son) relationship is entered into. (Freud's "Electra Complex" is probably the more appropriate term to use here.) This is not the difference that is at issue, however. There is another difference between the classical myth and Head's version of it to which I wish to draw attention: whereas the myth as passed down to us registers the deep sense of horror and revulsion at what happens when mother and son enter into a relationship (Jocasta hangs herself and Oedipus blinds himself), and this serves to reinforce the incest taboo, *The Cardinals* appears to suggest that an incestuous relationship might well be curative and beneficial.

Having introduced Mouse to the idea of an incipiently incestuous relationship with his sister, and having noted that she is neither shocked nor outraged, Johnny goes on to present to her details about their family background in a way which suggests that a sympathetic interpretation of the relationship between him and his sister is being solicited:

> After my father died my mother kept on getting children from various men. There were about twelve of us altogether. She was nearly always drunk too, so we just grew up like a lot of animals. My sister was a prostitute at the age of ten. She was the eldest in the family and only did it so that we could have

food to eat. She never complained, but at night she used to come and lie next to me and cry. One night she was stabbed to death. I think I would have never forgiven myself if I had withheld the kind of love she wanted from me. All that just makes me not care one hell about the laws and rules of society. They are made by men and women who know nothing about suffering. I had many reasons for asking you to come and live with me. You are the only person I can bear to have near me now. I can't take the sham and hypocrisy and false values any longer. (78)

The reasons for Johnny's sister being a prostitute are graphically rendered, and we are encouraged to understand and accept her for what she does. But this is only one part of the appeal being made here. The more important point is that she came to Johnny for the love that her parents and her society have denied her, and it is clear that "the kind of love she wanted" from Johnny was at least partially incestuous. The palpable gap in the text between "she used to come and lie next to me and cry" and "One night she was stabbed to death" represents the unsayable: that "the kind of love" between her and Johnny was not that which usually obtains between brother and sister. The "laws and rules of society" to which Johnny then alludes are clearly those concerning incest, and these we are encouraged to see as "sham and hypocrisy and false values." A powerful case for acceptance — or at least condoning — of incest is being made here. The idea of men taking advantage of a ten-year-old girl's poverty to indulge their pedophiliac tendencies is implicitly being weighed against the healing (albeit incestuous) love between a brother and sister.

If a case can be made for an incestuous relationship between a brother and sister in these circumstances, what about an incestuous relationship between father and daughter if the circumstances also justify it? As we saw, Johnny makes Mouse aware that the relationship between him and his sister was not "normal." He then goes on to say that if he had a daughter he would "probably make love to her too," and asks Mouse: "Does that shock you?" Her "No" (78) signifies that an understanding has been reached between them that societal norms are not universal, transcendent imperatives that must be unquestioningly obeyed. Each is prepared to entertain the idea that under certain circumstances the incest taboo can justifiably be transgressed.

We turn at this point to the prefatory note with which Head begins the novel: "*The Cardinals,*" she writes, "in the astrological sense, are those who serve as the base or foundation for change." Is the suggestion here that Mouse and Johnny are the cardinals that serve as the foundation for a very radical kind of change? That the incest taboo can be transgressed under certain circumstances?

In the end the author does not take these possibilities anywhere. Having flirted with the idea of making Johnny at least dimly conscious that the relationship he is entering into is incestuous, she retreats from the consequences of pursuing this possibility and provides a more conventional ending. The element of risk and danger is not entirely effaced, however: at the novel's conclusion we see Mouse and Johnny on the cusp of transcendence and oblivion, as they contemplate a relationship fraught with dangers known and unknown (principal among the latter, of course, being the incestuous nature of their relationship). Says Johnny: "Life is a treacherous quicksand with no guarantee of safety anywhere. We can only try to grab what happiness we can before we are swept off into oblivion" (137).

The incest theme is not the only area in which the novel falters. The "transgressions" alluded to can also be taken to refer to certain formal failings in the text as well. Evidence of the author's youthfulness is present in certain formal attributes of the text — the stilted and callow dialogue, the sometimes sketchy characterization and the bewildering and unaccountable mood-swings in the main characters. Another area of weakness is Mouse's behavior. Like Margaret in *Maru*, Mouse is passive and inert — a tendency she shares with some of Head's female protagonists which feminist critics have found disturbing. Here we have character as palimpsest — a slate-like surface on which assertive male characters inscribe their wills, without, however, ultimately being able to penetrate (Mouse remains both passive and chaste until the very end). The mutations in her name (all of which she unquestioningly accepts) are the most obvious example of this. Her passive acceptance of Johnny's bullying is less easy for the reader to accept, and the close juxtaposition of love and violence in his behavior towards Mouse is very disturbing.

In defense of her passivity it can be said that her identity and sense of self are in a constant state of evolution — a state common to most young adults perhaps, but one which is especially acute in the case of a person utterly bereft of the orienting matrices of a family history. Mouse inherits the double-edged sword that is existential freedom, but she experiences only too painfully the sharp edge of loneliness. All of this makes her an easy target for Johnny's aggression. Nonetheless, that she is never able to evolve beyond being the hapless victim of another's manipulations makes her an ambiguous heroic figure.

In *The Cardinals*, then, Head explores the possibility of transgressing one of society's most entrenched taboos. With the benefit of hindsight we can now see that, after this, it is unremarkable that she would go on to challenge other norms and values which form the cornerstones of society — that she would always swim against the current of literary fashion and social expectation. I wish to conclude by speculating on the reasons for Head's desire to transgress — or at least to explore the idea of transgression in her fiction.

Bessie Head was radically dislocated from any framework of societal norm and belief, and she was also deeply insecure. This meant that she was prepared to countenance extreme ideas; like her heroine Margaret in *Maru*, her upbringing meant that "almost anything could be thrown into her mind and life and she would have the capacity, within herself, to survive both heaven and hell."[28] One has to consider the deep psychological distress induced by Head's early childhood and adolescent experiences: being wrenched away from her biological mother (which she must have registered in some profound subliminal way); her rootless, alienating years as a foster-child; her induction into the severe and unnatural milieu of an orphanage run by repressed religious women; her sense of inadequacy as a teacher and her hurried abandonment of this career; her struggle to survive in Cape Town and Johannesburg in an era of increasing oppression by the State of people of color, oppression which included the promulgation and enforcement of a law that forbade sexual relations between people of different races — that made a person like Bessie, in fact, profoundly illegitimate (in every sense of the word). All of these experiences preceded, and clearly deeply influenced, her writing of *The Cardinals*.

Such extreme experiences engender extreme responses — including that of entertaining the notion that an incestuous relationship can be healing and beneficial. A disturbing thought arises from a consideration of her early life and work: throughout her life, and, most particularly, during her sexually active years from her early twenties onwards in South Africa, Head could never be sure that when meeting and being attracted to a man some years older than her (but not necessarily very much older), and becoming intimate with this man, that there was always the possibility — however remote — that she might be making love to her own father.

What better way to lay the ghost of these fears, to give shape to the frightening formlessness of a nightmare, than to confront, in an honest and

---

[28] Bessie Head, *Maru*, (1971), London, 1972, 16.

imaginatively rich manner — a manner which we have come to know as distinctive of Bessie Head — this potential encounter in the realm of fiction. Having experienced all she had, having endured the long years of loneliness, disorientation and fathomless anxiety, she may even have considered that finding her father in this way would have been a redemptive act — might, perhaps, have saved her.

DISARMING SILENCE: ETHICAL RESISTANCE
IN J. M. COETZEE'S *FOE*

Mike Marais

In *Shame*, Salman Rushdie describes silence as the "ancient language of defeat."[1] More recently, Dale McKinley has described it as the "voice of complicity."[2] These are fairly standard perceptions of silence, and partly account for the hostility with which J. M. Coetzee's *Foe* was received upon its publication in 1986.[3] During the period in question, the white minority government had declared a third state of emergency in South Africa and many readers expected the literature of the day to engage as directly as possible with the material realities of life under apartheid. Not only did *Foe* appear to disregard the political orthodoxy in South African literature that both complied with and generated such expectations by seeming to indulge in a form of postmodernist games-playing directed at the elitist predilections of a white intellectual coterie, but it also appeared to make a virtue of silence. Even those critics who sought to defend the novel against its many detractors by constructing correspondences between it and evolving political circumstances in South Africa were unable to make sense of this latter emphasis.[4]

In this essay, I argue, by contrast, that Coetzee uses silence to engage with history in *Foe*. (It should be noted, though, that this is a feature of *all* Coetzee's novels. However, the process is most evident in *Foe*, where its modalities are self-reflexively reflected upon.) I focus principally on two scenes in the novel, that is, Susan Barton's attempt to teach Friday lan-

---

[1] Salman Rushdie, *Shame*, London, 1984, 89.

[2] Dale McKinley, Review of *Hidden Agendas* by John Pilger, *The Sunday Independent*, 25 October 1998, 19.

[3] All parenthetical references are to the following edition of this novel: J. M. Coetzee, *Foe*, Johannesburg, 1986.

[4] For a survey of the critical reception not only of *Foe*, but also of Coetzee's other novels, see Teresa Dovey's introduction to *J. M. Coetzee: A Bibliography*, eds Kevin Goddard and John Read, Grahamstown, 1990, 1-14.

guage and the ending, in which a conception of silence emerges that is related to Emmanuel Levinas' understanding of ethics: namely that the absolute other's radical difference to the "same" invests the former with an oppositionality that enables him/her to resist the violent freedom of the autonomous subject.[5] In developing this argument, I show that silence enables an ethical authority that is to be distinguished from political power.

Towards the end of *Foe*, Susan Barton discusses Friday's silence with Foe in the following way:

> You err most tellingly in failing to distinguish between my silences and the silences of a being such as Friday. Friday has no command of words and therefore no defence against being re-shaped day by day in conformity with the desires of others. I say he is a cannibal and he becomes a cannibal; I say he is a laundryman and he becomes a laundryman [...]. No matter what he is to himself [...] what he is to the world is what I make of him. Therefore the silence of Friday is a helpless silence. (122)

This passage inscribes a tension in the novel between silence and freedom: in remarking on Friday's silence, Susan Barton remarks on her freedom. Moreover, she does so in a way that suggests a relation between freedom and violence. Freedom is here understood as the subject's freedom to violate the otherness of the other, to force the unknown into "conformity" with the known. Susan Barton's comments may therefore be compared with Levinas' view that the human subject is motivated by the wish to be free, and that s/he seeks to realise his/her free will, and thereby affirm him / herself, by annulling all that resists his/her powers, even when that resistance is merely a function of the existent's obscurity.[6] Differently put, the subject attains and assures his/her freedom by ensuring that otherness does not stand in his/her way. Knowledge is the principal means by which the subject achieves this end: s/he can only gain complete autonomy through a full comprehension of the world.[7] In this conception of subjectivity, knowledge consists in relating the alien entity to a system of *a priori* concepts and ideas. As a result of its intentional nature, consciousness reduces the other to its object and, in so doing, it achieves total correspondence between its representations and external reality. Given this epistemological

---

[5] See Emmanuel Levinas, *Totality and Infinity: An Essay on Exteriority*, trans. A. Lingis, Dordrecht, 1991. In terms of the phenomenological model of intentionality, the "same" consists of both the intentional *acts* of consciousness and the intentional *objects* that are constituted by these acts and, in turn, invest them with meaning.

[6] See Emmanuel Levinas, "Philosophy and the Idea of Infinity," *Collected Philosophical Papers*, trans. A. Lingis, Dordrecht, 1987, 49.

[7] *Ibid.*, 49.

procedure, which does not admit the possibility of being surprised by silence, the autonomous subject may be described as a self-sufficiency that does not care for other beings.

If placed in the context of this conception of autonomous subjectivity, it becomes clear that Susan Barton's principal criticism of Friday's silence, in the above passage from *Foe*, is that it does not have the *power* to *resist* the subject's careless freedom. Hence she contrasts Friday's silence with her own: while his is "helpless," hers is powerful. Through silence, she avers, she is able to assert her control over her story: "It is still in my power to guide and amend. Above all, to withhold" (123).

Despite Barton's criticism, the following passage (in which she, at Foe's behest, attempts to teach Friday language in order to make his silence "speak" [142]) implies that his silence may have an authority that does *not* derive from power:

> I reached out and took him by the chin and turned his face toward me. His eyelids opened. Somewhere in the deepest recesses of those black pupils was there a spark of mockery? I could not see it. But if it were there, would it not be an African spark, dark to my English eye? (146)

Clearly, Friday's silence *resists* Barton's attempts to make it "speak," and thereby points to his irreducibility to logocentric conceptuality. This resistance, together with the positioning of Barton *vis-à-vis* Friday, implies that the scene may be read in terms of Levinas' notion of the face. For Levinas, the "face to face" is the non-conceptual event of the subject's encounter with the other. It is "[t]he way in which the other presents himself, exceeding *the idea of the other in me*."[8] Levinas' description alludes to René Descartes' examination of the excessive dimension of infinity, that is, the fact that the *ideatum* of the idea of the infinite cannot be contained by the idea itself.[9] When one tries to conceive of infinity, the relation of adequation that usually pertains between idea and *ideatum* is ruptured and the latter *absolves* itself from the relation.[10] According to Levinas, it is this "idea of infinity, the infinitely more contained in the less" that "is concretely produced" in the event of the face to face.[11] Importantly, the infinitude of

---

[8] Levinas, *Totality and Infinity*, 50.
[9] See René Descartes, *Meditations on First Philosophy*, trans. and ed. E. Anscombe, London, 1969, 85-87.
[10] Levinas, *Totality and Infinity*, 48-52.
[11] *Ibid.*, 196.

the other *resists* the violent adequation of the other with the same — it "maintains the exteriority of the other with respect to the same."[12]

In the above passage from *Foe*, it is just such an infinite surplus that is produced by Susan Barton's inability to establish an adequate relation with the silent Friday. Friday's silence maintains his exteriority to the same and, in so doing, absolves him from the relation that Barton attempts to establish with him. The result of this absolution is that while she is in a relationship, it is to something that is indefinable. Using Levinas' terms, this relationship may be described as one "with the exterior [...] without this exteriority being able to be integrated into the same."[13] It is therefore an ethical relation, an "unrelating relation" between "separated beings," which respects, rather than elides, radical difference.[14]

In preventing exteriority from being integrated into the same, silence does therefore resist the autonomous subject's violent freedom. Moreover, in ensuring the irreducibility of Friday's otherness, it enables this otherness to *surprise* the subject and, as Levinas points out, in surprising the subject, the other challenges his/her autonomy.[15] Since the subject's freedom and power are grounded in a denial of otherness, s/he exists in a state of ontological solitude, that is, in a world that affirms his/her sense of self by reflecting back at him/her the very cognitive categories which s/he has imposed on it. In exposing the subject to what s/he has denied, the "epiphany" of the infinite disturbs this ontological solitude.[16] It confronts the subject with the impossibility of conceiving of him/herself in terms of freedom in unicity.[17] In the process, this interruption of subjectivity renders violence impossible. "Violent action," Levinas argues, "does not consist in being in a relationship with the other; it is in fact an action where one is as though one were alone."[18]

Susan Barton is thus mistaken when she states that Friday's silence is "helpless" and that it allows her to "turn" him "into" whatever she wishes. On the contrary, this silence ultimately precludes, even forbids, her from doing so by assisting in the production of infinity and thereby disturbing her ontological solitude. The effect on Barton of this challenge to her

---

[12] *Ibid.*, 196.
[13] Levinas, "Philosophy," 54.
[14] Levinas, *Totality and Infinity*, 295.
[15] *Ibid.*, 51.
[16] *Ibid.*, 51, 197-200.
[17] *Ibid.*, 51.
[18] Emmanuel Levinas, "Freedom and Command," *Collected Philosophical Papers*, trans. A. Lingis, Dordrecht, 1987, 18.

autonomy emerges clearly in her following complaint to Foe after her face-to-face encounter with Friday: "Mr Foe, I must have my freedom!" (147).

In that Friday's silence resists Barton's freedom, that is, prevents her from "acting as though alone" by confronting her with the undeniable fact of the face, it is a silence of authority. It must be emphasized, though, that the form of authority that is at issue here is one without power. After all, the other's challenge to the subject's freedom derives from an opposition without forceful resistance. Levinas explains this point as follows: "The infinite does not stop me like a force blocking my force; it puts into question the naïve right of my powers, my glorious spontaneity as a living being, a 'force on the move.'"[19] The other is that which resists the subject through an opposition that is radical to the extent that it derives from its exteriority to the same: it is not that which is opposed to the subject by its resistance. Hence Levinas states that "[t]he opposition of the face, which is not the opposition of a force, is not a hostility."[20] The other's resistance is, quite simply, "the resistance of what has no resistance — the ethical resistance."[21]

It follows that the authority of the other is premised on his/her weakness. S/he shows her/his infinity by means of that which is naked, exposed and defenceless: the face. Levinas argues that "The infinite paralyses power by its infinite resistance to murder, which firm and insurmountable, gleams in the face of the Other, in the total nudity of his defenceless eyes, in the nudity of the absolute openness of the Transcendent."[22] He goes on to say that "The being that expresses itself imposes itself, but does so precisely by appealing to me with its destitution and nudity — its hunger — without my being able to be deaf to that appeal."[23] The defenceless face of the other thus prevents the subject from violating him/her. By extrapolation, it is precisely the helplessness of Friday's silence, its sheer vulnerability, that opposes Susan Barton's careless freedom. Alternatively put, Friday derives authority, as opposed to force or power, from the weakness of his silence: his resistance is the resistance of that which has no resistance. The point here is that his utter helplessness *demands* responsibility

---

[19] Levinas, "Philosophy," 58.
[20] Levinas, "Freedom and Command," 19.
[21] Levinas, *Totality and Infinity*, 199.
[22] *Ibid.*, 199.
[23] *Ibid.*, 200.

from Susan Barton, it *demands* that she care and "be for the other" rather than for herself.

The complex notion of an ethical authority devoid of power is, perhaps, best explained in terms of Levinas' description of the ethical command of the other as that which "sound[s] in the mouth of the one that obeys."[24] Quite simply, the other has authority *because* the subject listens to, obeys, and articulates the command before s/he knows what the other orders him/her to do. Only if the subject is prepared to substitute him / herself for the other by being "for the other," can the other have this authority. By assuming responsibility for the other, the subject gives him/her the right to command. It is therefore by restructuring his/her subjectivity in terms of responsibility for the other and, in the process, forgoing an authority that is located in power, that the subject invests the other with an *anarchic* authority.[25]

The occurrence of a burden metaphor following Susan Barton's face-to-face encounter with Friday and her complaint to Foe that she has lost her freedom, points to the grounding of this notion of an ethical authority in self-substituting responsibility. After telling Foe that her responsibility for Friday is "becoming more than [she] can bear!" and that "[h]e is like the old man of the river!" (147), she recounts the story of Sinbad's encounter with the old man of the river:

> There was once a fellow who took pity on an old man waiting at the riverside, and offered to carry him across. Having borne him safely through the flood, he knelt to set him down on the other side. But the old man would not leave his shoulders: no, he tightened his knees about his deliverer's neck and beat him into a beast of burden. He took the very food from his mouth, and would have ridden him to death had he not saved himself by a ruse. (147-48)

The fact that this burden metaphor connotes ethical authority rather than political power is evident in the food image, which suggests not a reversal of the terms in a relation of dominance and subservience, but the autonomous subject's reconstitution of self by assuming responsibility for the other. Significantly, this image does not occur in Edward William Lane's translation of the Sinbad story.[26] However, it is used by Levinas in his argument that the subject's exposure to the other is characterised by a "pas-

---

[24] Emmanuel Levinas, *Otherwise than Being or Beyond Essence*, trans. A. Lingis, The Hague, 1981, 147.

[25] *Ibid.*, 45-59.

[26] *The Thousand and One Nights,* ed. Edward Stanley Poole, trans. E. W. Lane, London, 1859, III: 52-55.

sivity that cannot be taken up," and that this passivity "is an offering one-self that is a suffering, a goodness despite oneself," a "pain" or "persecu-tion."[27] He stresses this notion of self-effacement before the other with the following image: "To give, to-be-for-the-another, despite oneself, but in interrupting the for-oneself, is *to take the bread out of one's own mouth*, to nourish the hunger of another with one's fasting."[28] This "giving" involves a radical generosity exemplified by an act of effacement in which the self is possessed by the other. It is a giving which must transcend the circle of the self, and therefore not an act in which "the ego is affirmed," but one which "tears me from myself" and extends to the other without returning.[29] As Levinas points out, this movement away from the security of being to the insecurity of responsibility is accompanied by unendurable uncertainty and anxiety. It is for this reason that responsibility is a burden, that "noth-ing is more burdensome than a neighbour."[30]

From the Levinasian allusions in Coetzee's depiction of Susan Barton's intercourse with Friday in *Foe*, it is therefore clear that, rather than simply being a "language of defeat" or the "voice of complicity," silence may be in-terpreted in the novel as enabling a form of resistance that is grounded in ethical authority. Silence here is therefore associated with the ability of the other to resist violence and affect the autonomous subject in a way that brings about the substitution of careless freedom for the burdensome anxiety of responsibility for the other.

In *Foe*, the importance of silence is not confined to the presentational surface of the text. Indeed, it may be argued that the depiction of the effect of Friday's silence on Susan Barton self-reflexively reflects Coetzee's at-tempt to invest this novel with a silence that renders the reader responsible for the other. Thus, for instance, it becomes clear that Friday's silence mir-rors that of the novel as a whole when Foe, in referring to one of the "touches of mystery" in the story of the island and, by implication, in the novel itself (83-87), tells Barton that "In every story there is a silence, some sight concealed, some word unspoken [...] Till we have spoken the unspoken we have not come to the heart of the story" (141). It follows from the explicit parallel that this statement constructs between Friday's silence and that of the text, that the former implies the latter, indeed, *is* the latter. In terms of this foregrounding of textual silence, the ending of the

---

[27] Levinas, *Otherwise that Being*, 54-55, 101.
[28] *Ibid.*, 56, 142.
[29] *Ibid.*, 55.
[30] *Ibid.*, 88.

novel, in which an anonymous first-person narrator interacts with Friday and eventually attempts to vocalise his silence, invites being read as an allegory of reading.

In this image of reading, the first-person narrator kneels over Friday and there is a hint of violence in the phrase "I tug his woolly hair" (157), a hint which is further reinforced by the fact that Friday has a chain about his throat. Seemingly, the relationship here depicted is one in which the reader endeavours to master the text. Significantly, these details suggesting the violence of domination introduce the reader-surrogate's attempt to *speak* to Friday: "I tug his woolly hair, finger the chain about his throat. 'Friday,' I say, I try to say, kneeling over him, sinking hands and knees into the ooze, 'what is this ship?'" (157).

Clearly, this bid to articulate Friday's silence forms a parallel with the scene in which Susan Barton attempts to teach Friday language and, in my discussion of this earlier scene, I pointed out that the novel emphasises the failure of language to adequate otherness with the same during the face-to-face encounter. In the image of reading with which the novel ends, the conceptual force of language is again depicted as failing to establish a relation which correlates its terms: "But this is not a place of words. Each syllable, as it comes out, is caught and filled with water and diffused" (157). Tellingly, the reason for this failure to integrate Friday's exteriority into the same through language is revealed in the following sentence, which alludes to the non-conceptual event of the face-to-face and thereby suggests that the reader-surrogate's freedom in autonomy has been challenged by Friday's silence: "He turns and turns till he lies at full length, his face to my face" (157).

The fact that this image of reading in *Foe* is couched in the ethical terms of an encounter with the face, suggests that the relationship which it depicts is one in which the idea of infinity is "concretely produced." It is Friday's face and not force that opposes the autonomous reading subject's violence. And, in the sentences which follow and which describe Friday's response to the encounter, the efficacy of an opposition that is grounded in radical difference emerges:

> His mouth opens. From inside him comes a slow stream, without breath, without interruption. It flows up through his body and out upon me; it passes through the cabin, through the wreck; washing the cliffs and shores of the island, it runs northward and southward to the ends of the earth. Soft and cold, dark and unending, it beats against my eyelids, against the skin of my face. (157)

The reference to the reader-figure's eyelids in this passage is noteworthy. His/her eyes are shut and the suggestion is that they have been made quiet by the text's authoritative silence.[31] Indeed, the implicit opposition in this passage between vision and audition invests the reader-surrogate with that passivity which characterises the autonomous subject's exposure to the infinitude of otherness. The projective intentionality through which otherness is integrated into the same has made way for what John Llewelyn, after Maurice Blanchot, calls "attentionality," that is, waiting for the other, *listening* for the ethical command.[32]

Foe thus concludes with an image of a forceful relation modulating into a face-to-face encounter as the reader-surrogate subordinates him/herself to the authority of the otherness intimated by the text's silence. And because the opposition of the face is not grounded in force but radical difference, it follows that what is depicted here is not simply a reversal of the terms in the master-servant relationship of power. As I have argued, the authority of the other derives from the subject's epiphanic recognition of its otherness and self-substituting assumption of responsibility for it. Accordingly, the inequality of this relation is a function not of the exercise of power but of the assumption of responsibility.[33]

In suggesting that the literary encounter may be one in which the reader is inspired by infinity and thereby rendered responsible for the other, the image of reading with which *Foe* closes is supported by the allusion to William Wordsworth's *The Prelude* that is contained in the above quotation's reference to a slow, uninterrupted stream. In *The Prelude*, a strong contrast exists between reason, which experiences the world detachedly through vision alone, and an immersion in the world. This is particularly evident in the Mount Snowdon episode, where an openness to the world is imaged by the poet's quietening of the external eye and listening to the invisible subterranean stream:

---

[31] For a discussion of the significance of the Orphic gesture of "looking away" in the formulation of a literary aesthetic that is capable of drawing the other, see my paper entitled "Writing with Eyes Shut: Ethics, Politics, and the Problem of the Other in the Fiction of J. M. Coetzee," *English in Africa* 25:1 (1998), 43-60.

[32] John Llewelyn, *Emmanuel Levinas: The Genealogy of Ethics*, London, 1995, 53; see also Zygmunt Bauman, *Postmodern Ethics*, Oxford, 1993, 87-88.

[33] Compare Levinas' following description, in *Totality and Infinity*, of the asymmetrical aspect of the relationship of responsibility: "To recognize the Other is to give. But it is to give to the master, to the lord, to him whom one approaches as 'You' in a dimension of height" (75).

> There I beheld the emblem of a mind
> That feeds upon infinity, that broods
> Over the dark abyss, intent to hear
> Its voices issuing forth to silent light
> In one continuous stream; a mind sustained
> By recognitions of transcendent power,
> In sense conducting to ideal form,
> In soul of more than mortal privilege.[34]

In the context of *Foe*'s debate on interpretation, the point made by this allusion is, once again, that the masterful, intentional reader is exposed to infinity in his/her encounter with the text and, accordingly, that s/he becomes obedient, attentional.

The image of reading with which *Foe* ends therefore suggests the authority of the text's excessive silence, its ability to produce in the textual encounter the idea of the infinite which, in turn, interrupts the reader's subjectivity and inspires him/her to assume responsibility for, rather than foreclose on, the otherness that the text intimates. The novel's ending thus points to the possibility of an assignation between reader and text in which the ethical relation is *performed*. The *event* constituted by such an encounter would, of course, be grounded not in cognition but respect for the unknowability of the other.

Foe's self-reflexive meditation on reading clarifies the singular nature of the form of resistance that may be enabled by silence. Through its silence, the text aspires to inspire the reader with infinity: that is, it seeks to *perform* the ethical. It endeavours to expose the reader to that which will *concern* him/her and thereby become the means through which his/her relations with others in history will be affected.

Levinas' views on the entry of the ethical into the political explain how the ethical relation that the text endeavors to secure between reader and other is able to affect the reader's relations in the political domain. For Levinas, the ethical relation is not "clandestine." As he puts it, "The third party looks at me in the eyes of the Other."[35] Expressed differently, the relation to the other is also a relation to the community, to humanity as a whole. In Levinas' conception of the "entry" of the ethical into the community, the event of the face-to-face encounter has the consequence that the unequal, asymmetrical ethical relation comes to mediate those relations among peers that are already extant in the community. This, as Simon

---

[34] William Wordsworth, *The Prelude*, Harmondsworth, 1971, 14, lines 70-77.
[35] Levinas, *Totality and Infinity*, 213.

Critchley explains, is the implication of Levinas' assertion that "the reciprocal relationship binds me to the other man in the trace of transcendence."[36] The community that has been disturbed by the ethical is one that is "based on the inegalitarian moment of the ethical relation."[37] In entering the community, then, the ethical *alters* the political: it generates a community that is grounded in the irreducibility of the responsible relation of same to other, a relation which opposes totality by eliciting the constant interruption of infinity.

It seems clear that the image of reading with which *Foe* concludes, posits the possibility of an ethical community. Should, for instance, the actual reader's response to the novel follow the course of the reader-figure in the text, s/he will be concerned by the alterity that the text intimates. And, given the fact that "the third party looks at the subject in the eyes of the Other," the reader's proximity to the other will inevitably affect his/her relations in the order of the political. His/her relations with his/her peers will be mediated by his/her unequal relation to the other.

Ultimately, then, there emerges from Coetzee's *Foe* a conception of silence that is able to resist violence and thereby "engage" with apartheid history. Clearly, the mode of engagement that is self-reflexively adumbrated in this novel is very different to that which is found in most South African writing of the apartheid era. Unlike conventional forms of politically-committed writing that seek to oppose the violence of apartheid through resistance, Coetzee's novel's strategies of excession attempt to resist *all* violence by imparting a sense of the radical opposition of the absolute other. By exposing the reader to that which is exterior to the language of the same, *Foe* attempts to *concern* and so alter him/her. Differently put, this novel's attempt to affect the reader, and through him/her history, is not grounded in force, but in the ethical authority of the other — that is, in a form of authority that is divested of power.

---

[36] Simon Critchley, *The Ethics of Deconstruction: Derrida and Levinas*, Oxford, 1992, 227; and Levinas, *Otherwise than Being*, 158.
[37] Critchley, *The Ethics of Deconstruction*, 227.

"A GESTURE OF BELONGING":
CREATIVITY AND PLACE
IN SOUTH AFRICAN WOMEN'S WRITING

Gina Wisker

> Southern Africa might one day become the home of the storyteller and
> dreamer, who did not hurt others but only introduced new dreams that filled
> the heart with wonder.[1]

Against the daily horror of apartheid, the writing of women of South Africa offers an imaginative rebellion, a creative alternative or set of alternative envisionings of life and its values. Bessie Head, Miriam Tlali, Ingrid
de Kok, Gcina Mhlope and Zoe Wicomb all realistically and directly chart
the destructive daily lives of people under apartheid, and then defy the limits of mere description, exploring the destructiveness of imposed power
based on hierarchies of difference, exploring creative, sensitive relationships and expressions which imaginatively and spiritually overcome divisive prejudice.

It is the liberated and engaged imagination which both critiques the
destructiveness of oppression under racism, and offers new ways to live
and, more broadly, new ways of perceiving the world and the people in it.
The writing of South African women and the creative, hopeful spirit it engages with emerges despite the destructive silencing which apartheid imposed, its dehumanization limiting much of the writing of the period to a
documentary response. During apartheid, creativity and experimentation,
the power of the liberated imagination, were at odds with the daily horrors
of people's lives. As Elleke Boehmer points out:

> Narrative uncertainty, its suggestiveness and tease, were constrained within
> the deathly binaries of a long history of oppression and opposition.[2]

---

[1] Bessie Head, *A Woman Alone: Autobiographical Writings*, ed. Craig Mackenzie
Oxford, 1990, 103.
[2] Elleke Boehmer, "Endings and New Beginnings: South African Fiction in Transition," in *Writing South Africa*, eds Derek Attridge and Rosemary Jolly, Cambridge,
1998, 45.

Jolly and Attridge note of Boehmer's argument that:

> The unbearable reality of the apartheid world, she suggests, resists the nov-
> elistic imagination. There are some periods, it would seem, in which the task
> of imagining difference — temporally speaking and with regard to the other
> — is less possible than at other times.[3]

In her essay Elleke Boehmer explores fiction which operates as a record of
what is and has been, and *also* stands as a link into suggesting the possible,
the alternatives, and thus has an engaged role to play. It is important that
we recognize in South African writing the ability to record detail and
document, and still suggest that life could be other; thus harnessing both
the realistic detail and the creative imaginative leap, positing another
world.

Additionally, some South African writing both partakes of the qualities of post-modernism — fissures, fragmentation, oppositional structures
and versions, destabilizing of representation of self — and combines this
experimentation of form, this questioning of the established classical form
of the novel, or poetry, with ethical engagement and imaginative suggesti-
bility. My thesis in this discussion of selected South African women's
writing is that these writers combine often dichotomous responses and
forms to a creative imaginative end, and that they do this most particularly
when investigating and embodying the shifting relationship between iden-
tity/self and place/location. Miriam Tlali's characters in *Soweto Stories*
(1989) seek a home in crowded rooms, are dominated by bed bugs in a
transit hotel, terrorized out of temporary apartments and find solace writing in small spaces. Bessie Head's Elizabeth in *A Question of Power*
(1974) works through tormenting contradictions of identity in her room,
initially an arena for breakdown. In the village agricultural garden in
which she grows experimental vegetables and uses experimental farming
techniques, however, she finds a place to create, and from which personally to move on. Zoe Wicomb's sense of place in *You Can't Get Lost in
Cape Town* (1987) returns her to home and to the recognition of new versions of identity, based on memory and imaginative exploration.

In the work of Miriam Tlali, Bessie Head, Ingrid de Kok, Gcina
Mhlope and Zoe Wicomb in particular, imagery which enables an exploration of the ideas of identity and hope for creative change in the future re-
curs as that of geography, of the house and home space, and of journeying.
Of particular interest is the representation of Bessie Head's adoptive vil-

---

[3] Attridge and Jolly, *op. cit.*, 8.

lage, Serowe, in Botswana. Serowe is a border village which escaped colonialism and experienced the many travelers who passed over the border
out of South Africa, accommodating them into its own sense of identity,
never needing (except for the police response, of course) to identify their
difference as a reason for destruction, recognizing in fact that the "strangers" who passed through or stayed were versions of themselves, part of
their village identity, a part of their lives — not Others to be destroyed.
The familiarity of spaces, the accommodation of difference within a sense
of vital productive diversity and the importance of a sense of identity and
being at home, being in a place which allows you to expand and be yourself, is a crucial stimulus to the writer, and nurtures imagery of engaged,
imaginative works.

Bessie Head and Zoe Wicomb left South Africa to write, Wicomb
later returning several times and still traveling between her old and new
homes. Miriam Tlali and Ingrid de Kok stayed. The homeland of South
Africa is represented in their work and in that of their contemporaries, as
one where the regime was so oppressive as to deny basic human rights and
strangle creative, hopeful expression. We read of people, under apartheid,
consistently underpaid, dehumanized, their values denied and destroyed in
a historical divisiveness mythical in its all-encompassing grandness. Its
acting out of a cultural Otherising, rejection and destruction shocked the
rest of the world, partly because of the stirrings of tendencies to Otherising
or being Otherised which the rest of the world recognized, perhaps. Here
on a grand stage, a mythic drama of differentiation, destruction and exclusion was being played out: a grand narrative. The writing of Bessie Head
and other women writers provides a critically aware, creative and imaginative response to these contradictions and constraints.

Spaces and places in Africa are particularly resonant in terms of colonial and post-colonial discourse. Historically, reference to space and location recalls, for the colonizer and settler, the threat of the indigenous peoples who were, more often than not, either emptied out of the spaces of Africa in colonial discourse and representation, or figured as dangerous, different, to be denied and destroyed. J. M. Coetzee comments on this phenomenon in twentieth-century white South African poetry, arguing that:

> In all the poetry commemorating meetings with the silence and emptiness of
> Africa […] it is hard not to read a certain historical will to see as silent and

empty a land that has been, if not full of human figures, not empty of them either.[4]

Emptying the spaces of people in order to fill them with your own people and with your own representations is a popular stance for the colonizer. Coetzee sees it in twentieth-century poetry, and it is similarly popular as a stance in many nineteenth-century and early twentieth-century fictions which also seek to express Africa, including the South, as a woman, dark, potentially disempowering in her danger, but also rich and fertile, to be possessed. Mapping and labeling define and express the ownership of spaces. Joseph Conrad's *Heart of Darkness* (1902) is one text well known to explore this issue. It is a cautionary tale, pointing out the seductive dangers of Otherness expressed in the figure of Africa for the most (and least) enlightened of Europeans who intend to control, define and take from it. More recently, Ann McClintock comments on maps, the colonizer's controlling, naming and labeling vehicle: "the map is a liminal thing, associated with thresholds and marginal zones, burdened with dangerous powers."[5] The contradictions of colonial power are embodied in the dangers and promises which these maps represent. People are enabled to develop or prevented from developing their sense of identity in relation to the spaces and places which they inhabit and which have influenced them. In particular, a sense of national identity is formed by the social and geographical/physical environment: its presence in the popular imaginary of people present in the environment, and also those exiled or living in the diaspora.

For the women writers discussed here — at home, exiled in the diaspora, traveling, displaced, and/or returning — space, place and the people in that social context enable self-definition, the establishment and maintenance of an identity, a sense of belonging, and a place from which to grow, develop and improve in the imagination, a place from which to plan and build, create and project forward positive developments and alternatives. For many women the crucial space is the family home which nurtures or limits supportive, developmental relationships, love, education and personal growth in the community. Bound up with space, place and people is the security of identity from which to project a positive future.

---

[4] J. M. Coetzee, *White Writing: The Culture of Letters in South Africa*, Massachusetts, 1989. See chapter 9.
[5] Ann McClintock, *Imperial Leather: Race, Gender and Sexuality in the Colonial Context*, London, 28.

So the destructive movements of displaced job seekers and the families in Miriam Tlali's short stories, the invaded and destroyed, the misrepresented home and family spaces moved through in Ingrid de Kok's poems are matched by Bessie Head's imagining of a place/home in which to confront demons and to project Utopian visions — to recognize self and paint creative imaginings — to move forward. In the work of Zoe Wicomb the places and people among whom she grows up are seen to shape her protagonist, Frieda Shenton, and to be reclaimed and reshaped upon return from the UK. Wicomb's diasporan existence gives the perspective of distance enhanced by the newness of difference upon return. Wicomb creates "clearings in the bush" or in the Cape Town landscape where issues of identity, place and the creative, liberated imagination can be debated.

Gcina Mhlope's poetry conjures up the pain of displacement and poverty, where families are moved on and find it difficult to establish a sense of identity in any nurturing location, since none is forthcoming. Here the bare necessities of life are denied, and with it, identity and the power to imagine a new future, are dangerously threatened:

> Sometimes when it rains
> Rains for days without break
> I think of mothers
> Who give birth in squatter camps
> Under plastic shelters
> At the mercy of cold angry winds.[6]

The pain of enforced removals and enforced establishments of temporary living spaces are a destructive influence on women's lives. Attempting to bring up families, with the dangers and deprivations of dispossession and transience, and the conflicts between the values of the town and the rural village are subjects explored and dramatized by Bessie Head, Miriam Tlali, Zoc Wicomb, Gcina Mhlope, Ingrid de Kok and others, including the writers of COSAW (the Congress of South African Writers) collective whose work appears in *Like a House on Fire: Contemporary Women's Writing from South Africa* (1994). But even these transient living spaces have, through being inhabited by people, become communities whose existence enables a sense of identity to develop and, as was seen in the apartheid period, a community which engendered revolt and direct political action. The creative human spirit, under pressure, identifies with and occupies space unrecognized as nurturing by others. So Gcina Mhlope

---

[6] Gcina Mhlope, "Sometimes When It Rains," in *The Heinemann Book of African Women's Poetry,* ed. Ann Oosthuizen, London, 1987, 205.

pies space unrecognized as nurturing by others. So Gcina Mhlope actually found space, in Johannesburg, to write in a toilet (very definitely a new take on "a room of one's own"), and recalls this in her short story "The Toilet" (1987). The confining space gave her warmth, dryness, privacy and security:

> I was really lucky to have found that toilet because the winter was very cold. Not that it was any warmer in there but once I'd closed the door it used to be a little less windy. Also the toilet was very small — the walls were wonderfully close to me — it felt like it was made to fit me. I enjoyed that kind of privacy.[7]

With nowhere else to go, occasionally sneakily camping in her sister's room in the family house where she worked, Gcina Mhlope found sanctuary, made the best of what was available, however possibly disgusting, denied and avoided by others, and there was able to think, then write. When she found the door locked one morning, she was, significantly, still enabled to write, having had a supportive place to give herself a sense of belonging, safety and identity: a springboard for her creative efforts.

Gcina Mhlope's poem "Sometimes When It Rains" characterizes the sense of dispossession and displacement suffered by South Africans under apartheid which is dramatized in Miriam Tlali's stories. These people have little hope and no home:

> Sometimes when it rains
> I think of "illegal" job seekers
> In big cities
> Dodging police vans in the rain
> Hoping for darkness to come
> So they can find some wet corner to hide in.[8]

Miriam Tlali's work grows out of a period of protest writing in the grim days of the 1970s a period, however, of limited poetic license which enabled some freer speech:

> At the beginning of the 1970s a new spirit emerged with dramatic force. The youth of South Africa discovered a less vulnerable form of protest writing — a new form of power. For reasons that are hard to explain the poets and their writing enjoyed a form of official tolerance not accorded to any other kind of writer. This poetry became the only outlet for the increasingly grim

---

[7] Gcina Mhlope, "The Toilet," in *Sometimes When It Rains: Writings by South African Women,* ed. Ann Oosthuizen, London, 1987, 3.
[8] Mhlope, "Sometimes When It Rains," 205.

experience of the 1960's and 1970's. For the first time literary expression in our writing took on a completely political perspective.[9]

Miriam Tlali's people are frequently homeless, transient, moving through difficult spaces and trying to set up home there. One story features a traveller forced to spend a hellish night in a room with bed bugs ("Vigil with the flies and the bed bugs") — it is funny, but oppressive. "Fud-u-u-a!" deals with the threat of traveling on a train which must be done in pairs. Congestion does not seem to exist in the white-only coaches, nor does sexual pestering. These confined and threatening spaces are a direct result of racist separatism. While tourists are brought in to Soweto to study the local people, as if they were zoo animals in their own homes, on the trains their spaces are even more oppressed by practices of racism, power, and gender discrimination. It is said of Miriam Tlali that:

> She dared hold and express opinion. She dared not only to speak out against the dominance of male writing which had attended black literature from the very beginning. She struck out bold and fearless. She could not help but be noticed for she was not only among the first women novelists to resurface, but she was also the first woman novelist inside South Africa to take her place among the national gallery of our black literary figures [...]. She is among the very few writers which have refused to be intimidated and 'smoked' out of South Africa, by the harsh treatment which is reserved for black writers.[10]

Tlali's stories are influenced by several key places in terms of South African identity, development and community, including two of the settlements — Doornfontein in Johannesburg where she was born, and Sophiatown where she grew up — as well as Soweto where she has settled and which lends its name to the collection *Soweto Stories*. "Dimomona," a powerful tale of place and loss, is set in Sophiatown in 1932. Dimomona and Boitumelo Kgope "were tenants occupying one of a chain of ten rooms, each housing an average family of eight people" (44). What we see of their life, introduced here as merely poor, exemplifies the dehumanizing hardships and wicked absurdity of the apartheid laws. While the husband must work in the city, the wife must stay behind in the deprivation of the inaptly named "homelands," visiting him only to conceive their children, leaving the others behind. He, meanwhile, has to carry a pass book for identity purposes. His room is raided while he is on the toilet and, not carrying his pass book, Boitumelo is abused, manacled, marched by police

---

[9] Miriam Tlali, *Soweto Stories*, London, 1989. Introduction, xiv.
[10] *Ibid.*, xv.

whose accents and brutality give the event an air of nightmare: "condemned men" and "Offenders" (47) is how he and his colleagues, all
workers in the city but offenders against the pass laws, are characterized.

Boitumelo loses his freedom, his reputation and, on returning finally,
his job. Although he is an excellent worker, there is no leeway or compas-
sion from his employer who considers him rather feckless to have been
caught. The social distance between Boitumelo the worker and his employer is immense. The latter lives in a protected, rich, large house "the
big house with the towering palm trees and the blooming luscious garden"
(53), with two big black dogs trained to attack: "they were trained never to
tolerate a strange black face, especially, Boitumelo had told her" (54).
Generously the boss explodes, "Amazing how they always manage to get
themselves into gaol!" (55), with the insensitivity of the socially blind.
Broken and ill, once (unusually) he returns alive from prison, denied his
job, Boitumelo and family have to sell their few possessions and go back
to the land and further poverty, their lives ruined. The story is realistic, detailed and sensitive, giving insights into feelings and the utterly inhuman
laws and treatment of black by white. Miriam Tlali's clear vision presents
a tale which must have been typical.

Many white writers, although privileged merely because of their skin
color, spoke out too, and were silenced also, many leaving the country to
be able to speak freely. In the work of Ingrid de Kok and that of other
white writers (Coetzee, Nadine Gordimer, and others), we see there are
many white writers, teachers and others who spoke out against apartheid,
some of whom were imprisoned for their views. Ingrid de Kok, the Afrikaner poet, uses imagery of children, closed rooms and brutality to characterize the monstrous everyday destructiveness of life under apartheid. Brutality extends to everyone of every age in this regime:

> They took all that was child
> and in the dark closed room
> visions of a ripe split melon
> were at the tip of the knife
> they held to the child's dry tongue.
>
> [...]
>
> And this torn light,
> this long torn light
> will repair itself
> out of the filaments of children.

and all that is child will return to the house,
will return to the house.[11]

The image of a returning child expresses an imaginative hope for positive change in a situation of crisis and destruction of life and human values, in this case the record of police brutality in Victoria West. Ingrid de Kok's poetry consistently focuses on children as victims and on the inhuman, invading forces of the oppressors who move through, destroying, removing, fracturing homes and dreams and senses of identity. In "Small Passing," a poem to a woman whose baby was stillborn and who was told to stop mourning "for the trials and horror suffered daily by black women in this country are more significant than the loss of one white child," she interweaves images of loss, children leaving and returning home strangers, children shot. She creates here a sense of the unity of mothers — white and black — in their need to cherish, although fractured by prejudice and poverty and the demand to move on. The spaces are backyards and houses, and the space for a dead child needs recognition, would be marked by black and white mothers, in the heart and in the headstone. While the pain of the white mother is dismissed as minimal in comparison to the everyday pain of all black people, nonetheless, as Ingrid de Kok points out, mothers would be able to empathize across an unnatural division based on color and economics, and recognize that however privileged or unprivileged a mother is, the loss of her child is devastating, beyond social politics. It is a powerful poem about women's sense of the space and place of belonging, whatever the paucity of that place, and of a unity of nurturing and recognition across boundaries of color and economics. Her poetry touches on the sensitive difficulties of white South Africans of Afrikaner or European descent who are not the oppressors, and who find themselves marginalized and voiceless, their experience deemed irrelevant. Her perceptions create images of a South Africa of displacement and loss:

> See
> The newspaper boy in the rain
> will sleep tonight in a doorway.
> The woman in the bus line
> may next month be on a train
> to a place not her own.
> The baby in the backyard now

---

[11] Ingrid de Kok, "Al Wat Kind Is," in *The Heinemann Book of African Women's Poetry*, 184-85.

> will be sent to a tired aunt,
> grow chubby, then lean,
> return a stranger.[12]

Children are separated from parents, wives from husbands. Spaces are put between people who lose contact with their families and roots. From this position it is hard to develop hope and creativity. Mandela's daughter tried to find her father "through the glass. She thought they would let her touch him," and from the mothers she hears support: "Come with us to the place of mothers."[13] The stoicism and nurturing of ordinary people shines through in much of the writing of South African women and it is from this stoicism and nurturing that the roots of a creative imagination are seen to grow, against all odds.

Zoe Wicomb's *You Can't Get Lost in Cape Town* identifies even by its title the importance of the relationship between self, identity, and location. Her protagonist, Frieda Shenton, consistently focuses on the problems of trying to exist in the fissures of a society which has little place and space for Black or colored women, and feeling torn between the identification of home, which limits her, and the critiqued, vision of possibilities away from home, in the UK. She is defining herself in the gap between these two places, existing as a self which, to white people, is only an Other, although she "passes" for white when, for instance, seeking an abortion in the title story "You Can't Get Lost in Cape Town." Frieda locates herself in recalling her own past history, childhood, adolescence, student experience, and beyond, upon return from the UK. In the story, "You Can't Get Lost in Cape Town," Frieda emphasizes the pain of never being lost but never fully at home in a town which marginalizes you. However, the creativity, poetry, fiction and imaginative projection consistently move her beyond the constraints of racism and the extremely partisan law. She and her white lover, Michael, wish to marry and seek a place to be together, but know there is no place for them in South Africa as a mixed race couple, and no place at all for their unborn child, despite Michael's optimism:

> "We'll find somewhere," he would say. "A place where we'd be quite alone." This country is vast and he has an instinctive sense of direction. He discovers the armpits of valleys that invite us into their shadows. Dangerous climbs led by the roar of the sea take us to blue bays into which we drop

---

[12] Ingrid de Kok, "Small Passing," in *The Lava of this Land*, Illinois, 1997, 195.
[13] *Ibid.*, 181, 182.

from impossible cliffs. The sun lowers herself onto us. We do not fear the police with their torches. They come only by night in search of offenders. We have the immunity of love. They cannot find us because they do not know we exist. One day they will find out about lovers who steal whole days, round as globes.[14]

The daring, rebellious and secure tone of John Donne's "Sunne Rising" runs throughout this identification of hope and place. As lovers, their place is safe and hidden and they can control the sun. Even policemen, the enforcers of inhuman laws which would regulate love, cannot find them because their safety lies in the paucity of the racist imagination: no-one would even be able to imagine their existence. They have created something new and radical, powerful and beautiful, natural. The images of fruits, landscape and buildings of Cape Town resonate throughout this story, which evokes her home in which, pregnant with a mixed race child, Frieda feels particularly ill at ease. Able to relate identity, place and creativity with new hope, Zoe Wicomb is yet, like Bessie Head and the other writers considered here, also never lulled into a false sense of security. Theirs is a sense of paradox: repression and denial mixed with fruitful hope and the creative imagination which by working through the contradictions of life for women under apartheid, envisages alternatives and ways through.

Bessie Head's own position beyond the boundary of South Africa in Botswana, her adopted home, enables her to explore boundaries, spaces, places, social environments and the creative imagination's potential to suggest movement through pain, to change. Head's work does not deal directly with the incidences of prejudice, abuse and violence which she certainly experienced in South Africa herself. Instead, from her exiled position in Botswana, she was actually enabled to free her mind from the particulars and specifics and to deal, instead, with issues of the inhumanity of badly managed, oppressive power, internalized by the victims, warping them, preventing them from freeing their imaginations and perceptions of self and the world, destroying them. In this project, the interrogation of the destructive effects of racism are central, not least because Bessie Head was herself a victim of the Immorality Acts, her own mother confined to a mental home after (in her forties, a failed marriage and two sons, one now dead behind her) she became pregnant through a relationship with a black stable hand and was immediately exiled from the family. Bessie Head was

---

[14] Zoe Wicomb, *You Can't Get Lost in Cape Town*, London, 1987, 76.

acutely aware of the damage done through prejudice based entirely on skin color. But she can imagine and create alternative worlds without such absurd prejudice:

> With all my South African experience I longed to write an enduring novel on the hideousness of racial prejudice. But I also wanted the book to be so beautiful and so magical that I, as a writer would long to read and re-read it.[15]

She identifies *Maru* (1971) as having achieved this aim. In *Maru*, Bessie Head explores more broadly the issues of prejudice, oppression, exclusion and dehumanization based on difference. This is most creatively and positively explored, by concentrating on the most marginalized, a "Bushman," Margaret Cadmore, named after the missionary who brought her up, whose imaginative powers explore images in art, while in her daily life others reject, oppress and exclude her — or try to — because of their ingrained prejudice against the lowest of the low, the "Bushman." Through the Otherising which Margaret experiences, Head confronts the ignorance and damage of racism:

> The research I did among the Botswana people for *Maru* gave me the greatest insights and advantages to work right at the roots of racial hatred. I found out above all that the type of exploitation and evil is dependent upon a lack of communication between the oppressor and the people he oppresses. It would horrify an oppressor to know that his victim has the same longings, feelings, and sensitivities as he has. Nothing prevented a communication between me and the Botswana people and nothing prevented me from slipping into the skin of a Mosarwa person. And so my novel was built up in blinding flashes of insights into an evil that hung like the sickness of death over all black people in South Africa.[16]

And indeed, in reading *Maru* we are aware of the immediacy of this everyday racism which has been transferred from all Black people, to the "Bushmen," and to that singular creative individual, Margaret:

> If the white man thought that Asians were a low, filthy nation, Asians could still smile with relief — at least, they were not Africans. And if the white man thought Africans were a low, filthy nation, Africans in Southern Africa could still smile — at least, they were not Bushmen. They all have their monsters.[17]

---

[15] Head, *A Woman Alone*, 68.
[16] *Ibid.*, 69.
[17] Bessie Head, *Maru*, Oxford, 1971, 11.

Racism is exemplified in the village, but, more alarmingly, endemic in mankind's history as:

> wherever mankind had gathered itself together in a social order, the same things were happening. There was a mass of people with no humanity to whom another mass referred. Why, they are naturally like that. They like to live in such filth. They have been doing it for centuries.[18]

By identifying with Margaret as an oppressed and creative individual, as Other with whom we can relate, Bessie Head gets us right inside both the disgusting horror of racism's consequences, and creative ways of confronting it.

Bessie Head's sceptical religious response finds its firm home in a sense of the potential for goodness embodied in ordinary people who, enlightened and led by those who are neither superficial nor self-seeking in their power management, will care for others and ensure equality, will move creatively and positively towards the kind of sensitive change which is embodied in an individualistic way. She says:

> A discipline I have observed is an attitude of love and reverence to people. I had used the word God, in a practical way, in my books. I cannot find a substitute word for all that is most holy, but I have tried to deflect people's attention into offering to each other what they offer to an Unseen Being in the sky. When people are holy to each other, war will end, human suffering will end.[19]

Her tale is based on a true story. Margaret was brought up with kindness but in a rather distant relationship by Margaret Cadmore, the missionary's wife. Educated, talented, and newly graduated with a teaching qualification, Margaret finds that her work takes her into a town particularly prejudiced against the "Bushmen," the Masarwa, where the children single her out for disrespect — a difficult experience in her role as their teacher. Her spirit, however, remains strong and sensitive amid psychological and emotional hardships as well as the usual physical ones. Befriended by Dikeledi, the sister of Moleka who grows to love her, she has no trouble in finding and settling into her own home, which is a space resonant with importance for her, despite its simplicity and lack of furnishings. Margaret grows strong, peacefully inhabiting her own space, creative in her production of beautiful paintings which enable her to express her responses to the world around her and to those she cares for — an outward creativity from

---

[18] *Ibid.*, 68.
[19] Head, *A Woman Alone*, 99.

a safe space of self. This is the imaginative, positive position and statement Margaret is afforded. Her imaginative creative self suggests and enables responses of love and equality from those around her. It is a move
expressing the ability to ignore the negative, destructive powers of prejudiced others, and see alternative more positive ways of relating and being.

Margaret moves forward, and along the way enlightens Dikeledi,
Moleka, who loves her, and then Maru, who is destined to be chief. Maru
is also fully aware of the horrors of racism and sees a new world opening
up: his vision is enlightened too. He thinks:

> Should he bother to explain to her the language of the voices of the gods
> who spoke of tomorrow? That they were opening doors on all sides, for
> every living thing on earth, that there would be a day when everyone would
> be free and no one the slave of another?[20]

He envisages kings of tomorrow who do not need to rule with violence,
but with equality.

Margaret is surprised to be the object of the affection of two men, she
who "had no confusion of heart, only the experience of being permanently
unwanted by society in general." Her rescue of the mother goat and her kid
and then, when the mother is killed by the villagers, the kid alone, shows
her to be most in tune with those who suffer and are victimized. Her paint-
ing enables her to reveal and project her emotions, and to help Dikeledi
project hers. Margaret's care and creativity bring about a focusing change
in those who know her well. Maru is the powerful husband who seeks her
out against all prejudice, but then (paradoxically for those of us who are
European readers, and feminists perhaps) removes her to marry her and
live with her elsewhere, finding new simplicity — but no place to encourage real change back in the village. Some of the dangers of reading as
European feminists emerge here — resolutions which might annoy a European feminist might well please an African feminist. Feminism aside, issues of racial enlightenment emerge from the story. Margaret's marriage is
viewed as a window of opportunity for her people, the Masarwa or
"Bushmen," and this is expressed spatially as a wind of freedom blowing
through what was once the airless room of racial prejudice:

> When people of the Masarwa tribe heard about Maru's marriage to one of
> their own, a door silently opened on the small, dark airless room in which
> their souls had been shut for a long time. The wind of freedom, which was
> blowing throughout the world for all people, turned and flowed into the

---

[20] Head, *Maru*, 68-69.

room. As they breathed in the fresh clear air their humanity awakened [...] how had they fallen into this condition when, indeed, they were as human as everyone else? They started to run out into the sunlight, then they turned and looked at the dark, small room. They said: "We are not going back there."[21]

Perhaps grand scale change cannot happen, here, only localized change, but the celebrated imagination of Margaret and of the novel *Maru* offer a form of blueprint for changing perceptions and behaviors.

Another blueprint for change based upon the establishment of identity, of ontological security in relation to images of space and of location, emerges in *A Question of Power,* a fictionalized autobiographical account of Bessie Head's own breakdown when settled in Botswana. It is an imaginative record of the real and terrible experiences of exile and self-exile, schizophrenia and depression undergone by Bessie Head herself in Serowe when she first sought a new life in Botswana, but it is an even wider imaginative account than this personal suffering and breakthrough.

Elizabeth's own room and bed are the site of the playing out of immense psychological power struggles which represent the turmoil of her own mind, her divided self, and also represent the division of her country's self, embodied in her. She is torn between two male figures, whose daylight real representatives she hardly knows. Dan is the husband figure, tormenting her with sexual demands and power threats, while Sello is both a Buddhist monk in white, and a brown-suited restrictive, paternalistic force. Sello desires control over Elizabeth's soul, Dan over her body. As Paul H. Lorenz notes, this divided self is similar to the divided self of those oppressed under cultural colonization.[22] In Paolo Freire's words:

> The oppressed suffer from the duality which has established itself in their innermost being. They discover that without freedom they cannot exist authentically. Yet, although they desire authentic existence, they fear it. They are at one and the same time themselves and the oppressor whose consciousness they have internalized. The conflict lies in the choice between being wholly themselves or being divided; between ejecting the oppressor within or not ejecting him; between following prescriptions or having choices; between being spectators or actors; between speaking out or being silent, castrated in their power to create and re-create, in their power to transform the world. This is the tragic dilemma of the oppressed which their education must take into account.[23]

---

[21] *Ibid.*, 127.

[22] Paul H. Lorenz, "Colonization and the Feminine in Bessie Head's *A Question of Power*," *Modern Fiction Studies* 37:3 (1991), 596.

[23] Paulo Friere, *Pedagogy of the Oppressed*, New York, 1990, 32-33.

Lies, perverse sexual demands and oppressive power games dominate her sleeping and semi-sleeping moments, taking over almost her whole psyche until she can finally sort it out and refuse to be dominated by the destructive power of others, refuse to internalize it and let it play itself out in her. Elizabeth's body internalizes and dramatizes the power play of opposing forces. Working her way through this eventually leads to a new wholeness of self and identity.

She is visited in her waking dreams by:

> the wild-eyed Medusa [...] expressing the surface reality of African society. It was shut in and exclusive. It had a strong theme of power worship running through it, and power people needed small, narrow, shut-in worlds. They never felt secure in the big, wide flexible universe where there were too many cross-currents of opposing thought.[24]

Hélène Cixous' own equation of women's bodily awareness and liberating places and spaces fits well with the experiences of Bessie Head's Elizabeth, as identified by Paul Lorenz. Cixous comments on colonization and women's bodies as sites for oppression or liberation:

> Here they [= women] are, returning, arriving over and again, because the unconscious is impregnable. They have wandered around in circles, confined to the narrow room in which they've been given a deadly brainwashing. You can incarcerate them, slow them down, get away with the old Apartheid routine, but for a time only. At the same time as they're taught their name, they can be taught that their territory is black: because you are Africa, you are black [...] we have internalized this horror of the dark.[25]

Spatial images embody a sense of oppression, and the potential for freedom and new vision. Elizabeth works through her internalized oppression, finds the wholeness and power of her own body and identity, and then feels more at one with her land:

> If such a beauty and harmony built up in her outward circumstances it was totally at odds with the tormented hell of her inner world [...]. Half of her attention was turned towards the daily round of a vegetable gardener's life.[26]

This fictionalized autobiography is both a record of a personal breakdown, a crisis of identity Bessie Head suffered, and a metaphor for the drama of South Africa. Here, the location of the confined room enables the playing

[24] Bessie Head, *A Question of Power*, Oxford, 1974, 38.
[25] Hélène Cixous, "The Laugh of the Medusa," in *New French Feminisms*, eds Elaine Marks and Isabelle de Courtivron, New York, 1981, 247-48.
[26] Head, *A Question of Power*, 157.

out of power games and the reclamation of personal wholeness, of identity, while the location of the garden in Motabeng where Elizabeth nurtures experimental and highly successful vegetables, represents the project of new growth and development, a Utopian project come true. At the book's end, sexual fantasies and horrific power games finished, Elizabeth is restored to sanity and a new wholeness and oneness with identity and her sense of the location, with the whole of Africa. The gesture is one of belonging and nurturing:

> She had fallen from the very beginning into the warm embrace of the brotherhood of man, because when a people wanted everyone to be ordinary it was just another way of saying man loved man. As she fell asleep, she placed one soft hand over her land. It was a gesture of belonging.[27]

In her short stories Bessie Head explores differences — of class, education, country and town, and of gender. Her writing always opens a window onto the complexities of power and prejudice relations, showing Zora Neale Hurston's "triple burden" to be as true a description of the South African woman's life as it was of the African American woman's. Head's characters have to recognize that the Otherising which they experience is a product of the perception of the one in power — not a description of their real value — and to reject this Otherising without always rejecting the one who employs it, leading them instead towards recognition of this misperception, which is socially and culturally ingrained. And for themselves, they move on to gain their own sense of value, rejecting the binary oppositions and the ignorance from which gender and ethnic prejudices, among all others, spring. From this enlightened position a creative imaginative projection of other possibilities of living one's life, in a world sloughing off its immense deadening prejudices, emerge. The imaginative spirit of Bessie Head, Miriam Tlali, Zoe Wicomb and Ingrid de Kok frees itself from silence and mere record, positing alternative ways of living, and writing, as Rosemary Jolly and Derek Attridge put it of Miriam Tlali and Mongane Wally Serote: "There is a sense of a new space, a space filled with the potential to imagine difference differently."[28]

There are, however, dangers in the development and representation of self in the new South Africa, and these relate on the one hand to a potentially limiting, exclusive new version of nationalism, and on the other to

---

[27] *Ibid.*, 206.
[28] Attridge and Jolly, 11.

hopping on that other bandwagon, multiculturalism and post-colonialism. It is, they point out:

> also still jeopardized by the force of an inclusive nationalist rhetoric that ignores questions of power. As Rob Nixon puts it, "What is needed is an approach to difference that breaks with smiling multiculturalism and its ugly mirror image, apartheid, by recognizing that inequalities of power slice across the sites of identity."[29]

The house and home space and the geographical location negotiated in Head's work represent the sense of developing identity. This house and home space is set, in Head's case, in the geographical space of Serowe, when she was unable, as a poor single mother, to escape to the intellectually liberating diasporas of Paris or London, where many of the male writers settled. Her movement across the border into neighboring Botswana meant that she was still in Southern Africa, and could view the developments in her own land of origin with some little distancing, at an angle to it. Her own life there was consistently threatened by her refugee status, having to report weekly to the police and in fear of deportation when her mental state worsened. Rob Nixon describes her movement and settling: "Head's rural transnationalism began as an affliction, which she appropriated as an allegiance."[30] Her work developed to novels to the recording of oral history — largely of people whose lives resembled her own — boundary crossers in this village into which so many crossed — and this brought her into closer touch with the village in her last years.

Serowe is crucial to an understanding of Bessie Head's treatment of issues of ethnicity, gender, power and difference. She was, ironically, more at home in this border town which, relatively untouched by colonialism, was able to accommodate difference and assimilate it — so that the polarization of differences of color, caste, class and gender were not the chief deciding factors of life in Serowe as they were in daily life in South Africa. In her evocation of Serowe, especially in the short stories, *The Collector of Treasures* (1977), which she wrote alongside *Serowe, Village of the Rain Wind* (1981), Head could explore this concentration on relationships, myths, power games between the chiefs and people, and all from the safe geographical and imaginative base of identity which she adopted. She could develop a sense of identity in a space which was adopted, in one

---

[29] *Ibid.*, 32.
[30] Rob Nixon, "Rural Transnationalism and Bessie Head," in *Text, Theory, Space*, eds Kate Darian-Smith, *et al.*, London, 1996, 244.

which constantly enabled difference to move through it or settle in it without any need to reject or differentiate with violence and oppression. The representation of Serowe, the border village, is one which accords to the recognition of the stranger within ourselves — everything is recognizable as part of identity rather than a threat to it — quite the opposite to South Africa under apartheid. In Serowe, Head tells us:

> every new idea is absorbed and transformed until it emerges somewhere along the line as our traditional custom. Everything is touched by "our traditional custom" — British imperialism. English Independence, new educational methods, progress and foreigners, it all belongs.[31]

We are told, however, that:

> Serowe's customary accommodations arose out of the security of its peripheral and relatively fleeting subjection to colonialism, a heritage that allowed it to accommodate difference in a manner that could express, not disavow its identity.[32]

But of course:

> Head's work was apt to project a degree of social acceptance which, in her life, she knew only as a wavering prospect. Such determined optimism quietened in her fiction the cadences of desolation that distinguished her letters. If, to the last, Head's integration into Serowe on paper remained somewhat ahead of her integration in daily life, she at least acquired there a degree of allegiance and acceptance unimaginable in her early years in Botswana from the mid 1960s through to the early 1970s. Moreover, she had engineered for herself a spread of commitments that spanned writing as a vocation, the villages, the South African region, and those rural women who sought a greater share of Botswana's perceived cultural and economic life.[33]

Bessie Head's art is one of bridging which projects a rather idealized sense of unity which she did not experience in her daily life but it is an imaginative projection.

The women writers of South Africa discussed here negotiate paradox, alienation and hardship, inner torment and memories of brutal physical destruction. They record, and they move on, their very imaginative and creative act of recording itself providing a form of recuperation, retaliation, reinventing South Africa. Bessie Head, Zoe Wicomb, Gcina Mhlope, Ingrid de Kok and Miriam Tlali, women writers already under the triple burden

---

[31] Head, *A Woman Alone*, 70.
[32] *Ibid.*, 248.
[33] Nixon, *op. cit.*, 252.

of race, class and gender, write back and reclaim pride and wholeness, suggesting a future. In this they focus on space as a signifier of the shifting notion of belonging, identity and self. Their creative interpretation of the place for self is in locations which no longer reject them but open out and invite them. These locations now provide a home, a springboard. They can identify with place, establish identity, and encourage positive change from its creative safety.

CONSTRUCTING LIVES: BLACK SOUTH AFRICAN WOMEN AND BIOGRAPHY UNDER APARTHEID

Desiree Lewis

International protest against apartheid, especially during the seventies and eighties, was galvanized to a significant degree by the circulation of densely signifying information. This information was represented in photographic, film and written texts that narrated stories about the violence of the apartheid state and about the victimization and resistance of black South Africans in the face of it. One of the main roles of the British Aid and Defence Fund, which had an entire research department, or KAIROS, which operated from the Netherlands, was to function as a production base and archive for visual and written texts like film documentaries, newspaper reports of important events, leaflets and posters used in political meetings and demonstrations, and a range of anti-apartheid biographical projects.[1] The prominence of these texts and the explicit messages they encoded allowed non-South Africans to experience the urgency of South African politics. Thus, a key aim of the Anti-Apartheid Movement was to codify, distribute and in certain cases produce mediating and testimonial texts that could effectively transmit the stories of apartheid to readers who were physically, politically and culturally very far away from it.[2] It was around these narratives that non-South Africans could establish or confirm a stance of vigorous opposition to a repressive order or of solidarity with those who lived under it.

Among these mediating texts, biography can be an especially compelling genre because of its potential to explore collective and political processes through storytelling about individual lives. Biographical productions that dealt specifically with black subjects' responses to apartheid bur-

---

[1] IDAF operated in various countries, although in Britain it developed a large collection of material related to apartheid. This material is now located in the Maybuye Center at the University of the Western Cape in South Africa.

[2] IDAF produced a number of publications dealing with South African history and politics.

geoned during the late seventies and eighties, a high point in the apartheid state's clamp-downs as well as in anti-apartheid struggle in the country and protest abroad. Most of these projects had metropolitan audiences, and were often published by British or North American publishers. Focusing mainly on black women, they seemed to offer insight into lives that were marginalized within both racial and gender hierarchies. These texts exhibit diverse approaches, and range from the scholarly projects of well-known academics like Shula Marks or Belinda Bozzoli, through fictional productions like Poppie Nongena, to popularized life stories — exemplified by Carol Hermer's *The Diary of Maria Tholo*[3] or Diana Russell's *Lives of Courage*[4] — that straddle the conventions of journalism and fiction. At face value, these projects are evidently "progressive" and appear to make visible the lives of subjects who have been historically silenced. At the same time, the projects obliquely reinforce dominant images and social hierarchies. In what follows, I consider how two biographical projects, in many ways typical of broader "progressive" trends, indirectly echo the stereotypes about race, agency, power and knowledge that have been clearly associated with apartheid.

In exploring the textual codification of "lives" in certain South African biographical practices, I raise various questions about their uses of the signifier "black South African women." On one level, the selection of black women as biographical subjects challenges the traditional conservativism of a genre which has customarily valorized white male agency. On another level, however, the turning to black women as signifiers of communal and national processes often reveals writers' situation within dominant discourses, a situation which may contradict conscious writerly choices. The question raised consistently will be: why certain representations of subjects and not others? As Liz Stanley has argued:

> We should ask of biography the question "who says?" And who says is someone who has produced one more interpretation from amongst a range of possibilities, and who has produced it from one particular angle rather than any other. In other words, "the biographer" is a socially-located person, one who is sexed, raced, classed, aged, to mention no more, and so is every bit as much as an autobiographer is.[5]

---

[3] Carol Hermer, *The Diary of Maria Tholo*, Johannesburg, 1980.

[4] Diana Russell, *Lives of Courage: Women for a New South Africa*, New York, 1989.

[5] Liz Stanley, *The Auto/biographical I*, Manchester, 1992, 7.

The concerns above are raised in relation to two texts that reveal broader patterns in the evolution of anti-apartheid biography. Elsa Joubert's *The Long Journey of Poppie Nongena*,[6] first published in 1978 in Afrikaans as *Die Swerfjare van Poppie Nongema* and Shula Marks' *Not Either an Experimental Doll*[7] are, methodologically and stylistically, very different biographical productions. *The Long Journey of Poppie Nongena* is a self-consciously fictional reconstruction of a black woman's life by the Afrikaans novelist, Elsa Joubert. Publicized and read as a novel, it highlights overtly reconstructive processes in terms of subject-matter, form and style. In contrast, *Not Either an Experimental Doll* is an academic sociological work, concerned with detailed research and substantiation of sources and referring directly to personal accounts. Although aimed at different audiences and serving divergent functions, both encode familiar assumptions about "black South African womanhood," or about the transparency of interpretation in relation to the biographical subject. The attention to two projects which seem so radically different, one a popular fictional work marketed as a "sad story of a sad country, and of a humble black woman who never gives up," and the other, a seminal scholarly work by an influential historian, is aimed at exploring how deeply ingrained, yet also persuasive the manipulating procedures of biographical representation can be.[8]

In her study of women's writing and race in America, Diane Roberts suggests that white women have played a key role in disseminating popular American images of blacks and race relations. Although women have been restricted to cultural spheres, rather than to central political and social arenas, they have engaged with key political issues. Roberts writes:

> Women's books — *Uncle Tom's Cabin, Gone With the Wind*, and many in between — have been elaborators and transmitters of many of the most powerful representations of blacks in western culture. And because the debate over slavery, and later the debate over segregation, has been argued by men publicly, in government, in speeches, but as often (and perhaps with more power) by women in published appeals and in fiction.[9]

A similar role for white women has existed in South Africa, with well-known women writers like Sarah Gertrude Millin, Daphne Rooke, and

---

[6] Elsa Joubert, *The Long Journey of Poppie Nongena*, Johannesburg, 1980.
[7] Shula Marks, *Not Either an Experimental Doll*, Natal, 1987.
[8] Alan Paton, Foreword to *The Long Journey of Poppie Nongena*.
[9] Diane Roberts, *The Myth of Aunt Jemima: Representations of Race and Region*, New York, 1994, 7.

more recently, Elsa Joubert, and Nadine Gordimer playing prominent, although often unacknowledged roles in transmitting particular images of black South Africans and certain views of race relations. The reception of Elsa Joubert's well-known work in particular illustrates the intervention of a cultural text into political life. Jack Cope captures its history when he writes:

> The book created a furore and went through edition after edition. As a serial in a national Afrikaans Sunday newspaper, it found an entirely new readership. Passed from hand to hand, nicked out of special supplements [...] A well-known professor at the University of Stellenbosch started a controversy by venturing an opinion through the press that this was a book for every Afrikaner to read as an object lesson.[10]

Yet what political meanings does the text underscore? In the following analysis, I deal with the ways in which Poppie , the biographical subject, is encoded through a discourse of strong motherhood, and the way this discourse feeds into dominant power relationships. Defying passivity, the strong mother image appears to be an empowering one. In their discussions of this image in the American context, however, African-American feminists have identified its repressive and coercive implications.[11] Michelle Wallace, for example, argues that a range of stereotypes like "mammy," "Sapphire," "matriarch" and "Aunt Jemima" straddle one persisting myth, the myth of the black Superwoman as mother, and writes: "It seemed to me that the evidence was everywhere in American culture that precisely because of their profound political and economic disadvantages, black women were considered to have a peculiar advantage."[12] Wallace provides a way of examining the contradiction between celebrating power and coercing a prescribed role, between affirming strength, while locating this strength in a framework of oppressive causes and effects.

Poppie in Joubert's novel is located within a lineage of strong black women: her grandmother, ouma Hannie, her mother, Lena and her own daughters. The main characteristic of these women is their capacity, in the face of formidable obstacles, to raise their families, support their children

---

[10] Jack Cope, *The Adversary Within*, Cape Town, 1982, 196.

[11] For a survey of views, see Patricia Hill Collins, *Black Feminist Thought: Knowledge, Consciousness and the Politics of Empowerment*, New York, 116-37.

[12] See Michelle Wallace, *Black Macho and the Myth of the Superwoman,* New York, 1978; and her "Variations on Negation and the Heresy of Black Feminist Creativity," in *Reading Black, Reading Feminist*, ed. Henry Louis Gates, New York, 1990, 56.

and create and conserve their constantly vulnerable homes. The celebration of womanhood starts with the representation of Poppie's grandmother, the old woman who raises her during early childhood. Described as a matriarchal figure, ouma Hannie seems to exercise independent and authoritative control. The following extract, for example, underscores her imperious authority and independence: "Ouma Hannie was very strict with her children. She wasn't at rest till they were married with lobola money, as well as in church. Then she setted in the location of Upington and took in the grandchildren [...] and reared them as she had reared her own."[13]

Celebratory descriptions like these underplay evidence elsewhere that oppressive circumstances usually compel ouma Hannie to play an instrumental role in her extended family. As the narrative proceeds, it becomes evident that her children are either unemployed or unable to take care of their children because they need to search for work. That ouma Hannie often endures an exhausting role as family head is especially evident in references to her relationship with her unemployed son. In many of these, however, she is represented only as an indulgent and compassionate mother: "He'd come home drunk, singing [...]. Then ouma Hannie would say: Pengi, you're making a noise, my head can't stand it. Then he'd say: But listen, man listen I'm singing to you" (14).

According to the logic of her life story, Poppie imbibes a sense of duty and selfhood from her grandmother. Yet this learnt altruism is seen to acquire the status of myth, a kind of sacrosanct inevitability, unmarked by contradiction. It is this mythologized notion of women's customary identity which is lauded in ways like the following: "Ouma Hannie was strict with Poppie [...]. She must be home before sunset. That was the custom of her people [...]. This is what Ouma taught us. It is our duty to go" (55). This extract covertly mythologizes identity: Poppie is first introduced as a subject who is spoken about and acted upon, and then described through first-person narration in which Poppie speaks not only for herself but for an "us" defined as an extension of her.

When Poppie grows older, her mother looks after her in Lambert's Bay. Lena's status, as a self-sacrificing breadwinner and nurturer, is delineated even more emphatically than ouma Hannie's. She is described mainly in terms of what she does, and how she acts, rather than through how she feels or responds. The over-riding impression of Lena, as of ouma

---

[13] Joubert, *The Long Journey of Poppie Nongena*, 13. All further references are contained in the text.

Hannie, is of her constantly managing to find jobs, providing for her family, and eluding the laws which prevent her from securing basic human needs. Like her mother, Lena, Poppie is represented mainly in terms of her everyday actions, her tasks, routines and literal movement. Poppie does things and experiences events, rather than feels or responds psychologically. It is striking that in her fictional reconstruction of an individual's life, Joubert seems relatively uninterested in textualizing the private and emotional life of her subject, the very realm which novelistic practice usually foregrounds. Where this private and emotional life does surface, it is invoked only to be suppressed: Poppie transcends private reflection through maintaining a stoically self-sacrificing role. Generally, the moments of private agonizing — precisely the moments when Poppie responds ambiguously to prescribed roles — surface in the text as "epiphanies" from which Poppie emerges resolved to immerse herself in altruistic duty.

The identification of turning points is an important means by which biographers transform the flux of their subjects' lives into coherent narratives. Joubert's marking of turning points frames Poppie's life experiences to naturalize her interpretation of her subject's development. When she is a young child, Poppie is seen to derive pleasure from reading and writing, the realm of discursive power and authority from which she is alienated. Immediately following the reference to Poppie's pleasure in this activity, however, she stoically submits to prescribed duties:

> There was a puzzle page and we took a pencil and joined up little dots according to numbers, and then could see the picture of a dog or a lion or an elephant taking shape. Ag, we liked that so much. I looked after mama's children until I was thirteen, because at thirteen the factory took children to work as cleaners. (48)

Later, when Poppie marries, she broods about the consequences of wifehood: "Then when all the people have gone to bed and his kinsmen have left, the man comes to you with the words that have rained down on you, because you know you have not married only the man, you have married into his family. From now on you are under their roof" (74). The narrator does not, however, pursue Poppie's reflections: her cryptically represented misgivings about marriage are displaced when the narrative bluntly shifts to a description of how she is favorably received by others: "The in-laws were satisfied with Poppie's work, and Stone was satisfied. If you have children one day, he would say, you must bring up your children in just the same way as your ouma brought you up" (75). A similar suppression of

Poppie's emotion occurs in a description of her response to forced removals. When Poppie's work permit in Cape Town is withdrawn, there is a brief although poignant description of her anguish. Very abruptly, however, her thoughts turn to a determination to cope:

> They tore up my papers in front of me. They took me from the house my husband built for me. They took me from my husband and my mama and my brothers. They can do what they will, but I am not dead yet. Now I go forward. I go forward with what I have kept, and that is my children. And the first thing I must do, is to see that my children get their schooling. (203)

The portraits of women's fortitude, then, suggest that they naturally and spontaneously adopt their roles and obligations. Conflicts and feelings associated with these roles are displaced or marginalized, and the impression created is of the "invincible strength and genius of the Black mother, as bogus as the one of the happy slave."[14]

Another index of Joubert's use of the structuring principle of strong motherhood revolves on the contrasts established between women and men. Each of the central women figures is explicitly contrasted with a weak and dependent man. Thus, descriptions of oompie Pengi stress his dissipation, irresponsibility and dependency, with these weaknesses foregrounding the virtues of his mother, ouma Hannie. Lena, Poppie's mother is similarly juxtaposed with two of her sons: Plank and Jakkie. Like oompie Pengi, Plank drinks heavily and is often financially dependent on his mother. There are few references to the interaction between them; instead, descriptions dwell on the way his behavior differs from his mother's. When the drunk Plank tries to hide from the police in a fowl-run, for example, the reader is given a detailed report:

> His body dragged on the earth, his jacket dragging up round his neck. The fowls were going mad inside the fowl-run and while they were dragging him outside some of them sat on him and shit on his clothes. He did not fight, his only fight was to keep his body like a dead man. Chicken feathers were in his hair and he spat and blew to get the down out of his mouth. (131)

Jakkie, Lena's younger son, is an activist. Yet his activism is often described as having the same consequences as his brother's excessive drinking. When Jakkie flees from the police, for example, his mother is arrested and the account peculiarly suggests that her arrest is a consequence of Jakkie's "selfishness," rather than of a repressive political environment. The

---

[14] Renita Weens, "Hush, Mama's Gotta Go Bye Bye: A Personal Narrative," *Sage* 1:2 (1984), 27.

central gender contrast in the text, however, is Poppie in relation to her sickly husband, Stone Nongena. Stone symbolically becomes a dependent child in relation to his wife as mother-figure. After his death, Poppie experiences another of the epiphanies which inspire her resolve to endure: "Poppie lay for a week and then she got up and said: The children need money. I must go and work. Where else will my children get their food?" (250). Although Joubert may base her accounts on information provided by her subject, it is striking how information is structured into a pattern of emasculated, dependent or selfish men as they throw into relief the absolute virtues and strengths of women.

The image of the black woman as strong mother has been a prominent one in black South African literature and politics. Certain critics have traced the origins of this image to the imperatives of black women's peripheral involvement in political activism or the maintenance of families.[15] Less has been made, however, of the origin of this image outside of black communities and in a wider society. Employment opportunities for black South African women have historically restricted many to domestic service. South African domestic servants have often occupied uniquely intimate positions in South African households and in broadly servicing white South African families. With laws restricting their mobility and rights to live in urban areas, black South African live-in domestics have had to forsake their own families and communities to take up pivotal positions in "surrogate families" by whom they are employed. This role demands the suppression of a private and personal self, with duties associated with motherhood and wifehood being shaped entirely by economic and political imperatives.

In *July's People*, her novel about master-servant relationships, Nadine Gordimer interrogates the veneer of intimacy which often obscures employer-servant servant-employer relationships in South Africa, and the absurdity of the employer's stereotypical view of the ever-dutiful, diligent and obliging servant. The following description from the novel, in particular, indicates how easily this figure is fixed as a stereotype:

> A white schoolgirl is coming across the intersection where the shops are [...]. In step beside her is a woman of the age blacks retain between youth and the time when their sturdy and comfortable breasts and backsides become leaden weight, their good thick legs slow to a stoop — old age [...]. When the black woman makes to move against the traffic light suddenly

---

[15] Many South African feminists have developed this idea. One of the first and most influential is Cherryl Walker, *Women and Resistance in South Africa*, London, 1982.

gone red, the white girl grabs her hand to stop her, and they continue to hold hands, loosely and easily, while waiting for the light to change. Then they caper across together.[16]

The myth of the black woman as strong mother and nurturer, ever-sacrificing, ever-dutiful and denying her own pain and thoughts, seems to reach back in the South African cultural imagination to the familiar figure of the reliable, ever-present domestic servant. Both her status, as "mother" whose services are bought (and from whom absolute duty can therefore be expected) and the familiar stereotypes of her humility, loyalty and duty seem to come into play when we examine South Africa's prominent images of the unconditional love, loyalty, fortitude and strength of black women as mothers.

That these images are inextricably entangled with *redefinitions* of motherhood by black women themselves cannot be denied. It is often difficult, if not impossible, to trace cultural images to definitive power relationships. Considering one of the more oppressive sources of the black-woman-as-strong-mother image, however, does help to indicate its potentially coercive effects. This is particularly important when the image is such a seductive one, when it seems so explicitly to celebrate an active and empowering identity for a politically subordinate group. As Michelle Wallace cautions, however:

> Even more important than whether black women believe the myth or whether some women engage in superlative accomplishments (which they obviously do) is the way the dominant culture perpetuates the myth, not to celebrate the black woman but as a weapon against her. "She is already liberated" becomes an excuse for placing her needs last on the shopping list in town. Also very important is the way in which otherwise liberal or marginal constituencies [...] consent to or actively conspire with the dominant discourse in this process.[17]

Elsa Joubert has claimed that her novel is based on facts gleaned from interviews with Poppie Nongena and members of her family, that her own role would simply be that of "a tape-recorder, a mouthpiece."[18] Yet the methodological feature immediately apparent in Joubert's *Poppie* is the overtly manipulating role of a fictionalizing story-teller in relation to her

---

[16] Nadine Gordimer, *July's People*, Johannesburg, 1981, 30.

[17] Wallace, *Black Macho and the Myth of the Superwoman*, 61.

[18] See Margaret Lenta, "A Break in the Silence: *The Long Journey of Poppie Nongena*," in *Momentum: On Recent South African Writing*, eds Margaret Daymond, J. Jacobs, and Margaret Lenta, Natal, 1984, 148.

subjects' voices: it is clear that Joubert has taken tremendous license in shaping, connecting and highlighting particular themes, as well as in exploring the details of her informants' thoughts and interpretations. Although based on interviews with her subject and those close to her, Joubert's text is heavily preoccupied with animating and lending narrative vitality to her subject.

This often leads to abrupt and unmarked shifts between, for example, the present and past tenses or different narrative voices. As the writer strives to capture immediacy and realism, Poppie is seen to tell her own story in the first person, or else to reminisce conversationally as though the reader were listening to her actual speech: "Even now when my brothers and I are together, we speak Afrikaans, that's what we like to speak, that comes naturally, ja" (15). Elsewhere, Joubert deploys an unidentified narrator who uses Poppie's register and speech style, but also summarizes and dramatizes incidents in her subject's life — as in the following: "This was the time when Poppie's mama came from De Aar, where she was in service with white people, to have a rest in ouma's house. She told ouma that the father of her children was no more. He had died in the war" (33). The abrupt and unacknowledged shifts signal the conflict between the writer's need to establish structural and interpretive control on the one hand, and to sustain the impression of Poppie's unmediated life story and perception on the other. Why has Joubert taken such pains to create an impression of her subject's actual voice, and what are the effects of the narrator's impersonation?

Joubert wrote the novel at a moment of stark racial polarization in South African politics, a time when white and black South Africans inhabited diametrically opposed worlds. For a writer who admits to having come from "a conservative Afrikaans family,"[19] this polarization was particularly extreme. Joubert has claimed that "Her need to talk was as great as my need to listen [...]. It meant much to me to be led into her life, step by step, to be introduced to a world that had been so strange to me."[20] The idea of being led "step by step" to a world that is "strange" implies that one of her primary concerns is to learn about a world from which she is distanced. Yet does the biographical subject speak to the biographer, or does the biographer confirm her sense of "a world that had been so strange to me"?

---

[19] *Momentum: On Recent South African Writing*, eds Margaret Daymond, J. Jacobs and Margaret Lenta, 58.
[20] *Ibid.*, 61.

One of the patterns to which the narrative returns is Poppie's perception of traditional Xhosa life. During childhood and early adulthood, Poppie is clearly seen as belonging to a hybrid tradition which combines urban life, Christianity and Xhosa practices. The Xhosa ethos she inhabits is seen to have a culturally distinct nobility, as indicated in descriptions like the following:

> On Saturdays we liked to go to the cattle and goat kraals just outside the town to pick up dung and fill the tins and old dishes ouma gave us [...]. We make patterns in the wet dung, down on our knees with the palms of our hands, drawing wide circles with great sweeps away from out bodies, and back again. We Xhosa people call these patterns indima or hand spoor. (27)

While this description marks Poppie's life as culturally different, it is the comforting difference of a fetishized notion of "custom." Poppie, then, is located in a culturally different world which reinforces the passive and exoticized spectacle of "another culture." Elsewhere, however, Poppie becomes the witness to a world connoted as primitive. When Poppie confronts the rural Ciskei environment in which she is eventually forced to buy a house, she is consistently shown to be alienated, horrified or alarmed. The reader is encouraged to identify with her alienation, as in the following description:

> The floor and the walls were filthy. As her eyes grew accustomed to the half dark, she saw children of different ages crawling over the cement floor. She bent to pick him up and as she bent the old woman used her foot to shove him back to that part of the room where she had spread newspapers, where the children remained to urinate and defecate. The stench in the room was strong. (292)

At certain points, the different cultural world is rendered even more emphatically "primitive" and mysterious. One example is when Poppie's implied apprehension is filtered into a description of circumcision:

> On the first day in the bush the boys are cut. They cut the foreskin off their penises [...]. The bush ceremony is like baptism in the river. He must first confess, everything bad he has done must be told. If he has slept with his sister, he must confess. Else his wound won't heal. If he slept with other girls, it's not so bad [...]. Other sins are worse, that's why this confessing is strictly private for the men alone. The women never hear what is said. (272)

A similar apprehension, configured through Poppie, is marked in representations of traditional medicine. There are a number of these encounters, and the biographer's hand in selecting archetypal and graphic pictures of "tradition" becoming overtly apparent. When Poppie visits a witchdoctor, for example, the biographer captures her response in the form of an outsider confronting an enigmatic "tradition"; thus the reader can comfortably inhabit Poppie's vantage point and follow her gaze at a secret world:

> The lean-to was his surgery, where he kept his medicines. On the shelves were canned-fruit bottles with roots and bits of shrubs and leaves and seedpods in them, and next to the bottles coils of hair and jackal tails and bones and broken animal skeletons, on the floor in a corner an intact snake skin. (146)

In a curious conflation of narrated subjects and first-person narration, the emphasis is placed on the witness (who literally looks and with whom we are encouraged to look) who ratifies the primordial scene here.

In a fascinating index of how the biographer uses her subject as mediator, Poppie is seen, momentarily, to "disappear" into a realm to which she elsewhere bears witness. During a spell in the Ciskei, she joins a group of dancers and is implied to be temporarily immersed in a world of "primitive tradition":

> From where she sat, she started to crawl on all fours [...]. The pull was the same she had felt in her dreams [...]. She had forgotten that she was Poppie, mam-ka-Bonsile, mama-ka-Thandi [...]. She felt: If I can dance, I will throw all my troubles from me, I'll leave them behind, I'll be safe, I'll come to that dark land where I will feel no pain. (282)

Here Poppie's experience is explicitly connoted as descent, lapse, regression, a moment when the biographer turns to particularly stark stereotypes, yet also seems threatened by the powerlessness to represent. In an abrupt reassertion of biographical control, however, the description of Poppie's lapse is curtailed when the narrative suddenly shifts to the crying of her child. Poppie ceases to be the elusive insider within, and once again becomes the insider as outsider, a witness whose testimony can be translated to the reader and Joubert. Poppie therefore occupies an insider/outsider position which is established in the text as a stable and comforting one. She is seen to have access to the world of "tradition," "custom," and in the words of the text, "the people of the land," but is not seen to speak for it. By constructing this location, Joubert is able to guarantee her interpretation of an "othered" world.

Poppie's role as a witness who is outside yet appears to be authentically inside "black life" is evidenced also in representations of her perceptions of black political activism. Like many images and events associated with the "people of the land," this world is explicitly marked as demonic. In one central description of black politics, the narrative dwells on the way older people are victimized by fiery young activists:

> The children stopped people on the streets and if they smelt of liquor, they would beat them up with sticks from the Port Jackson trees on the dunes. When the old drunks came on the street, they ran from the groups of children, because the children wanted to know: Where did you buy the wine? Who sold it to you? The old men were scared to say we got it at such and such a house, because they knew they'd send trouble to that house. But they would be beaten till they told and then the children would go to the shebeen house and burn it down. (315)

Poppie, then, becomes the authenticating and authorizing figure who leads the reader on a journey towards recognizing official perceptions of black political activism. Her role in a process which is ultimately one of confirming a dominant image (black protest as demonic, anarchic and brutal) is underscored in the journey she undertakes towards the end of the text. Here Poppie and a friend flee from one black township to another in the middle of a battle involving township residents, migrant workers and the police. This odyssey allegorizes Poppie's inbetween status, with the narrator again exploiting the subject's gaze to provide graphic accounts of scenes of carnage, death and lawlessness. At the same time, underscoring the scene, the writer reminds us of Poppie 's role as witness: "That Sunday, after Johnnie and his girl had left, the thing started, Poppie tells, I saw it all" (331).

Throughout the text, Poppie's vision of black life is ultimately the vision of the biographer, a vision emanating from media reports and official views about the anarchy of political protest, from conventional stereotypes of the exoticism or barbarism of "tribal life and custom." Simply claiming that Joubert problematically speaks for Poppie touches on only part of the problem with the text's politics of representation. What is crucial is how the biographical subject is used for authentication and becomes transparent, a medium through which the biographer confirms preconceived views of a "strange world."

A similar strategy is manifested in Carol Hermer's The *Diary of Maria Tholo*. Like Poppie, Maria Tholo is cast as the outsider within, the experiencing spokesperson who, on the fringes of black life, communicates to an outside world. Compared to Joubert, Hermer appears to play a far less intrusive role: her short commentaries punctuate Tholo's own narrative. Yet authenticity is achieved with almost as much artifice as is the case with Poppie Nongena. In her preface, Hermer writes: "This book is taken from a series of weekly, tape-recorded interviews conducted over a year starting February 1976" but later claims "The diary format was chosen to lend immediacy to the events."[21] The implication is that Hermer constructed Tholo's "diary" around the interviews. The diary, ostensibly a form for directly communicating personal reflections, becomes a fiction which constructs authenticity.

Related methods of constructing "authenticity" coexist with similar roles for the biographical subjects. Like Poppie Nongena, Maria Tholo is ostensibly a speaker from whom the culturally ignorant reader learns about the life of a different world. What the reader often sees, however, are familiar dominant images, as exemplified in the following:

> The policemen crowded together to stop them entering the gate. And then as if a switch had been pulled the girls started wailing. You know how Africans can scream. "Wah, wah, wah. It's not a dog that's been buried. We want to see our comrade. We want to see our fellow-student." The people around took up the chorus and the next moment it was just pandemonium, with everybody screaming.[22]

Discussing the unique status of the "I" in biographical and autobiographical discourse, Norman Denzin spells out the implications of what may seem obvious:

> Behind the pronoun stands a named person — a person with a biography. When, as a writer and a speaker, this person appropriates these words and this pronoun (I, you, he, she, me), he or she brings the full weight of his or her personal experience to bear upon the utterance or statement in question. The personal pronoun thus signifies this person making this utterance. It becomes a historical claim.[23]

Joubert manipulates her subject by conspicuously blurring different narrative voices. The manipulation is usually less overt in social science and historical projects. Through the allusions to a witnessing/experiencing subject whose voice is "scientifically" captured," these projects make seductive claims to authenticity. Many of these projects were written between the late seventies and the early nineties, and include: *Women of Phokeng* (1991); *Sibambene: The Voices of Women at Mboza* (1987); *We Make Freedom* (1984); *A Talent for Tomorrow* (1985) and *A Snake with Ice Wa-*

---

[21] Carol Hermer, *The Diary of Maria Tholo*, Johannesburg, 1980, ix and x.
[22] *Ibid.*, 25.
[23] Norman Denzin, *Interpretive Biography*, London, 1989, 21.

ter: Prison Writings of South African Women (1992). A time of general polarization between white and black South Africans, this period gave rise to mounting interest in "finding out about black South African experiences." Many biographers have claimed to be primarily concerned with the voices and experiences of their women subjects, voices and experiences usually drowned out in male-centered studies of black politics. Thus, Belinda Bozzoli writes at the end of *Women of Phokeng*:

> We are often told that the great men and great events theory of history is inadequate, but we are not often allowed to see what the alternatives are. Here the women give us their version of how things look from below, how history is constructed in their eyes.[24]

In view of these articulated intentions, it is remarkable how little space is actually devoted to women's voices, and how extremely obtrusive and insistent the interpretive role of the biographer is. A lengthy introduction is followed by decontextualized and often very brief comments by interviewed women, all of these being linked to the interpretive frame of the author. Her sovereign position is blatant in the following comments from her introduction: "Of course these testimonies need to be read with a critical eye and with enough knowledge of the context to make it possible to sift through the gold of true evidence from the bulk of ideology, poor memory, and willful misleading that occurs."[25]

Revealingly, many of the biographical projects produced in the eighties have been multibiographies, studies of the lives and texts of groups of women. On one level, biographers may choose to deal with groups to counter a bourgeois and male-centered bias towards the autonomous and masterful subject. On another level, studies of groups more easily allows the silencing of individual idiosyncrasies and agencies. That this effect may well inform the prominence of multibiographies is suggested by the conspicuousness of this form at a particular historical moment.

The casting of women as figures through whom broader social processes can be explored reveals the inevitably *autobiographical* impulse of biography. It also lays bare a familiar symbolic casting of women in relation to groups. In their influential study of relationships between gender and ethnicity, nation or race, Nira Yuval-Davis and Floya Anthias present a number of ways in which women are involved in constructions of com-

---

[24] Belinda Bozzoli, *Women of Phokeng*, Johannesburg, 1991, 242.
[25] *Ibid.*, 7.

munal identities.[26] Two of these are specifically cultural: as participators in
the ideological reproduction of the collectivity and transmitters of culture;
and as signifiers of ethnic/national differences — as foci and symbols in
the construction, reproduction and transformation of ethnic/national discourses. These perceptions of "woman" cohere in the symbolic roles of
women in many South African texts, apparently focusing on women, but
also about black communal and historical processes. At the same time that
biographers appear to challenge the invisibility of black women's perceptions and interpretations in social science texts, they confirm notions of
"woman" as a symbolic figure for constructing various representations of
community. In many biographical projects, "black South African woman"
becomes a vacant cipher, "real" only in linking the life within the text to
the biographer's textualized world beyond it. The "intimacy" signaled by
the presence of the biographical subject is entirely contradicted by the way
this subject underwrites "someone else's experience [...] to a seemingly
endless process of translation and transference."[27]

A consequence of the symbolic casting of black women is the displacement of the voices of biographical subjects. But we could also specu-
late about how it constructs gendered notions of black political responses.
The eighties, the period at the end of a protracted struggle against an in-
transigent Afrikaner Nationalist Government, was an important moment of
international opposition to apartheid. Much of this solidarity was mobi-
lized through media representations of black South African suffering, endurance and resilience, tropes easily linked to images of women. This cluster of tropes became part of a globalized discourse of opposition to apartheid. Producers of women's biographical projects like Carol Hermer and
Diana Russell, South Africans living abroad, have been close to the
sources of this discourse.[28] It would be silly to suggest their self-conscious
involvement in global anti-apartheid image-construction. To some extent,
however, the global paternal anti-apartheid discourse fixated on images of
black South Africans as victims, images reinforced by describing the fem-
inized behaviors and responses of black women.

---

[26] Nira Yuval-Davis and Floya Anthias, *Woman-Nation-State*, London, 1989, 7.

[27] Ann duCille, "The Occult of True Black Womanhood: Critical Demeanor and
Black Feminist Studies" *Signs* 19:3 (1994), 622.

[28] Hermer has actually described how an original project to research one family's
life history was transformed: "Then came June 16 and Soweto [...]. Though at first
Maria's flood of stories was incidental [...] it soon became clear that we were compil-
ing a unique historical record." See Hermer, *The Diary of Maria Tholo*, 9.

Shula Marks' *Not Either an Experimental Doll* was begun when she accidentally discovered a body of correspondence belonging to Mabel Palmer, a prominent educator and organizer of Natal University's "Non-European Section." The correspondence chronicles Palmer's mentoring of a young black woman, known in the text as Lily Moya, between 1949 and 1951, when their relationship broke down. The edited correspondence also includes the letters of Sibusisiwe Makhanya, a black social worker whom Palmer asked to help her in assisting Lily. Although clearly a non-fictional sociological study, *Not Either an Experimental Doll* captures a powerful sense of the "tragedy" of Lily's experiences. Divided into the editor's introduction, the correspondence, and an epilogue, the story spans several years, covering the young Lily's first exposure to Palmer, and the ensuing correspondence between Lily, Palmer and Makhanya; and then the researcher's discovery of Lily Moya in the 1980s.

Lily, first appealing to Palmer for assistance to further her education and release her from an arranged marriage, is "taken up" by Palmer, who becomes increasingly involved in her affairs: finding her a position as a student at Adams College, lending her books, and later financing her education. As Lily's appeals for emotional support increase, Palmer's sympathy wanes, and she becomes progressively more impatient with Lily's inability to "stand on [her] own feet." Writing that she has been betrayed or become the victim of a conspiracy, Lily performs badly at school and demonstrates growing animosity towards her teachers and peers. She eventually leaves Adams, does not follow up Palmer's plan to move her to another school, Marianhill, and leaves for Johannesburg. From here she writes to Palmer that "You badly handled me back" and that she "is very ill."[29] In the epilogue, the biographer recounts her eventual discovery, three decades after the time of the correspondence, of an aged, heavily drugged Lily, a diagnosed schizophrenic and chronic mental hospital patient. Overall, the text establishes an interpretive frame which privileges Palmer's points of view and discursive location. It forecloses those of Lily, whose race, age and discursive resources are so radically different from Palmer's. The reader is persuaded to take up a collaborative position both with the biographer, and with the biographer's "normative" subject. Thus, the subtitle's promise of access to "the separate worlds of three South Af-

---

[29] Marks, *Not Either an Experimental Doll*, 186. All further references are contained in the text.

rican women" and Marks' remarks that "This was — and is — Lily's book," are questionable, to say the least (195).

In "Can the Subaltern Speak" Gayatri Spivak discusses the representation of third-world women in relation to the practice of sati, showing how their location in colonial and gender hierarchies leads to their being positioned only as objects in intersecting discourses. Spivak concludes: "The subaltern as female cannot be heard or read."[30] Lily's position in *Not Either an Experimental Doll* presents theoretical and political concerns that Spivak raises about the silencing of the subaltern subject. In the following discussion, I explore what I shall term Lily's "autograph" to consider her agency and an interpretive framework which questions her designation as object and inevitable victim. The concept "autograph" is used by Marilyn Brownstein in her exploration of the life-texts of Virginia Woolf and Walter Benjamin. "Autograph" registers subjectivity "not as part of the search for an authentic identity, but rather [with] the potential of the life-writer to reproduce a discursive occasion that is open-ended and therefore an occasion on which subjectivity may be restored to history."[31] Autograph is also a term which suggests both authority and the truncation of the subject's self-representation. Following Bernstein, I see this truncation registering a space where language signifies beyond lexicon or linguistic orders, moments when images elusively imply thoughts, and patterns of idiosyncratic memories in the subject's self-representation.

In charting Lily's autograph, I concentrate on how her status as "victim" is constructed in discourses which construct an "other" in the service of dominant subjects' stories of selfhood. I focus on two sites of interpretation in the text, and the extent to which they reinforce each other. One is established by the testimonies of Mabel Palmer, a woman who apparently selflessly devotes her time, money and energy to "helping" a politically subordinate Lily. The second revolves around the scholarly activity of the text's producer, whose authority depends on her successful and persuasive representation of a subject about whom there seems so little evidence, yet about whom she is able to write at length.

In her letters to Mabel Palmer, Lily repeatedly speaks as the recipient or potential recipient of Palmer's attentions. Her references to poverty, orphan-hood and victimization by men define a compound marginality: "I

---

[30] Gayatri Spivak, "Can the Subaltern Speak? Speculations on Widow-Sacrifice," *Wedge* (1985), 130.
[31] See Marilyn Brownstein's essay in *The Seductions of Biography*, eds Mary Rhiel and David Suchoff, New York, 1996, 186.

am an orphan with no property, a student, born on the 31ˢᵗ August 1933. All along I had been learning as a day scholar student, due to financial embarrassment" (58). Palmer repeats this image of Lily, and in letters to others, echoes Lily's self-narrative: "She is a little native girl of 16 years of age who lives near Umtata, and who is burningly anxious to continue her education. She is an orphan and her native guardian does not feel he can afford to send her to school" (75). At some point, however, Palmer expects Lily to flourish, in ways similar to Sibusisiwe Makhanya, as a black woman who succeeds in the public domain, and who takes up a position of authority and agency within dominant discourses. At the same time that she positions Lily as the object of her patronage, then, she also expects Lily to act independently. The messages which Lily interprets can, therefore, become impossibly contradictory: on one hand she is instructed to be independent, while on the other she is told that she is irrevocably dependent, inferior. In a letter which Marks identifies as the turning point in Lily's experience, Palmer responds to Lily's request by stating:

> The best way that you can help me is by staying at Adams and doing as well as you can both in your work and getting on with the other students, and that would be the best return you can make for the kindness I am showing you. The kindness does not necessarily involve any personal or intimate friendship. Indeed such an intimate friendship is impossible and could only be achieved on the basis of equal interest and experience, which does not exist between you and me. (137)

An acute awareness of the political implications of her relationship with Palmer seems to be an important explanation of Lily's radical withdrawal from the public and "politically empowering" activities described in the text. Throughout her letters, Lily is immersed in what Palmer describes as the thoughts of a very "self-centered and indeed selfish young woman" (137). Yet the "self-centeredness," here defined as trivial, often revolves around an attentive perception of how others see her and how she is expected to behave. Constantly yearning for displacement, preoccupied with doing what she has not been allowed to do, and occupying new physical and psycho-existential spaces, Lily insistently registers her social entrapment and initiates various forms of rebellion. That her focus on the self and constant questing can be read politically, however, is entirely invalidated by Palmer. Thus, she impatiently writes: "Pull yourself together; stop thinking that you can have everything you want; do not turn into a self-centered little snob or I shall have cause to regret that I offered you the help that rescued you from you natural position in life" (139).

For Palmer, and indeed for Marks as biographer, the letters are glaring, indisputable evidence of Lily's unreasonable diffidence, her inability (and not refusal) to take up the opportunities provided by her benefactor. The evidence of victimization appears to be irrefutable in the face of, for example, the concluding lines of Lily's first four letters: "I beg for your sincere sympathy" (55); "I should be very glad if you would answer to my humble requests" (56); "I'm sure I'll please you in any way in my character" (59); "please be sympathetic" (59). Yet can this be read only as evidence of Lily's victimization, her suffering the circumstances of political oppression and discursive entrapment? One of the most persuasive illusions in *Not Either an Experimental Doll* is the impression, created by the reproduction of Lily's letters, that the reader has access to her private thoughts, and that since her private letters so insistently inscribe her abject status, they constitute indisputable evidence of Lily's self-perception as a victim. Yet the status of the letters as evidence of Lily's innermost thoughts is far from absolute. In fact, all the reproduced letters can be read as fictive productions — shaped by particular contexts and directed at intended readers — of specific writing personae. Palmer consistently writes in the position of her public persona of educator and patron: she frequently sends her letters to Lily to others; she explicitly situates her exchanges with Lily in the broader pattern of her educational and political work; she is generally aware of the position of her letters in a public domain. In contrast, Lily constructs her letters to Palmer very much within the framework of an inter-personal exchange, an exchange in which she constructs a particular persona for an address to a specific correspondent.

Feminist critics like Judith Butler have dealt with the way that the persona, a performance of self which exaggerates culturally ascribed positions, can, for marginal subjects, constitute a covert awareness of imposed positions.[32] While the adoption of masks may take the form of overt subversion, as in the case of iconoclasts like Brenda Fassie, it is important to consider how the letter form, with the spaces it provides for performance, may signal a silent but implicit disavowal of an adopted mask.[33] Consequently, Lily "operates out of fragments of the self, out of memory's ech-

---

[32] See Judith Butler, *Gender Trouble: Feminism and the Subversion of Identity*, New York, 1990.

[33] Brenda Fassie is a well-known figure in black popular music, especially kwaito. Her performances and image can be read in similar ways to Madonna's and illustrate self-consciously flamboyant and ironic poses of femininity.

oes of strategies designed to cope with environmental particularities."[34] Lily's letters, far from confirming her complicity, can be seen to register covert resistance. Here it is especially important to consider the young black woman's use of the English language, for her a second language learnt in authoritarian institutions and underpinned by repressive codes of deference and submission. The idea of the autograph, (what is not directly said but underpins what is said), becomes a crucial way of reading into Lily's persona. In considering Lily's letter-writing voice as a fragment of self, it is also important that her life extends to relationships, conflicts and encounters which neither Palmer nor the biographer have access to. This other life is often hinted at, yet is never identified as the context of inaccessible information about Lily. For Marks, it is simply homogenized as the "undoubtedly pathogenic nature of her environment, a frightening amalgam of the cruelties structured by colonialism and individual circumstance" (204).

In the same way that the status of Lily's letters can be explored as textual productions of a self in relation to her correspondent, so should Palmer's be seen as evidence of her discursive production of subjectivity. Palmer frequently refers to her sense of duty in relation to Lily, writing, for example: "I would be very much to blame as an older woman who has been fairly successful in the field of education if I neglected your appeal. You can depend upon it that I will not do so if I can find any way of helping you" (68) or "I am a very busy woman with a great deal to do for my own students" (77). In the course of the correspondence, this sense of duty intensifies, with Palmer, despite the growing evidence of Lily's failure to live up to her expectations, increasing her attentions to Lily.

While she continually expresses impatience and disillusionment, her attentions to Lily appear to increase as the latter shows less evidence of "developing." When Lily performs particularly badly at Adams College, Palmer makes zealous efforts to move her to Marianhill. When Lily eventually disappears, Palmer writes to inquire about her whereabouts; when Lily leaves for Johannesburg, she sends her a gift and concludes her letter with: "I shall always be interested in hearing what happens to you" (191). At a time when Palmer appears to be most exasperated by Lily's ingratitude, therefore, she seems most compulsive in her attentions towards her. This points to another way of interpreting the relationship of dependency: Lily becomes a crucial means by which Palmer confirms her sense of self

---

[34] Brownstein, *op. cit.,* 188.

as, among other things, socially responsible (in opposition to Lily's "self-ishness"), articulate, in relation to Lily's inarticulateness, reasonable in relation to Lily's irrationality, successful, in relation to Lily's failure. The "positive" self displayed in the behavior and letters of Palmer, then, can be interpreted politically as effects of a discursive process through which Palmer names herself in relation to Lily's shortcomings.

In her interpretation, Marks usually echoes the representations of Palmer. Apart from presenting the reader with the "indisputable" evidence of Lily's letters, this is achieved largely through constructing models of successful self-realization, in particular through the introductory biographical portrait of Mabel Palmer. Before reading her letters, the reader is enjoined to become complicit with the biographer's perception of her: "As we shall see, a devastating common sense and a lack of sensitivity, coupled with quite extraordinary generosity in both time and money, characterized Mabel Palmer's relationship with Lily Moya" (7). At other points Palmer is congratulated in phrases like: "One can only sympathize with Mabel's somewhat harassed reply" (18) or "And Mabel did interest herself in Lily's case. With accustomed energy she set about enquiring of her friends and acquaintances what the most suitable arrangements for Lily would be" (19).

In an illuminating cross-reference to Sibusisiwe's Makhanya's process of "empowerment," Marks describes this black woman's relationship with her former patron, Mabel Carney. As a student in New York, Makhanya met Carney and regularly visited her home. Following a series of visits, Carney confronted her about her intrusions. Marks recounts her initial response: "Mortified, Sibusisiwe rushed home and wept." Shortly afterwards, however, Makhana is described as asking Miss Carney's forgiveness, and the description that follows recounts Makhanya's numerous achievements. The test of self-realization which Makhanya faces is seen as the test which Lily fails. Although Lily writes a letter in which she apologizes to Palmer for imposing on her, her work deteriorates, and she continues to appeal to Palmer. Like Palmer, Marks defines Makhanya as a subaltern subject successfully liberated by her patron. That Makhanya's judgment of Lily ("You gave her a splendid chance and she has abused it" [190]) endorses Palmer's, strengthens the model of development for measuring success here. The reader is persuaded that what must be questioned is not the model, but the subject who fails.

The complicity of the reader with the text's point of view is engineered not only through the emphasis on Palmer's point of view, but also by marking the authoritative status of the text and its generic "historicity." Where *Not Either an Experimental Doll* may use methods as controlling as those of Poppie, its authority is inscribed by the numerous and conclusive discursive markers of factual documentation. One of these is the list Marks provides to acknowledge the tradition of scholarship in which she is situated. The text becomes the product not only of an individual researcher, but of a canon of authoritative research. Authority is also established through a meticulous referencing procedure, with the many footnotes that gesture beyond the text assuring the reader that the text is anchored in a real world out there. While maps and photographs serve the same function, at least two photographs expose the gap between a quest for "reality" and the elusiveness of this "reality." One is a photograph of a young girl, captioned "Snapshot of an unidentified girl. This picture was found among Mabel Palmer's papers and may well be the one Lily promised to send her." Here the writer's desire for evidence gets in the way of conclusiveness, and the reader is reminded that what the text presents can only be what the biographer is able to gain access to. Another is the photograph of a homestead with the caption "The Moya family looked very like this." The homestead may suggest Lily's, but the photograph does not capture her own home. Again, there is a suggestion of the biographer's unfulfilled pact with the reader. Visual representation, however, has the power to persuade more compellingly than writing, so that these admissions to approximations of truth are outweighed by the quantity of visual representation.

Marks' strategy for persuading the reader not only of her authority, but also of her noble intentions convinces the reader of the "neutrality" of her text. The writer goes through the formal motions of self-reflexivity,[35] while in the epilogue, she writes: "For all the joy of discovery, it has proven painful to come to terms with Lily's subsequent story" (197). Invocation of pain (the sympathetic biographer's proximity to her subject) sits oddly with the admission of "joy," the triumph of "capturing" her subject. But it is this joy which surfaces clearly in Marks' story, disclosed only in her epilogue, of Lily's madness. No clues to this outcome are given in the introduction; the biographer withholds the knowledge to shape a plot that artfully turns life-text into "tragedy." Assured of her power to create suspense and expectations from the reader, Marks poses the question: "What

---

[35] Examples include the epigraph and occasional self-interrogation like "After considerable soul-searching — was I after all another Mabel Palmer, a 'misguided do-gooder?'" (196).

happened to Lily Moya?" and recounts the biographer's triumphant discovery in her quest narrative. This story takes an unexpected turn when
Marks reads a letter, published in response to her inquiries about Lily's
whereabouts, in a newspaper. This letter temporarily unsettles the biographer and concludes: "The crowning fatuity of your article comes when you
express a desire to talk to [Lily]. By what right? And why assume she
wishes to talk to you? In conclusion, forget about it. Sales will be small
and you would be well advised to mind your own business" (195-96).

But the displacement of authority is brief, and the biographer rein-
states sovereignty when she confirms that the writer of the letter could not
have been Lily. At this stage, Marks gives full reign to historicizing zeal,
exploring such subjects as the history of Sophiatown, possession by ances-
tral spirits and psychiatric services available to Africans. Lily's madness
provides the closure which Marks' quest seems to contradict: it offers the
writer's ending to a story about an elusive subject who, when discovered,
is trapped in silence. In a similar way that Palmer persistently writes to and
about the figure of a Lily who becomes increasingly weak, powerless and
silent, so does the biographer endlessly discover the silence and victimization of her passive subject. Even as Marks sets out to unsettle a conventional tradition of history, her writing remains defined by that history and
its assumptions about the interpreter's rationality and definitive agency.

Within the framework established by asserting Palmer's straightfor-
wardly well-meaning intentions, the traces of Lily's overt, although cryptic
signs of struggle with ascribed subject positions are ignored or marginalized. One particularly telling example is when Palmer asks Lily to write a
short story on "The Life of a Native Girl in a Reserve," or if not wherever
else you live" (87). Lily responds briefly, and includes the following provocative commentary: "I'm very sorry for not producing you a good draft
to 'The Life of an African Girl.' I have not been a good traveler or very
observant to such a subject, you will see little of my experience only based
to what our people say of our girls and what we ought to do" (89). Palmer
writes to Lily that "you only write interestingly and amusingly when you
are writing about yourself. When I asked you to describe to me the life of a
girl on a native reserve, your article was not very satisfactory" (138). This
comment, and what it reveals about Palmer's crudely stereotypical perception of Lily and the black woman's tacit resistance to this, seems a crucial
site for inquiry. Yet Lily's dense, although obscure commentary is paid
scant attention, and Marks, almost echoing Palmer's assumptions about rationality, contents herself with commenting in a footnote that Lily never

produced the requested story. By the end of the correspondence, Lily's anger towards Palmer, "I was never meant to be a stone but a human being with feelings, not either an experimental doll" (186), becomes a random outburst, confirmation of Lily's illogical response and of her characteristically erratic behavior.

Lily has desires and subjectivity that signal agency, even though they do not reveal a "specific endorsement of agency in the traditional sense — with its attributes of both action as well as intention."[36] Where it is possible to read Lily's behavior and letters as interrupting a power relationship, the questions constantly posed in the text pivot on Lily's failure: Why did Lily not take up the opportunities presented for her? Why did Lily never become a successful and powerful black woman like Sibusisiwe Makhanya?

It could be argued that Marks, simply by writing about a subject like Lily, goes a long way towards challenging the idea that only the narratives of socially successful subjects are worth documenting. Yet when agency is relentlessly located within the act of interpreting others, rather than in their responses; or measured against dominant norms of success; positions of authority within dominant structures or platforms, or fluency with language, speaking from positions within the dominant discourse, then disruptive moments of rebellion can easily be ignored. The life text of a subordinate subject, far from contributing to new knowledges, can simply reinforce the basic assumptions of old ones. While the coding and manipulation in *Not Either an Experimental Doll* are particularly revealing about problems with speaking for subaltern subjects, they also lay bare many assumptions about life-writing generally. Biography conventionally assumes the neutrality of the biographer: her ability to "capture" a life so that interpretation becomes transparent. The limitations of the biographer are hidden or disguised, and conventions that persuasively signal accuracy, authenticity and realism conceal the artfulness of the text. The profusion and range of biographical writing about black South African women seems to offer an important intervention into life-writing traditions that have been not only white-centered but also male-centered. Yet disempowering images and hegemonic interpretations persist in the apparently emancipatory practice of "making black women's lives visible." Thus a commonsensical and traditional feminist principle, the need to write about hitherto unex-

---

[36] Rajeswari Rajan, *Real and Imagined Women: Gender, Culture and Postcolonialism*, New York, 1993, 12.

plored subjects, seems a far less radical imperative than the need to interrogate the biographical method itself. In this way, biographers might develop forms of self-reflexivity in which they make transparent or become
alert to the processes through which they construct their subjects' lives.

Apartheid clearly generated tremendous international concern about a
dispensation that, from viewpoints including ethics, religion and politics,
was abhorrent. Narratives about lives under apartheid have consequently
functioned as discursive sites for readers within the country and especially
beyond it to confirm *their* sense of self, their norms and values. Scholarly
productions such as *Not Either an Experimental Doll* and Belinda Bozzoli's *Women of Phokeng*, have been widely circulated abroad and have
considerably influenced an international academic community's sense of
what it has meant to be a black South African under apartheid. Other texts,
such as *Poppie Nongena* or *Lives of Courage* have had general appeal for
non-specialist readers in South Africa as well as in Britain and North
America. It is important to approach these texts not simply as works that
offer information about marginal subjects, but as discursive productions
which interpellate readers in specific ways. Thus the telling of stories of
apartheid through narratives of individual lives is revealing not so much
about these lives or apartheid, as it is about the codification of apartheid as
spectacle and about the way this codification has stereotyped black South
African subjects.

Biography inevitably involves the reconstruction of an(other). Yet:

> As more and more scholars cross over to write about the lives of non-
> traditional subjects, it should encourage us, as biographers and readers of
> biography, to pause and examine the values we both place and practice
> upon. As more and more emphasis is placed on recognizing those subjects
> previously ignored, writers of life texts need to examine the values that are
> placed and practiced on the life of the "Other."[37]

The need for biographical criticism and a reassessment of its traditional
methods is especially significant in view of the fact that "biography," as a
general practice of life-writing, is not only an academic or high cultural
practice, but a significant aspect of popular cultural practice. When we
consider the construction of individual lives in, for example, television
documentaries, magazine profiles or newspaper columns, it becomes clear
that biography is an influential site of cultural politics and prescribed identities and roles. Furthermore, the meanings of life stories often give shape

---

[37] *The Seductions of Biography*, 87.

to or become stories of national culture and identity. With the official displacement of overtly oppressive apartheid life stories (like Jan van Riebeek's discovery of the Cape), new life stories which may continue to reproduce the covertly oppressive myths of traditional power relationship, are an important subject for inquiry.

DISCONTINUITY-IN-RELATIONSHIP: APARTHEID IN THE SOUTH AFRICAN SHORT FICTION CYCLE

Sue Marais

> In an ultimately unfathomable world, one should have the lucidity and good nature to salute all systems, including history, as obsessive mistakes. (Patricia Tobin)

> People in misdeveloped twisted lands may not be able to dominate what really happens to them; but they can at least control the stories they tell about how they want what happened to them remembered. (Ariel Dorfman)

Short story cycles are defined by Boris Tomashevsky as collections which are "arranged according to some unifying principle."[1] Valerie Shaw claims that the "overall unity" of the cycle form is achieved "through linked episodes rather than any sustained narrative or thematic movement."[2] And Timothy C. Alderman writes that the cycle consists of "separate stories (sometimes novellas, sketches, or parables, sometimes interspersed with poetry or even essays) that form a dynamic relationship with each other and with the reader [...] the integrated collection is known above all for its tension between cohering, centripetal forces and separating, centrifugal forces."[3] Forrest L. Ingram, the foremost English researcher of the form in its twentieth-century manifestations to date, explains that a cycle is "a set of stories so linked to one another that the reader's experience of each one is modified by his [sic] experience of the others," and a balance is maintained between "the individuality of each of the stories and the necessities of the larger unit."[4] Subsequently Ingram expands on this latter idea:

---

[1] Boris Tomashevsky, "Literary Genres," *Russian Poetics in Translation 5: Formalism — History, Comparison, Genre*, trans. L. M. O'Toole, Oxford, 1978, 82.
[2] Valerie Shaw, *The Short Story: A Critical Introduction,* London, 1983, 159.
[3] Timothy C. Alderman, "The Enigma of *The Ebony Tower*: A Genre Study," *Modern Fiction Studies* 31 (1985), 135.
[4] Forrest L. Ingram, *Representative Short Story Cycles of the Twentieth Century: Studies in a Literary Genre*, The Hague, 1971, 13 and 15.

> Central to the dynamics of the short story cycle is the tension between the one and the many [...]. Every story cycle displays a double tendency of asserting the individuality of its components on the one hand and of highlighting, on the other, the bonds of unity which make the many into a single whole. (19)

It is on the basis of its characteristic "dynamic pattern of recurrent development" that Ingram claims that the cycle should be recognized as a "unique literary genre" in its own right, as distinct from the novel or the "mere" collection of discrete and autonomous short stories.[5]

More pertinent here, however, is the recognition that the inherent dualism of the cycle form — the tension between "the one and the many" — singularly equips it to depict the opposing impulses in any society towards unity and diversity or integration and alienation, that is, to represent the interaction between the individual and the community, and any particular community and its "others." In discussing Sherwood Anderson's *Winesburg, Ohio*, for example, Ian Reid points out that the text evinces "a superficial appearance (and indeed the ideal possibility) of communal wholeness, and an underlying actual separateness."[6] Reid argues that other cycles are informed by the same "structural and stylistic principle" of "discontinuity-in-relationship," and that they "express fundamentally a similar sense of groping search by isolated characters ('lives flowing past each other,' in Anderson's phrase) for an elusive feeling of community."[7] James G. Watson makes a similar point when, in regard to the cyclical fictions of Thomas Wolfe, he comments: "the heroes of these pieces search endlessly through their own inner distances for a door to community that, for them, does not exist."[8]

In many cycles, however, the integrative or centripetal strategies employed foreground notions of a unified (if internally fraught and externally threatened) community, a community which "usually can be said to constitute the central character of [the] cycle."[9] The "community persona" thus comes to accrue a prominence over and above the sum of its individual constituents or members, and the particularities and peculiarities of the geographical locale depicted appear to have a deterministic influence on

---

[5] *Ibid.*, 203.
[6] Ian Reid, *The Short Story*, London, 1977, 48.
[7] *Ibid.*, 49.
[8] James G. Watson, "The American Short Story: 1930-1945," in *The American Short Story 1900-1945: A Critical History*, ed. Philip Stevick, Boston, 1985, 140.
[9] Ingram, *op. cit.*, 22.

its inhabitants: identity and location are interlinked.[10] Accordingly, the short story cycle has had a long association with regionalism as a literary mode. Mary Louise Pratt comments, for example, that it is:

> on the regional periphery that the short story cycle has been most likely to make its appearance [...]. To some extent such cycles do a kind of ground-breaking, establishing a basic literary identity for a region or group, laying out descriptive parameters, character types, social and economic settings, principal points of conflict for an audience unfamiliar with the region itself or with seeing that region in print.[11]

The link between the cycle form and regionalism is a function of the fact that, as Reid points out, many cycles "locate their unity of place in some rural region" (Reid, 49) and this "topographical unity" (Shaw, 158) lends itself to the evocation of details of local color. Having cited Robert Rhode's contention that "If successfully used, local color strengthens the setting by adding to the impression of actuality," Mary Rohrberger concludes that regionalism, understood to signify "fidelity to a particular geographical section carefully and truthfully depicting the region and manners and morals of the people living there," is in turn allied with realism and with Henry James's concept of "solidity of specification."[12] The link between the cycle form, realism and regionalism is made explicit by Shaw, in her discussion of "Places and Communities" in the short story: "The device of grouping tales and stories set in the same location" is aimed at creating "a persuasive effect of realism."[13] In such collections, she maintains, "the reader is acclimatized to conditions in a circumscribed locality and so becomes familiar with a particular way of life."[14]

Generically speaking, then, the short story cycle would appear eminently suited to a verisimilitudinous depiction of regional communities as self-contained entities and, especially, to communities in which social cohesiveness is in some sense jeopardized or strained by internal and/or external forces. Pratt, for instance, points out that Reid's concept of "discontinuity-in-relationship" "suggests why the short story cycle rather than the novel might be chosen to portray, for example, the disorder of frontier so-

---

[10] Trudi Emily Adendorff, *South African Short Story Cycles*, Durban: University of Natal, unpublished MA dissertation, 76.

[11] Mary Louise Pratt, "The Short Story: The Long and the Short of It," *Poetics* 10 (1981), 187-88.

[12] Mary Rohrberger, "The Question of Regionalism: Limitation and Transcendence," in *The American Short Story*, ed. Philip Stevick, 147-48.

[13] Shaw, *op. cit.,* 158.

[14] *Ibid.,* 159.

ciety, or of traditional societies disintegrating in the face of moderniza-
tion."[15] It also suggests its particular appositeness to the South African
context — a society torn and traumatized by the conflicting tendencies towards "apart-heid"/segregation and "een-heid"/unity. André Brink captures this germaneness when he writes: "in many respects the centrifugal
forces in the situation are countered by a centripetal dynamic. This operates on both spatial and temporal levels."[16]

Prominent examples of the affinity displayed by the modern cycle
form for regionalism and for the representation of marginalized communities and alienated individuals within communities are, as indicated earlier,
Anderson's *Winesburg, Ohio* (1919), together with James Joyce's *Dub-
liners* (1914), John Steinbeck's *The Pastures of Heaven* (1932), and William Faulkner's *The Unvanquished* (1938) and *Go Down, Moses* (1942).
Locally, a similar inclination is evident in Pauline Smith's *The Little Karoo* (1925), Herman Charles Bosman's *Mafeking Road* (1947), Bessie
Head's *The Collector of Treasures* (1977), Ahmed Essop's *The Hajji and
Other Stories* (1978), Njabulo Ndebele's *Fools and Other Stories* (1983),
Miriam Tlali's *Footprints in the Quag: Stories and Dialogues from Soweto*
(1989), and the first section, "Women at Work," of Sindiwe Magona's *Living, Loving, and Lying Awake at Night* (1991). Trudi Adendorff maintains
that the first four of the above-mentioned cycles, which she subjects to a
sustained analysis, all exemplify "a noticeable degree of integration"
which may be attributed to the "writer's evocation of a particular place or
region, and its community,"[17] and that, in these texts, "the reader's awareness of the character of the region and its community is formed through
the process of recurrence and development, a process which transforms the
region and the community into the sustained personae of the cycle."[18] In
the case of the latter five cycles, produced by black writers under apartheid, this is a resistant persona, constructed as an expression of solidarity
in response to the forced and arbitrary dissolutions of individual identity
and family and other social groupings imposed by the apartheid state.

Ndebele, in *Rediscovery of the Ordinary*, articulates the impulse guiding this corrective and regenerative project when he claims that:

---

[15] Pratt, *op. cit.*, 188.
[16] André Brink, "Reinventing the Real: English South African Fiction Now," *New
Contrast* 21:1 (1993), 45.
[17] Adendorff, *op. cit.*, 2.
[18] *Ibid.*, 144.

our literature ought to seek to move away from an easy pre-occupation with demonstrating the obvious existence of oppression. It exists. The task is to explore how and why people survive under such harsh conditions. The mechanisms of survival and resistance that the people have devised are many and far from simple. The task is to understand them, and then to actively make them the material subject of our imaginative explorations [...] the task of the new generation of South African writers is to help to extend the material range of intellectual and imaginative interest as far as the subject of life under oppression is concerned. It is to look for that area of cultural autonomy and the laws of its dynamism that no oppressor can ever get at; to define that area, and, with purposeful insidiousness, to assert its irrepressible hegemony during the actual process of struggle.[19]

Ndebele's own collection provides a compelling example of the assertion of the inherent value of a community *despite* its existence as an apartheid construct, and a refusal to subscribe to or internalize exactly those oppressive or incapacitating stereotypes which the State desired to perpetuate.

A related impulse motivates Tlali's collection, since the collection constitutes something of a response to Lauretta Ngcobo's assertion, in the Introduction, that "[t]he sabre of white apartheid rule cuts divisions even among people of one race."[20] Eva Hunter, for example, describes Tlali's text as "calling on Soweto's inhabitants to look into themselves to reform those responses that are destructive."[21] And Tlali herself writes: "it was important for the struggle that we be one thing."[22]

In terms of Bessie Head's distinctive oeuvre, Rob Nixon argues that if what he terms her "regional transnationalism" was initially:

a symptom of her viciously administered life, it was one of her singular achievements to transform that regionalism into a groundbreaking literary vision [...]. Head saw local history not least as a mechanism for survival. Serowe promised Head a redeeming alternative to the threatening histories to which she had been exposed: familial blankness, a predestined female history of atonement for a transgressive life, and systematic racial conquest.[23]

---

[19] Njabulo Ndebele, *Rediscovery of the Ordinary: Essays on South African Literature and Culture*, Johannesburg, 1991, 158-59.

[20] Lauretta Ngcobo, "Introduction," in Miriam Tlali, *Footprints in the Quag: Stories and Dialogues from Soweto*, Cape Town, 1989, xvi.

[21] Eva Hunter, "'A Mother is Nothing but a Backbone': Women, Tradition and Change in Miriam Tlali's *Footprints in the Quag*," *Current Writing* 5:1 (1993), 60.

[22] Tlali, *op. cit.*, 79.

[23] Rob Nixon, "Rural Transnationalism: Bessie Head's Southern Spaces," in *Text, Theory, Space: Land, Literature and History in South Africa and Australia*, eds Kate Darian-Smith, Liz Gunner, and Sarah Nuttall, London, 1996, 244-46.

Having quoted Head's own comment, "I decided to record the irrelevant,"[24] Nixon points out that her strategy obviously invites comparison
with Ndebele's emphasis on the redemptive force of the ordinary, and
concludes:

> Head's most affecting prose arises from her quickness to redeem the irrele-
> vant, the common, the ordinary and, in the etymological sense of "earthly,"
> the mundane. [Her] animation by the ordinary was partly a reaction against
> the tremendous violence of South Africa which had fallen, like a dead hand,
> across her imagination. In fleeing apartheid, she rejected both the imagina-
> tive priority of such extraordinary violence and the functionalist imperatives
> of most South African literature, both of which she rejected as dehumanis-
> ing. Like Njabulo Ndebele [...] if for somewhat different reasons, she broke
> with the literary tradition of the titanic clash, often staged between charac-
> ters who are little more than ciphers representing self-evident moral ex-
> tremes.[25]

An examination of Magona's text reveals that the informal community of
black domestic workers described in "Part One: Women at Work" — alien
residents of a white suburb in East London — in a sense constitutes a single, dominant persona: what Anne McClintock, in a different context, describes as "a dynamic, collective continuum of voices and identities [...]
distinct and [...] inseparable."[26] Thus, though this section has a sequential
plot-line, with the central protagonist-narrator Atini's journey from her rural home in the Transkei to the city acting as a framing device, Atini's
story and the interpellated first-person narratives of her co-workers involve
a significant degree of "repetition-with-variation": the collage has a reit-
erative structure in terms of its recurrent motifs and themes, and its poly-
phonic yet univocal quality. As Atini herself wonders: "And here in the
city, are all these women wearing the same blanket or do my eyes fail to
see the different pattern?"[27] Subsequently, she concludes: "But, deep
down, all the words tell the same story."[28] Isabel Hofmeyr comments that
the ways in which the personal stories of domestic workers have generally
been told in South Africa (that is, via biographical interviews and the mediation of a white woman interviewer): "prevents informants from express-

---

[24] *Ibid.*, 246.

[25] *Ibid.*, 249-50.

[26] Anne McClintock, "'The Very House of Difference': Race, Gender and the
Politics of South African Women's Narrative in *Poppie Nongena*," in *The Bounds of
Race*, ed. Dominick La Capra, Ithaca, 1991, 215.

[27] Sindiwe Magona, *Living, Loving and Lying Awake at Night*, Cape Town, 1991,
55.

[28] *Ibid.*, 59.

ing their experience through alternative fictive conventions derived from popular, oral story telling traditions that are, for example, *not necessarily chronological.*"[29] "Women at Work" represents just such a representation, through a cyclical and oral format, of black working-class women's story/stories, and of their communal solidarity.

Juxtaposed against those cycles by black writers which project a sense of community defined by and yet resistant to both the ideology and the material repercussions of the apartheid state, however, are those by white writers, predominantly, which foreground notions of unrealized or failed community, that is, the pre-eminently divisive and polarizing reality of apartheid. These narratives evidence a sense of increasing estrangement, impotence and, somewhat paradoxically, dispossession — they exemplify what Brenda Cooper has dismissively characterized as "the sad, tired, dated and, ultimately, draining paradigm of the angst of the homeless, placeless, white English-speaking, disaffected South African."[30] The titles of some of these volumes reflect this sense of displacement and marginalization, for example, Denis Hirson's *The House Next Door to Africa* (1986), Peter Wilhelm's *Some Place in Africa* (1987), and Damon Galgut's *Small Circle of Beings* (1988).

The contrasts between the two groupings delineated above would thus seem to corroborate Malvern van Wyk Smith's pessimistic contention that South African literature inevitably divides up into two opposing and ultimately irreconcilable camps — white writing and black writing — which are premised on the polarities dread/optimism, wilderness/community and appropriation/resistance.[31] Van Wyk Smith writes, for example, that, in the post-Sharpeville era:

> a fierce affirmative dialectic of township solidarity, humanity and organicism developed, issuing in an aesthetic of urban values and communal praxis, in sharp contrast to a traditional white aesthetic of the private encounter with a redemptive wilderness. Fundamentally this is an aesthetic of optimism rather than pessimism, productive of a literature of celebration rather than dread.[32]

---

[29] Isabel Hofmeyr, "An Important and Imaginative Anthology," *Staffrider* 9:4 (1991), 132 (emphasis added).

[30] Brenda Cooper, "Yet Another Search for Identity," *Contrast,* 6:3, 1987, 90.

[31] See Malvern van Wyk Smith, *Grounds of Contest: A Survey of South African English Literature*, Cape Town, 1990.

[32] *Ibid.*, 98.

In the late eighties, however, the short fiction cycle was to develop in innovative directions which eschewed such simplistic binaries.

Ingram points out that the depiction in graphic, ostensibly realistic detail of a single locale in many cycles does not detract from its symbolic significance: setting becomes a "symbolic landscape, meticulously described, but displaying details which primarily reinforce one or more dimensions of the thematic or mythic movement of the cycle."[33] In the local context, this is apparent when the region depicted and its inhabitants are accorded a somewhat idyllic and nostalgic significance, as is evident in Pauline Smith, for example.[34] In cycles produced by black writers during the height of apartheid, setting and community accrue a politically-motivated impetus as an expression of solidarity and cultural cohesion / value which transcends or eludes the imposed confinement and derogation of segregated ghettoes, whereas those produced by white writers embody disjunction and an agonized sense of atrophied individual and collective identity.

Ingram's contention above goes some way towards recognizing the fact that, despite the supposed or actual referents in real geographical space of locales such as Winesburg, Dublin, Salinas Valley, Yoknapatawpha County, the Little Karoo, the Groot Marico District, Serowe village, Fordsburg and Lenasia, Charterston Location, Soweto and East London, these are fundamentally *"imagined* communities."[35] This has already emerged implicitly in the use of such previously-cited comments on regionalism and the cycle form as Pratt's "seeing that region *in print*" and Rhode's "the *impression* of actuality", to which might be added Rohrberger's phrase "a specific *literary* geography."[36] Each of these formulations draws attention to the *fictionalization* of a common locality and its inhabitants — their existence as literary constructs.

Similar recognitions of artifice in the representation of community and region in South African cycles are to be found in J. M. Coetzee's contention that what Pauline Smith, as a "pastoral novelist," was attempting to preserve of a "rural order" in her narratives set in the Little Karoo was "a

---

[33] Ingram, *op. cit.,* 21.

[34] See J. M. Coetzee, *White Writing: On the Culture of Letters in South Africa*, Johannesburg, 1988, 63-81.

[35] See Benedict Anderson, *Imagined Communities: Reflections on the Origin and Spread of Nationalism*, London, 1991, 6 (emphasis added). Anderson obviously uses this term to refer to nations, that is, larger entities than those communities discussed here.

[36] Rohrberger, *op. cit.*, 158 (emphases added).

social stability that she idealized, even *fabricated*,"[37] and Dorothy Driver's comment that Smith "*constructs* in her fiction a spatial and temporal setting — what Tony Voss calls the "anonymous 1890s" — that permits her to avoid confronting racial issues."[38] Lionel Abrahams, in a related vein, describes the setting of Herman Charles Bosman's stories in terms which invite an analogy with Faulkner's Yoknapatawpha County:

> however convincingly Schalk Louren's Groot Marico and the rest of his world looks and sounds and smells like the actual platteland, it is in fact substantially a geographic phantom, an aesthetic invention. The regionalism, the realism of these stories is only apparent, a cloak, a sort of ectoplasm to render visible a population of creatures whose native home is the author's imagination.[39]

Thus, it would appear that the early (exclusively white) examples of the cycle form in South Africa witness a relatively un-self-conscious fictionalization — sometimes even elegiac romanticization — of the nexus of identity and place. In the peak years of the apartheid epoch, as has become evident earlier, among both black and white writers, such disingenuity is problematized, since notions of "belonging" and being dispossessed are patently a result of systemic social engineering premised on the elaborated fallacy/fiction of "race": so-called "group areas" — and identities — are an obvious function of arbitrary human interventions and constructions. By the mid-eighties to the early nineties — the period of late apartheid — however, the discursive underpinnings of *all* concepts of locality and identity, of "them" and "us," and of processes of inclusion and exclusion, were to become a prominent theme in both the literary and critical/academic spheres, as is evident in the following comment:

> Land, in all its forms of possession and tenure, is deeply linked with personal and social identity; its boundaries are not established by "natural" barriers — rivers, mountains, and the like. They are discursively produced; they secure notions of community and polity and impinge on fundamental conceptions of "near" and "far," "neighbour" and "stranger," those who are "us," and whose word for that may translate as nothing more than "human" itself, as against those who are "other."[40]

---

[37] J. M. Coetzee, *op. cit.*, 6 (emphasis added).

[38] Dorothy Driver, "God, Fathers, and White South Africans: The World of Pauline Smith" in *Women and Writing in South Africa: A Critical Anthology*, ed. Cherry Clayton, Johannesburg, 1989, 77 (emphasis added).

[39] Lionel Abrahams, "Foreword," in *The Collected Works of Herman Charles Bosman*, ed. Lionel Abrahams, Johannesburg, 1981, 10.

[40] Nick Visser, "Positions: Wits History Workshop," *Pretexts* 2:1 (1990), 76.

This period heralds a new phase in the South African short fiction cycle, in which the literary conventions of realism and regionalism are supplanted by reflexivity and experimentation.

In 1990 Tony Morphet maintained that, from the mid-eighties, a new phase had entered South African literary practice in which irony operated more subversively by being "*translocative* across the lines of the multiple discourses that are constructing the cultural nodes and spaces of the society."[41] Morphet ascribed this new "settlement" to the influence of "poststructuralist and postmodern theorisations," and maintained that it was characterized by the increasing currency of the notion of textual and intertextual mediation, and a concomitant focus on questions of discursivity, narrativity and representation in apparently disparate disciplines:

> Whether history is, or is not, also only a text is still under dispute; but what is no longer tenable is the view that it is accessible to us in some way beyond or behind texts [...]. Similarly, the relations between language, texts, discourses and historical subjects have been broken open in a way that makes it impossible to speak in the way that [Albie Sachs and Njabulo Ndebele] do of "our people" as though they were in some sense coming already formed into history from the outside.[42]

Morphet was not alone in identifying this shift and pinpointing certain of its characteristic features: during roughly the same period a significant number of local writers, critics and academics registered the emergence of a new mode of writing in South Africa. Kelwyn Sole, for example, claimed that "Formal innovations and interesting new types of approach to the interface between the individual and the community, between the private and the political, have been apparent inside the country for a while,"[43] and Gareth Cornwall identified what he termed "better writing [...] which registers response to a decentered and less symbolically simplified society [...] we're entering that phase now."[44]

This perceived shift was signposted, as indicated above, by an interrogation of notions of authority, subjectivity and origin(ality), and by the increasing use of the type of metafictional strategies and "destabilizing devices" or "defamiliarizing vocabularies"[45] commonly associated with

---

[41] Tony Morphet, "Cultural Settlement: Albie Sachs, Njabulo Ndebele and the Question of Social and Cultural Imagination," *Pretexts* 2:1 (1990), 103.

[42] *Ibid.*, 102-103.

[43] Kelwyn Sole, "Interview," in *Exchanges: South African Writing in Transition*, eds Duncan Brown and Bruno van Dyk, Pietermaritzburg, 1991, 84.

[44] Gareth Cornwall, "Interview," in *ibid.*, 17.

[45] Van Wyk Smith, *op. cit.*, 126; and Lars Engle, "The Novel without the Police,

postmodernist writing: interpellated reader-and author-figures, cross-generic hybridisation, parodic intertextuality, and a refusal of closure, amongst others. Van Wyk Smith explained the appeal of such strategies:

> apartheid represents a social text that tried to write us all into a particular scenario [...] the only authorised story [...]. In such a context the disruptive, transgressive, deconstructive strategies of poststructuralism and postmodernism hold obvious procedural and thematic attractions for any oppositional writer. Not only can the individual witness ("my truth: how I lived in these times, in this place") be inserted into the national story as a transgressive sub-plot, but the national narrative itself, plus all the protest narratives which have been generated in opposition to it, may now be subjected to the discontinuities, the indeterminacies, and the provisionalities of a discursive mode that fundamentally resists all master myths.[46]

Whether the escalating use of such strategies was a function, as Morphet claims, of the importation of theories from abroad, or of socio-political and cultural changes occurring in South African society itself during the period of transition — or a combination of both — is a moot point, but what is unequivocal is that considerable consensus existed concerning those texts that were considered representative of the new mode and, significantly, many of these are short fiction cycles.

Morphet, for example, claimed that Ivan Vladislavic's *Missing Persons* (1989) constituted the "best and most recent example" of this contemporary form of work in which "the intersections of different discourses open up not only the cross-cutting tracks of history but also the problematic relations between subjectivity and location."[47] The collection offers tantalizing intimations of coherence, whilst frustrating recuperation in terms of received notions of narrative cause and effect. Moreover, the stories it contains describe surreal yet curiously familiar urban landscapes, littered with drek and populated by characters Sherwood Anderson might well have referred to as "grotesques."[48] As Alf Wannenburg commented in an early review: "Vladislavic's world [...] has many familiar features, but in mindscapes strange to me [...] in such a country the signposts are frequently ambiguous, the intention elusive."[49] These "mindscapes" reflect the parameters and perennial preoccupations of South African psyches /

Pretexts 3 (1991), 117.

[46] Malvern van Wyk Smith, "Waiting for Silence; or, The Autobiography of Metafiction in Some Recent South African Novels," *Current Writing* 3 (1991), 93.

[47] Morphet, *op. cit.*, 103.

[48] Sherwood Anderson, *Winesburg, Ohio*, New York, 1976, 22.

[49] Alf Wannenburg, "Review: *Missing Persons*," *New Contrast* 71 (1990), 82.

psychoses, which are in turn subjected to a deconstruction via a dissolution of the boundaries between history and fantasy, fact and fiction, the personal and the public, the comic and the tragic, culpability and innocence, and reality and nightmare.

Two other texts, cited by Brink as evidencing "exciting signs of renewal and invention," display a similar defiance of conventional generic categories and narrative expectations to *Missing Persons* and, again, both of these are short fiction cycles: Zoe Wicomb's *You Can't Get Lost in Cape Town* (1987) and Joël Matlou's *Life at Home and Other Stories* (1991).[50] Brink refers to the "successive chapters" of the former as being able to be read "as separate stories" and remarks, of the latter, that it is "arguably the most remarkable fiction by a black South African writer for years. Like Wicomb's text it can be read either as a series of short stories or as a (very short) novel."[51] Earlier, Matlou's text had received a similar recognition from Morphet, who claimed that it comprised:

> the first stories from a black writer in English to employ a profoundly reflexive authorial strategy [...]. The ultimate paradox is that [Ndebele's] evocation of the pre-modern "storyteller" should emerge from the storms of the 1980s as a post-modern "fabulist" — both of them speaking under the sign of "the ordinary."[52]

In the nineties there has been a proliferation of cyclical texts which similarly employ self-reflexive devices: Maja Kriel's *Original Sin and Other Stories* (1993), Shaun De Waal's *These Things Happen* (1996), and Vladislavic's subsequent collection *Propaganda by Monuments and Other Stories* (1996), for example. In a general sense, then, it would appear that the inherent dualism or hybrid character of this genre — its position somewhere between the novel and the short story proper — lends it to the type of metafictional interrogations and technical innovations referred to earlier, and that in South Africa, specifically, the cycle form has proved especially appropriate to a rendering of the tensions inherent in a multifarious and fractured society in the process of attempting to transform itself into a unified but culturally heterogeneous democracy. Moreover, it is surely not surprising that in a deeply ruptured society, such as this, where the national/historical narrative is in the process of being radically altered or "rewritten"/imagined, that narrative fiction tends to reflect an acute

---

[50] Brink, *op. cit.,* 60.
[51] *Ibid.,* 53.
[52] Tony Morphet, "Ordinary-Modern-Post-Modern," *Theoria* 80 (1990), 140.

sense of the storied nature of reality. Elleke Boehmer, for example, maintains that South Africa "needs new kinds of stories [...] new forms of thinking about reality,"[53] and Brink writes of the necessity to "reinvent the real."[54]

Van Wyk Smith, however, dismisses much of such writing as follows:

> All these texts competently wield the metafictional techniques of post-modernism, but in their very success they also witness to a literature of dread that increasingly inscribes its own and its culture's imminent demise on the recorded reality [...]. Ingenious as [various] recent South African post-modernist fictions are, and however graphically indicative of the violent psychological and social dislocations which generate them, they do lay themselves open to Mphalele's charge of fostering a rhetoric of desolate places at the expense of community.[55]

I would argue that certain kinds of cycles interrogate the very binaries on which arguments such as Van Wyk Smith's rest, and that their self-reflexivity serves to increase the reader's consciousness of the ways in which national narratives and personal (hi)stories are constructed or "written." In other words, they sensitize the reader to the reality that subjectivity and location are contingent on narrative and linguistic codes and conventions, that these are subject to the abuses of power, and as constructs they may be changed: a politics of location and identity is indistinguishable from an aesthetics of location and identity. It is my contention that this realization goes some way towards enabling the endeavor described by Michel Foucault:

> The problem is not of trying to dissolve [relations of power] in the utopia of perfectly transparent communication, but to give one's self the rules of law, the techniques of management, and also the ethics, the ethos, the practice of self, which would allow these games of power to be played with a minimum of domination.[56]

It would seem self-evident that any such attempt at an "anti-hegemonic strategy" is not only desirable or commendable but imperative in the so-called "post-apartheid" South Africa.[57]

---

[53] Quoted in Fiona Goncalves, "Narrative Strategies in Mia Couto's *Terra Sonambula*," *Current Writing* 7:1 (1995), 60.

[54] Brink, *op. cit.*, 47.

[55] Van Wyk Smith, *op. cit.*, 123-28.

[56] Quoted in Rory Ryan, "Some Processes and Functions of Literary Knowledge Production in South Africa," *AUETSA Conference Papers*, 1991, 592.

[57] Cornwall, *op. cit.*, 16.

NOTES ON CONTRIBUTORS

DESIREE LEWIS lectures at the University of the Western Cape, South Africa. Her current research focuses on South African biography and autobiography.

CRAIG MACKENZIE lectures at the Rand Afrikaans University. His publications include *Bessie Head: An Introduction* and *A Woman Alone*, a collection of Head's autobiographical writings. He is also the editor of the journal *English in Africa*.

MIKE MARAIS is a Lecturer in English at the Rand Afrikaans University. He has published a number of articles in *English in Africa, Current Writing*, the *Journal of Commonwealth Literature,* and *Journal of Literary Studies*.

SUE MARAIS lectures at Vista University, Soweto. Her research interests include South African short fiction. She has published in *English in Africa*.

JUDIE NEWMAN is Professor of American and Postcolonial Literatures at the University of Nottingham. Her publications include *The Ballistic Bard: Postcolonial Fictions, Nadine Gordimer, John Updike, Saul Bellow and History,* and numerous essays on American and Postcolonial novelists.

VASU REDDY is a Lecturer in the Department of Afrikaans and Dutch at the University of Natal. He has published chapters in *South African Human Rights Yearbook*, and *The Greatest Taboo: Homosexuality in the African Diaspora* as well as articles in the *South African Journal of African Languages*, and the *Journal of Literary Studies*.

DAVID SCHALKWYK is Senior Lecturer in English at the University of Cape Town. His articles have appeared in such journals as *Research in African Literatures, English Literary Renaissance*, the *Journal of Southern African Studies, Journal of Aesthetics and Art Criticism,* and *Shakespeare Quarterly*.

KELWYN SOLE is a Senior Lecturer at the University of Cape Town. He has published in *Research in African Literatures, TriQuarterly, English in Africa, World Literature Today,* and *Current Writing*. He has also published two collections of poetry that have been translated into French and Italian.

GINA WISKER is Principal Lecturer and Head of Women's Studies at the Anglia Polytechnic University. Her publications include *Insights into Black Women's Writing, It's My Party: Reading Twentieth-Century Women's Writing*, and *Fatal Attractions: Rescripting Romance in Fiction and Film* (with Lynne Pearce). She is currently working on a book on postcolonial and African American women's writing.

NAHEM YOUSAF is Senior Lecturer in English at the Nottingham Trent University. His publications include *Alex La Guma: Politics and Resistance*, and, as co-editor, *George Orwell*.

INDEX

The English Book and its Marginalia
Colonial/Postcolonial Literatures after
Heart of Darkness

Asako Nakai

Amsterdam/Atlanta, GA 2000. IX,210 pp.
(Textxet 35)
ISBN: 90-420-1364-8   EUR 41,-/US-$ 38.-

This book is about books that recount the story of encountering another book. There are various versions of the story told and retold from the heyday of imperialism up to the present day (Homi Bhabha calls it the trope of 'the discovery of the English book'); by considering each of these versions carefully, we may also give an alternative account of twentieth-century 'English literature' as the site of an intercultural discourse. This project is very much inspired by debate on postcolonial theory, namely, the debate between Said and Bhabha. Part I is devoted to the discussion of Conrad, especially of *Heart of Darkness*, and investigates how the novella has continually been reproduced to the extent that it represents 'the English Book' of colonial/postcolonial literatures. The chapter on Hugh Clifford (Ch.3) is virtually the first intensive critique of his novels, such as *Saleh* (1908), with a particular focus on their intertextual relations with Conrad's texts. Part II examines how the story of the English Book is repeated and revised in the texts of the following authors: Joyce Cary, Isak Dinesen, V. S. Naipaul, Kaiko Takeshi, and Ngugi wa Thiong'o.

Editions Rodopi B.V.
USA/Canada: One Rockefeller Plaza, Ste. 1420, New York, NY 10020,
Tel. (212) 265-6360,
Call toll-free (U.S. only) 1-800-225-3998, Fax (212) 265-6402
All other countries: Tijnmuiden 7, 1046 AK Amsterdam, The Netherlands.
Tel. ++ 31 (0)20 611 48 21, Fax ++ 31 (0)20 447 29 79
Orders-queries@rodopi.nl   www.rodopi.nl

The Star You Steer By
Basil Bunting and British Modernism

Edited by James McGonigal and Richard Price

Amsterdam/Atlanta, GA 2000. 298 pp.
(DQR Studies in Literature 30)
ISBN: 90-420-1214-5   Bound EUR 68,-/US-$ 64.-

This book explores Basil Bunting's continued reputation and influence in modern British poetry, and also the impact of a peculiarly 'Northern' inflection of Modernism (which Bunting largely defined) within the varieties of contemporary poetry being written now. The editors asked a variety of English, Scottish, Welsh and American poets and academics to reflect upon the themes, implications, impact or example of Bunting's work in the centenary year of his birth, looking back on the beginnings of Modernism at the start of the twentieth century into which he was born, or forward into the twenty-first century in which he continues to be read and learned from: a true poetic star to steer by.

The resulting collection of fourteen new essays reveals the continued ability of Bunting's poetry both to delight and to challenge. Topics covered include the nature of influence; Celtic and Northumbrian contexts for the modern English long poem; prosodic patterns in early Bunting; Bunting as a reader of his own work; narrative sources in his poetry; the problem of patronage; his 'rueful masculinity'; women poets and Bunting; radical landscape poetry; his translations from the Persian Hafiz and the Roman Horace; economic and social tensions in his work; the poet as 'makar'; and a previously unpublished selection of his letters from the 1960s to the 1980s, commenting upon his own and others' poetry and on the political condition of Britain in those years.

The collection will be of interest to teachers and readers of twentieth century English and American poetry, and to those exploring the processes of literary translation. Contributors include David Annwn, Richard Caddel, Roy Fisher, Victoria Forde, Harry Gilonis, Ian Gregson, Philip Hobsbaum, Parvin Loloi, James McGonigal, Richard Price, Glynn Pursglove, Harriet Tarlo, Gael Turnbull, and Jonathan Williams.

Editions Rodopi B.V.
USA/Canada: One Rockefeller Plaza, Ste. 1420, New York, NY 10020,
Tel. (212) 265-6360,
Call toll-free (U.S. only) 1-800-225-3998, Fax (212) 265-6402
All other countries: Tijnmuiden 7, 1046 AK Amsterdam, The Netherlands.
Tel. ++ 31 (0)20 611 48 21, Fax ++ 31 (0)20 447 29 79
Orders-queries@rodopi.nl   www.rodopi.nl

Essays on the Song Cycle and on Defining the Field

Essays on the Song Cycle and on Defining the Field. Proceedings of the Second International Conference on Word and Music Studies at Ann Arbor, MI, 1999.

Edited by Walter Bernhart and Werner Wolf in collaboration with David Mosley Amsterdam/Atlanta, GA 2001. XII,253 pp. (Word and Music Studies 3)

ISBN: 90-420-1575-6   EUR 57.-/US-$ 53.-
ISBN: 90-420-1565-9   EUR 23.-/US-$ 21.-

This volume assembles twelve interdisciplinary essays that were originally presented at the Second International Conference on Word and Music Studies at Ann Arbor, MI, in 1999, a conference organized by the International Association for Word and Music Studies (WMA).

The contributions to this volume focus on two centres of interest. The first deals with general issues of literature and music relations from culturalist, historical, reception-aesthetic and cognitive points of view. It covers issues such as conceptual problems in devising transdisciplinary histories of both arts, cultural functions of opera as a means of reflecting postcolonial national identity, the problem of verbalizing musical experience in nineteenth-century aesthetics and of understanding reception processes triggered by musicalized fiction.

The second centre of interest deals with a specific genre of vocal music as an obvious area of word and music interaction, namely the song cycle. As a musico-literary genre, the song cycle not only permits explorations of relations between text and music in individual songs but also raises the question if, and to what extent words and/or music contribute to creating a larger unity beyond the limits of single songs. Elucidating both of these issues with stimulating diversity the essays in this section highlight classic nineteenth- and twentieth-century song cycles by Franz Schubert, Robert Schumann, Hugo Wolf, Richard Strauss and Benjamin Britten and also include the discussion of a modern successor of the song cycle, the concept album as part of today's popular culture.

 **Editions Rodopi B.V.**

USA/Canada: One Rockefeller Plaza, Ste. 1420, New York, NY 10020,
Tel. (212) 265-6360, Call toll-free (U.S. only) 1-800-225-3998, Fax (212) 265-6402
All other countries: Tijnmuiden 7, 1046 AK Amsterdam, The Netherlands.
Tel. ++ 31 (0)20 611 48 21, Fax ++ 31 (0)20 447 29 79
Orders-queries@rodopi.nl   www.rodopi.nl

National Stereotypes in Perspective
Americans in France, Frenchmen in America

Ed. by William L. Chew, III

Amsterdam/New York, NY 2001. X,433 pp.
(Studia Imagologica 9)
ISBN: 90-420-1365-6   EUR 82,-/US-$ 77.-

Since the late 18th century, when they first entered into an alliance during the American Revolution, the French and Americans have had a long and sometimes stormy relationship based on a complex mix of mutual admiration, cultural criticism, and sometimes downright disgust for the "other." The relatively new interdisciplinary field of imagology, or image studies, allows us to place the dynamics of such a relationship into perspective by grounding its analysis firmly in the study of national stereotypes, in the process providing new insights into the mentality of the observer. For if anything, image studies demonstrate again and again that national character is not–as assumed uncritically for centuries–an innate essence of the "other", but rather a self-serving functional construct of the observer.

For the table of contents please refer to our website

Editions Rodopi B.V.
USA/Canada: One Rockefeller Plaza, Ste. 1420, New York, NY 10020,
Tel. (212) 265-6360, Call toll-free (U.S. only) 1-800-225-3998, Fax (212) 265-6402
All other countries: Tijnmuiden 7, 1046 AK Amsterdam, The Netherlands.
Tel. ++ 31 (0)20 611 48 21, Fax ++ 31 (0)20 447 29 79
Orders-queries@rodopi.nl   www.rodopi.nl

The Conning of America
The Great War and American Popular Literature

Patrick J. Quinn

Amsterdam/Atlanta, GA 2001. 261 pp. (Costerus NS 136)
ISBN: 90-420-1475-X   EUR 46,-/US-$ 43.-

The Conning of America examines for the first time from a literary perspective the propaganda writings produced in the United States during the period of World War I. This American propaganda literature was written in two distinct stages: the first stage was written by the pro-War establishment based on the East Coast of the United States before American entry into the conflict. It attempted to vilify Germany and her Allies while at the same time showing England, France, and Russia as the victims of a well-planned organized German plan for world domination—beginning with the invasion of neutral Belgium. The literature urged the United States to prepare for a German invasion of America and to be wary of German-Americans, who most likely were spies in the employ of the Imperial German government. The second stage of propaganda literature occurred when America declared war on the Central Powers in April 1917.
While still using the blood thirsty militaristic Hun as a symbol of German inherent evil, the propaganda literature began to portray the Americans as the saviors of European culture. American boys were being sent to Europe on a spiritual mission to purify decadent European culture, while at the same time their sacrifice would rejuvenate and sanctify American values in the fire of the conflict in order for America to take her proper place in the new post-war order.

Editions Rodopi B.V.
USA/Canada: One Rockefeller Plaza, Ste. 1420, New York, NY 10020,
Tel. (212) 265-6360, Call toll-free (U.S. only) 1-800-225-3998, Fax (212) 265-6402
All other countries: Tijnmuiden 7, 1046 AK Amsterdam, The Netherlands.
Tel. ++ 31 (0)20 611 48 21, Fax ++ 31 (0)20 447 29 79
Orders-queries@rodopi.nl   www.rodopi.nl

Writing the Early Modern English Nation
The Transformation of National Identity in Sixteenth- and Seventeenth-Century England.

Edited by Herbert Grabes
Amsterdam/Atlanta, GA 2001. XV,199 pp. (Costerus NS 137)
ISBN: 90-420-1525-X   EUR 37,-/US-$ 34.-

While there is overwhelming evidence that nationalism reached its peak in the later nineteenth century, views about when precisely national thinking and sentiment became strong enough to override all other forms of collective unity differ considerably. When one looks for the historical moment when the concept of the nation became a serious – and subsequently victorious – competitor to the monarchic dynasty as the most effective principle of collective unity, one must, at least for England, go back as far as the sixteenth century. The decisive change occurred when a split between the dynastic ruler and "England" could be widely conceived of and intensely felt, a split that established the nation as an autonomous – and more precious – body. Whereas such a differentiation between king and country was still imperceptible under Henry VIII, it was already an historical reality during the reign of Queen Mary.

That the most important factors in this radical change were the Reformation and the printing press is by now well known. The particular aim of this volume is to demonstrate the pivotal role of pamphleteering – and the growing importance of public opinion in a steadily widening sense – within the process of the historical emergence of the concept of the nation as a culturally and politically guiding force. When it came to the voicing of dissident opinions, above all under Queen Mary and later during the reign of King James and Charles I, the printed pamphlet proved to be a far superior form of communication.

This does not mean that books played no role in the early development and dissemination of the concept of an English nation. Especially the compendious new English histories written at the time did much to support the growth of cultural identity.

Editions Rodopi B.V.
USA/Canada: One Rockefeller Plaza, Ste. 1420, New York, NY 10020,
Tel. (212) 265-6360,
Call toll-free (U.S. only) 1-800-225-3998, Fax (212) 265-6402
All other countries: Tijnmuiden 7, 1046 AK Amsterdam, The Netherlands.
Tel. ++ 31 (0)20 611 48 21, Fax ++ 31 (0)20 447 29 79
Orders-queries@rodopi.nl   www.rodopi.nl

Exploding Aesthetics

Edited by Annette W. Balkema and Henk Slager
Amsterdam/Atlanta, GA 2001. 188 pp. (Lier en Boog Series 16)
ISBN: 90-420-1325-7   Bound   EUR   41,-/US-$ 38.-
ISBN: 90-420-1315-X   Paper   EUR   18,-/US-$ 17.-

Today, many visual artists are giving the cold shoulder to the static, isolated concept of visual art and searching instead for novel, dynamic connections to different image strategies. Because of that, visual art and aesthetics are both forced to reconsider their current positions and their traditional apparatus of concepts. In that process, many questions surface. To mention a few: Could the characteristics of an artistic image and its specific manner of signification be determined in a world which is entirely aesthetisized? What would be the consequences of a variety of image strategies for aesthetic experience? Would it be possible to develop a form of cultural criticism by means of artistic activities in a culture awash in images?

In order to answer such questions, aesthetics as a philosophy of art needs to transform its field into a critical philosophy of topical visual culture. As an impetus to such a reinterpretation of the visual working area, the L & B Series organized three symposia evenings under the title "Exploding Aesthetics", in cooperation with De Appel Center for Contemporary Art, Amsterdam. Besides the presentations and discussions from these symposia, this volume includes various arguments, positions, and statements in both articles and interviews by a variety of visual artists, designers, advertising professionals, theorists and curators. The participants are: Mieke Bal, Annette W. Balkema, Peg Brand, Experimental Jetset, Liam Gillick, Jeanne van Heeswijk, Martin Jay, KesselsKramer, Friedrich Kittler, Maria Lind, Wim Michels, Nicholas Mirzoeff, Planet Art, Joke Robaard, Annemieke Roobeek, Remko Scha, Rob Schröder, Henk Slager, Richard Shusterman, Pauline Terreehorst, Wolfgang Welsch and Marie-Lou Witmer.

Editions Rodopi B.V.
USA/Canada: One Rockefeller Plaza, Ste. 1420, New York, NY 10020,
Tel. (212) 265-6360, Call toll-free (U.S. only) 1-800-225-3998, Fax (212) 265-6402
All other countries: Tijnmuiden 7, 1046 AK Amsterdam, The Netherlands.
Tel. ++ 31 (0)20 611 48 21, Fax ++ 31 (0)20 447 29 79
Orders-queries@rodopi.nl   www.rodopi.nl

Telling Stories.
Postcolonial Short Fiction in English

Edited by Jacqueline Bardolph. Finalized for publication by André Viola with Jean-Pierre Durix.

Amsterdam/Atlanta, GA 2001. XV,477 pp. (Cross/Cultures 47)
ISBN: 90-420-1534-9   Bound EUR 114,-/US-$ 106.-
ISBN: 90-420-1524-1   Paper EUR 34,-/US-$ 32.-

The present volume is a highly comprehensive assessment of the postcolonial short story since the thirty-six contributions cover most geographical areas concerned. Another important feature is that it deals not only with exclusive practitioners of the genre (Mansfield, Munro), but also with well-known novelists (Achebe, Armah, Atwood, Carey, Rushdie), so that stimulating comparisons are suggested between shorter and longer works by the same authors. In addition, the volume is of interest for the study of aspects of orality (dialect, dance rhythms, circularity and trickster figure for instance) and of the more or less conflictual relationships between the individual (character or implied author) and the community.

Furthermore, the marginalized status of women emerges as another major theme, both as regards the past for white women settlers, or the present for urbanized characters, primarily in Africa and India. The reader will also have the rare pleasure of discovering Janice Kulik Keefer's "Fox," her version of what she calls in her commentary "displaced autobiography'" or "creative non-fiction." Lastly, an extensive bibliography on the postcolonial short story opens up further possibilities for research.

 **Editions Rodopi B.V.**
USA/Canada: One Rockefeller Plaza, Ste. 1420, New York, NY 10020,
Tel. (212) 265-6360, Call toll-free (U.S. only) 1-800-225-3998, Fax (212) 265-6402
All other countries: Tijnmuiden 7, 1046 AK Amsterdam, The Netherlands.
Tel. ++ 31 (0)20 611 48 21, Fax ++ 31 (0)20 447 29 79
Orders-queries@rodopi.nl   www.rodopi.nl